Kieler Studien · Kiel Studies 322
Horst Siebert (Editor)
Kiel Institute for World Economics

Springer
Berlin
Heidelberg
New York
Hong Kong
London
Milan
Paris
Singapore
Tokyo

Holger Brauer

The Real Exchange Rate and Prices of Traded Goods in OECD Countries

Springer

Dr. Holger Brauer
Offenbacher Landstraße 7
60599 Frankfurt am Main
holger.brauer@feri.de

ISSN 0340-6989

ISBN 3-540-00430-0 Springer-Verlag Berlin Heidelberg New York

Cataloging-in-Publication Data applied for
A catalog record for this book is available from the Library of Congress.
Bibliographic information published by Die Deutsche Bibliothek
Die Deutsche Bibliothek lists this publication in the Deutsche Nationalbibliografie;
detailed bibliographic data is available in the Internet at <http://dnb.ddb.de>.

Springer-Verlag Berlin Heidelberg New York
a member of BertelsmannSpringer Science+Business Media GmbH

http://www.springer.de

© Springer-Verlag Berlin · Heidelberg 2003
Printed in Germany

Hardcover-Design: Erich Kirchner, Heidelberg

SPIN 10911143   42/2202-5 4 3 2 1 0 – Printed on acid-free paper

Preface

The subject of purchasing power parity has received widespread attention in the discipline of economics. For single goods, the law of one price only holds under certain conditions which are rarely satisfied in the real world. The reader may well have experienced numerous examples for price differences across borders while being on vacation, and these differences usually depend upon the exchange rate. The most noticeable example, however, are nontradable goods, and labor in particular. One might be tempted to ask whether this observation justifies an analysis such as it is done in this study, since the ongoing process of globalization should reduce any existing differentials by arbitrage. The conclusion from this study will be that it does justify it, not despite globalization, but because of it.

On the one hand, lowering barriers for trade forces price differentials to melt down for those goods for which a nearly perfect market exists. On the other hand, costs of nontradable inputs into production such as labor are floating between countries, even when accounted for productivity differentials. These extremes set the stage on which enterprises have to decide over prices and production. The exchange rate is a major, but not the sole determinant for production cost differentials between countries. Even in currency unions like the European Monetary Union, countries may differ in price competitiveness due to differences in their labor markets or productivities. In either case, the real exchange rate is affected, which compares some price or cost index over countries, depending upon its particular definition. The concept of the real exchange rate thus constitutes the pivotal element in this study, and it proved to be a very useful one.

The basic inspirations for this study came from Prof. Dr. Dr. h.c. Horst Siebert, to whom I am particularly indebted. I very much benefited from having the opportunity to review my work with him on a regular basis. My special thanks go to Prof. Dr. Gerd Hansen, who contributed some very essential suggestions with respect to the empirical methods. I also got many inspirations from numerous fruitful discussions related to my work which I had with my colleagues, of whom I only name PD Dr. Oliver Lorz, at the risk of being unfair to lots of others which also deserve to be mentioned here. Many thanks also go to

Nicole Rimkus, who was an indispensable help in drafting the tables and figures and improving the layout of this work. Britta Thun took great care of turning the manuscript into a finished product. Finally, I would like to thank Melanie Grosse for thoroughly reviewing the manuscript in the editorial process. With her valuable comments and suggestions she took on much of the work which ought to be done by me. However, it goes without saying that I am the sole responsible for any remaining errors.

Bad Homburg, January 2003   Holger Brauer

Contents

A. Aim of the Study   1

B. Various Approaches to Price Comparisons of International Goods under Production Costs Shifts between Countries   4

    I.   The Real Exchange Rate and Purchasing Power Parity   6

    II.   Cost and Exchange Rate Pass-Through   10

    III.   Pricing to Market   15

C. Theoretical Determinants for the Degree of Pass-Through and Pricing to Market   19

    I.   Modeling Framework   20

    II.   Nature of the Shock   23

       1.   Exchange Rate Changes   24

       2.   Domestic Cost Changes   30

    III.   Demand Characteristics   33

       1.   Price Elasticity of Demand   33

       2.   Consumer Switching Costs   35

       3.   Substitutability between Product Varieties   38

       4.   Summary: The Impact of Demand Characteristics on Price Adjustments   52

    IV.   Production Characteristics   53

       1.   Number of Firms   53

       2.   Market Share   58

       3.   Transport Costs   59

       4.   Intermediate Inputs   64

    V.   Summary: What Determines the Link between Relative Costs and Relative Prices?   72

    VI.   Appendix   73

       1.   Derivation of Equation (C.2)   73

       2.   Coefficients in Equation (C.53) and (C.54)   76

       3.   Role of γ in the Duopoly Model C.III.3   76

4. Derivation of Equations (C.74) and (C.75)   80
5. The Duopoly Prices with $\gamma = 0$ as a Special Case of the General Number-of-Firms Model   81

D. Empirical Results for the Degree of Pass-Through in Domestic and Export Markets   83

I. Country-Specific Findings for the OECD   84
  1. A First Evidence from Charts   84
  2. Evidence from Descriptive Statistics on Price Variability   90
  3. Accounting for the Determinants of Price Setting by Regression Analysis   101

II. Sector-Specific Results for Western German Manufacturing   114
  1. The Classification of Sectors According to the Type of Good   114
  2. Evidence from Descriptive Statistics on Time Series of Prices   118
  3. Evidence from Real Exchange Rate Effects on Relative Prices   125
  4. Explaining Sectoral Differences   133

III. Appendix   142
  1. Figures   142
  2. Tables   144

E. The Impact of Cost Competitiveness on Relative Export Prices and World Market Shares   152

I. Defining Competitiveness   152
  1. Is Competitiveness an Issue for Policy?   152
  2. The Measurement of Competitiveness   154

II. Country Results for Cost and Price Competitiveness and National Export Performance   155
  1. The Empirical Picture   155
  2. Quantifying the Impact of Relative Unit Labor Costs on Relative Export Prices   160
  3. Evidence for the Relation between Relative Unit Labor Costs and Export Performance   163

III. Sectoral Implications of Real Exchange Rate Movements   164
  1. The Real Exchange Rate and Comparative Advantage   164

    2. Empirical Results for Sectoral Cost Competitiveness and
       Sectoral World Market Shares   166

  IV. Appendix   172

F. The Law of One Price and Adjustments of Real Economy   178

  I.   Does the Law of One Price Hold Asymptotically for Export
       Prices and for Unit Labor Costs?   179
      1. The Motivation for Unit Root Tests   179
      2. The Empirical Approach   183
      3. Empirical Results   184

  II. The Role of Profit and Investment as Adjusting Tools to Real
       Exchange Rate Disequilibria   187
      1. The Approach of Campa and Goldberg   187
      2. How the Competitive Structure of Goods Markets
         Determines the Evolution of Profits   192
      3. The Role of the Demand Elasticity for the Magnitude of
        Profit Fluctuations   196
      4. Some Empirical Evidence on Real Exchange Rates, Profits,
        and Investment for Main Industrial Sectors   198

  III. An Integrative Approach of Modeling the Decision to Enter and
       Exit in the Export Market and Price Setting   202

**G. Concluding Remarks: Is the Real Exchange Rate an Issue for
    National Policy?**   208

References   212

List of Tables

Table 1: The Impact of Various Shocks on Instantaneous Pass-Through, Adjustment of Export and Domestic Prices, and Price Drift for Nonsubstitutable Goods   33

Table 2: The Impact of Various Demand Parameters on the Strength of Adjustment in the Relevant Prices or Price Ratios due to an Exchange Rate Shock   52

Table 3: Variance Pass-Through for Individual Countries   97

Table 4: Pricing to Market and Its Determinants across Countries   99

Table 5: Country-Specific Error-Correction Regressions for Import Prices   105

Table 6: Pooled Error-Correction Results for the Determinants of Import Price Pass-Through across Countries   107

Table 7: Country-Specific Error-Correction Regressions for Export Prices   111

Table 8: Pooled Error-Correction Results for the Determinants of Export Price Setting across Countries   112

Table 9: A Selection of German Manufacturing Sectors and Sectoral Pricing Behavior   120

Table 10: Classification of Goods According to Homogeneity and Pass-Through   121

Table 11: Sectoral Error-Correction Results for Import Prices   129

Table 12: Sectoral Error-Correction Results for Export Prices   131

Table 13: A Selection of German Manufacturing Sectors and Relative Pass-Through of Import Prices Relative to Export Prices   135

Table 14: The Impact of Structural Determinants on Pass-Through   138

Table 15: The Impact of Structural Determinants on Pricing to Market   140

Table 16: Variances and Correlations between Relative Unit Labor Costs, Relative Export Prices, and Relative Consumer Prices   161

Table 17: Panel Data Estimation of World Market Shares against Relative Unit Labor Costs   169

Table 18: Time Series Correlations between Relative Export Prices of
Selected OECD Countries   181

Table 19: Time Series Correlations between Relative Unit Labor Costs of
Selected OECD Countries   181

Table 20: Unit Root Tests for Relative Export Prices and Relative Unit
Labor Costs   184

Table 21: Panel Unit Root Tests for Relative Export Prices and Relative
Unit Labor Costs   186

Table 22: The Impact of a Currency Appreciation on the Components of
Marginal Profit and Investment   194

Table 23: The Impact of Shifts in Relative Unit Labor Costs on Profits   200

Table 24: The Impact of Shifts in Relative Unit Labor Costs on Relative
Expenditure on Research & Development   201

Table A1: Augmented Dickey–Fuller Test for Unit Roots Applied to the
Price and Real Exchange Rate Series across Countries   144

Table A2: Augmented Dickey–Fuller Test for Unit Roots Applied to the
Differenced Series of Prices and Real Exchange Rates across Countries   145

Table A3: Germany's Country-Specific Import Share with Respect to
Total Imports in the Respective Sector   146

Table A4: Germany's Country-Specific Export Share with Respect to
Total Exports in the Respective Sector   148

Table A5: The Correspondence between Sector Classifications and SITC
Trade Categories used in Chapter D   150

Table A6: Tests for Integration Applied to the Sectoral Relative Import
and Export Prices and Relative Unit Labor Costs   151

List of Figures

Figure 1: Various Approaches to International Price Comparisons   5

Figure 2: The Classification of Goods According to Integration of Markets and Type of Competition   13

Figure 3: The Link between Cost Competitiveness, Price-Cost Ratios, and Relative Prices   16

Figure 4: The Relationship between Exchange Rate Shocks, Changes in Relative Production Costs, Pass-Through, and Export Price Adjustments   26

Figure 5: The Relationship between Domestic Cost Shocks, Pass-Through, and Export Price Adjustments   31

Figure 6: Pass-Through Elasticities with Increasing α 34

Figure 7: Cost Pass-Through Elasticities with Increasing α 35

Figure 8: Pass-Through Elasticities with Increasing γ 36

Figure 9: Cost Pass-Through Elasticities with Increasing γ 38

Figure 10: The Interrelationship of Different Price Elasticities to an Exchange Rate Depreciation   41

Figure 11: The Impact of an Increase in σ on Pass-Through, the Export and Home Market Price Adjustments, and the Export Price Drift   47

Figure 12a: The Impact of Substitutability on Import Price Pass-Through, Domestic Price Adjustment, and Relative Producer Prices when Margins Are Small ($\alpha \rightarrow 1$)   49

Figure 12b: The Impact of Substitutability on Import Price Pass-Through, Domestic Price Adjustment, and Relative Producer Prices when Margins Are Large ($\alpha = 4$)   49

Figure 13: Exchange Rate Pass-Through and Pricing to Market with Increasing α 50

Figure 14: Import Prices of Manufactured Goods and Foreign Unit Labor Costs   85

Figure 15: Volatility of Import Prices of Manufactured Products and Foreign Unit Labor Costs   87

Figure 16: Export and Domestic Producer Prices, Home and Foreign Unit Labor Costs   88

Figure 17: Movement of Import and Domestic Prices by Type of Good   116

Figure 18: Unit Labor Costs and Prices in Selected Sectors of German Manufacturing   117

Figure 19: Price Correlation (*CORPMPD*) and Pass-Through (*SDPM/SDPXF*) across Sectors   121

Figure 20: The Theoretical Relationship between Substitutability and Pass-Through by Type of Good   123

Figure 21: The Correlation of Import Prices (*CORPMPD*) versus the Correlation of Export Prices (*CORPXPD*) with Domestic Prices   124

Figure 22: A Comparison of Relative Unit Labor Costs, Relative Export Prices, and OECD Market Shares for Selected Countries   157

Figure 23: The Transmission of Relative Cost Shifts into Export Prices   178

Figure 24: The Simultaneous Determination of Export Capacity and Export Prices   206

Figure A1: Pass-Through Elasticities with Increasing γ   77

Figure A2: Pricing to Market with Various Natures of Exchange Rate Changes   78

Figure A3: Pass-Through into Import Prices for Further Selected Sectors   142

Figure A4: A Comparison of Relative Unit Labor Costs, Relative Export Prices, and OECD Market Shares for Further Countries   172

List of Variables

Chapter B

$A,\dots,D$	particular country
e	shortcut for nominal exchange rate e^{rs}
e^{rs}	nominal exchange rate in terms of currency units of country r for one currency unit of country s
h	linear combination of relative prices and the nominal exchange rate
i	subscript for product variety
k	nonzero constant
M	markup factor defined as the ratio of producer prices over marginal costs of production
MC	marginal costs of production
p^{rs}	price of a product produced in country r and sold in country s measured in currency units of country s
p^{r*s}	price of a product produced in country r and sold in country s measured in currency units of country r
P	aggregate price level
r	exporting country index
$RERC$	real exchange rate based on production costs
$RERC^{rs}$	real exchange rate based on production costs, measured as the ratio of production costs in country s relative to country r, transformed by the exchange rate e^{rs}
$RERP$	real exchange rate based on consumer price indices
$RERP^{rs}$	real exchange rate based on consumer price indices, measured as an index of prices in country s relative to country r, transformed by the exchange rate e^{rs}
s	importing country index

ϑ	weight parameter

Chapter C

A, B	particular country
c	production costs
e	shortcut for nominal exchange rate e^{rs}
e^{rs}	nominal exchange rate in terms of currency units of country r for one currency unit of country s
E	elasticity
h^d	input coefficient for intermediate inputs bought from domestic firms
h^f	input coefficient for intermediate inputs bought from foreign firms
h^w	input coefficient for labor costs
i, j	variety of goods
m	margin of variable unit profit
M	markup factor
n	number of producers and varieties in one country
N	total number of producers and varieties in all countries
p	price index
p^{rs}	price of a product produced in country r and sold in country s measured in currency units of country s
p^{r*s}	price of a product produced in country r and sold in country s measured in currency units of country r
r	exporting country index
R	residual expenditure, i.e., money left for all expenditures other than those for the differentiated goods considered
s	variable: market share
s	superscript: importing country index

t	variable: transport costs
t	subscript: time index
U	utility function
w	wage rate
x_i	quantity purchased of variety i
x_t	quantity purchased at time t
Y	money of representative agent for consumption
α	parameter in the demand function representing the reservation price
β	parameter in the demand function
γ	parameter in the demand function representing switching costs
λ	discount rate in the intertemporal value function of the producer
Π	variable profit defined as revenue from sales minus variable costs for the producer
Π_{i1}^{rs}	variable profit defined as revenue from sales minus variable costs for variety i for the producer in country r who sells to country s at time $t = 1$ in currency units of country r
Π_{i2}^{rs}	variable profit defined as revenue from sales minus variable costs for variety i for the producer in country r who sells to country s at time $t = 2$ in currency units of country r
Π_{it}^{rs}	global variable profit for the producer in country r who sells to country s, defined as sales minus variable costs of variety i in the current and in the next period in currency units of country r
σ	parameter in the demand function representing substitutability

Chapter D

A, B	particular country
c	production costs, approximated by unit labor costs

CORPMPD	correlation coefficient between relative changes of import prices and relative changes of domestic prices
CORPXPD	correlation coefficient between relative changes of export prices and relative changes of domestic prices
CPXRULCR	correlation coefficient between changes of relative export prices and changes of relative unit labor costs (calculated from first differences in logarithms)
D	dummy variable
e	shortcut for nominal exchange rate e^{rs}
e^{rs}	nominal exchange rate in terms of currency units of country r for one currency unit of country s
E	index of relative unit labor costs
$g - 1$	error-correction adjustment coefficient
i	country index
i	sector index in (D.30)–(D.33)
j	index of all trade partners of country i
k	third markets of countries i and j
LNPM	import price (in logarithms)
LNPPI	domestic producer price (in logarithms)
LNPX	export price (in logarithms)
LNREER	real effective exchange rate (in logarithms)
LNRER	logarithm of the real exchange rate
LNRULCM	relative unit labor cost series in import price regressions for Germany constructed by using German sectoral import shares (in logarithms)
LNRULCX	relative unit labor cost series in export price regressions for Germany constructed by using German sectoral export shares (in logarithms)
N	number of countries included in the regression sample
NER	nominal exchange rate in U.S. dollars

p^{rs}	price of a product produced in country r and sold in country s measured in currency units of country s
p^{r*s}	price of a product produced in country r and sold in country s measured in currency units of country r
PENE	import penetration ratio calculated as the ratio of imports to total domestic demand
PSHARE	share of a country's production relative to all OECD countries
RD	R&D expenditure by establishment normalized by the total manufacturing average in each country
RDOUT	ratio of R&D expenditure to gross output
s_j^k	market share of a producer from country j in market k
S_l^k	sales from country l in market k
SDPM/SDPXF	ratio of the standard deviation of import prices to the standard deviation of foreign export prices (calculated from first differences in logarithms)
$seas_i$	seasonal dummy variable for quarter i
SIZE	average employment per establishment normalized by the total manufacturing average in each country
ULC	normalized unit labor costs
VARPM	variance of import prices (calculated from first differences in logarithms)
VARPMR	variance the of relative import prices, with the relative import price being the import price relative to the domestic price (calculated from first differences in logarithms)
VARPXR	variance of relative export prices, with the relative export price being the ratio of export price to domestic producer prices (calculated from first differences in logarithms)
VARULC	variance of domestic unit labor costs (calculated from first differences in logarithms)
VARULCF	variance of foreign unit labor costs computed in domestic currency units (calculated from first differences in logarithms)
VARULCR	variance of the ratio of domestic to foreign unit labor costs (calculated from first differences in logarithms)

VRPU	variance ratio of relative export prices to relative unit labor costs (calculated from first differences in logarithms)
VRPXPD	ratio of the variance of export prices over the variance of domestic producer prices (calculated from first differences in logarithms)
W_{ij}	weight attached by country i to country j
XDEP	export dependency defined as the share of exports relative to domestic production
XSHARE	export share of a respective country relative to all OECD countries
v_i	country-specific fixed effects
φ	pass-through coefficient
φ_e	exchange rate pass-through coefficient
φ_c	cost pass-through coefficient
ϕ	parameter indicating the weight of foreign costs in the export price adjustment

Chapter E

A,..., C	particular country
c	unit labor costs as a proxy for total production costs
C	aggregate unit labor cost index
CCU	correlation coefficient between relative consumer prices and r relative unit labor costs (calculated from first differences in logarithms)
CPU	correlation coefficient between relative export prices and relative unit labor costs (calculated from first differences in logarithms)
CRPC	ratio of *CPU* over *CCU*
E	elasticity
i	country index

j	index of competitor countries of country i
k	target market index
LNRULC	relative unit labor costs (in logarithms) defined as the ratio of unit labor costs of a country relative to the weighted average of all OECD countries (in logarithms)
p	export price
P	aggregate export price index
s	sector
t	time index
x	real export quantities
X	aggregate real export quantity index
z	export share of a particular industry

Chapter F

A, B	particular country
e	shortcut for nominal exchange rate
e^{AB}	nominal exchange rate in terms of currency units of country A for one currency unit of country B
f	short form for $f\left(K_t, L_t^A, L_t^B\right)$
F	fixed costs
g	capital cost adjustment function
i	country index
I	investment
K	capital stock
L	labor input, being representative for all variable inputs
M	markup factor
MC	marginal costs
OP	operating profit

p^{AB} (p^{AA})	price of a product produced in country A and sold in country B (A) measured in currency units of country B (A)
$RULC$	relative unit labor costs defined as the ratio of unit labor costs of a country relative to the weighted average of all OECD countries
s	importing country
s_L	labor share
s_K	profit share
t	time index
V	firm value
VUC	variable unit costs
w	factor price for variable inputs
x	quantity sold in home and export markets
$XDEP$	export dependency defined as the share of exports relative to domestic production
Z	short form for a term defined in (F.28)
Γ	short form for a term defined in (F.21)
δ	depreciation rate of the capital stock K
θ	logarithm of labor productivity
ι	parameter in the investment function
ν	parameter in the investment function
ξ	logarithm of the ratio of total costs over variable costs
Ξ	constant
Π	gross profit
ρ	adjustment coefficient
υ	pass-through coefficient
$\exists[.]$	expectation operator

$\mathfrak{I}_\tau$ information set at time τ

ϖ discount rate

List of Abbreviations

CES   constant elasticity of substitution

DW   Durbin–Watson statistic

EMS   European Monetary System

EMU   European Monetary Union

ERPT   exchange rate pass-through

GLS   generalized least square

GP   Güterverzeichnis für die Produktionsstatistik

iid   independently and identically distributed

ISIC   International Standard Industrial Classification

OECD   Organisation for Economic Co-operation and Development

PPP   purchasing power parity

PTM   pricing to market

R&D   research and development

SE   standard error of a regression

SITC   Standard International Trade Classification

SUR   seemingly unrelated regressions

ULC   unit labor costs

VEC   vector error correction

A.   Aim of the Study

Globalization has many features. One of them is without doubt the increasing global exchange of tradable goods, both material and immaterial. Another aspect is the growing importance of multinational enterprises, which can easily shift production toward locations where it is cheapest to produce and which sell their products in several national markets by applying some kind of profit optimization framework to each market separately. Both of these aspects are important catalysts for the unfolding of locational competition, which states that, with capital being internationally mobile, countries compete against each other with respect to their share of business investment. This share is related to the countries' share of production or exports in the world market.

This study focuses on two questions. The first one is whether countries price their traded goods only on basis of their specific costs of production, or whether conditions in the relevant target market or the world market also affect price setting. This issue is particularly important with regard to the frequently observed shocks caused by shifts in nominal exchange rates or production costs between countries on the one hand, and the law of one price which is expected to hold for identical goods on the other hand, although some modifications have to be made due to imperfect product homogeneity or transport costs.

Because one important insight delivered later in Chapters C and D is that the pass-through of costs into prices relevant for the buyer is incomplete, the second question arises as to how market shares respond when national cost differentials occur vis-à-vis the trade partner or the rest of the world. To the extent that prices are set according to sales market conditions rather than to costs in the originating country, reflecting the fact that single producers enjoy only little pricing power, exports should be less affected by changes in the real exchange rate, at least in the short term, even though elasticities of export demand with respect to relative prices may be sufficiently large. The real exchange rate is conceived here as the level of costs in the producing country relative to the trade partner's level, when both are made comparable in the same currency by means of the nominal exchange rate.

This muted pass-through into prices which apply to the importer of the good might explain why the observed mean reversion of exchange rates to their respective purchasing power parities is so slow for pairs of countries linked by flexible exchange rates. When trade flows do not respond reasonably in the short term to shifts in the real exchange rate and thus fail to affect demand and supply in the foreign exchange markets, they do not contribute to restoring the nominal exchange rate to a level consistent with purchasing power parity. The incomplete exchange rate pass-through might also explain why there is the empirical puzzle of a high correlation between national savings and investments. Suppose a country wants to save for higher future consumption. It can do so if its periodic trade balance is in surplus. In order to achieve a current account surplus, however, a real depreciation of its national currency is warranted in order to increase its international price competitiveness, so that it can sell the surplus of production over national demand on the world market. To the extent that margins of exporters are adjusted to shifts of domestic costs or of the exchange rate, and prices in the destination markets are quite inflexible, relatively large nominal exchange rate changes are necessary to achieve a shift in relative international export prices and a change in the trade balance.

This work is organized as follows: Chapter B gives a brief introduction into the basic theoretical concepts which are of relevance, before Chapter C sets out a thorough analytical approach to determine the magnitude of pass-through, the relevance of market-specific price setting, and the proportion by which national producers alter their export prices relative to their competitors when they experience a relative cost shift. Factors which determine these elasticities depend on product attributes, the market structure, and demand properties. In Chapter D, it is investigated empirically whether pass-through and pricing to market differ between countries or economic sectors. It is found that the size and openness of countries is relevant as well as the average firm size and the degree of product differentiation.

The implications for explaining national export performance of countries are investigated in Chapter E. It is found that export price differentials between countries, which are the relevant pivotal element in the transmission process toward export demand shifts between countries, reflect differences in national costs. However, this price dependency is only partial, particularly in the short term and for large intercountry shifts of competitiveness, so it is of interest to investigate the implications for the evolution of market shares. Some puzzling evidence suggests that country-specific export shares are affected in the event of strong and long-lasting real exchange rate changes, even though this can hardly be explained on the basis of export price setting alone. One important hypothesis in this respect is that the strategy of absorbing cost shifts in the producers' profit margins helps stabilize a country's market share only temporarily, whereas in the long run, production processes reallocate away from locations where cost shifts in the upper direction occur toward more favorable sites. In Chapter F, some pieces of arguments, both theoretical and empirical, are presented to back this hypothesis. One valuable finding from panel unit root tests is that a long-run tendency of unit labor cost differentials between countries to be reversed is detected, but this tendency of restoring disequilibria is stronger when the test is repeated with export prices instead of unit labor costs, thus highlighting the role of globalization of product markets for the adjustment process in the real sector. Chapter G concludes.

B.   Various Approaches to Price Comparisons of International Goods under Production Costs Shifts between Countries

Before distinguishing between different methods of using prices it should first be argued why prices are of any interest for assessing globalization or competition on world markets at all. The standard Heckscher–Ohlin theorem tells us that a country that opens up to trade faces the price vector on world markets instead of the formerly autarky price vector. It is this new price vector which is the input for both production and consumption schedules, and welfare analysis suggests that the resulting reallocation of resources leads to a welfare gain for the economy as a whole. The intuitive explanation is quite simple: the world price vector acts as a sort of reference price as long as any arbitrary amount of goods can be traded into the country or out of the country. Thus, the value of production is maximized if the producers adjust the marginal rate of substitution at world prices. The relative shadow prices of production in the respective country and in the rest of the world are identical, and production in the country is now done in an efficient way, which would not necessarily happen if domestic prices are hindered to adjust to world prices.

The interest in comparing prices from an international point of view has sparked off different approaches in the economic literature. The first approach is the literature on the *law of one price*, which suggests that prices of the same goods should be identical when converted into the same currency. To the extent that this relationship holds we speak of internationally integrated markets. However, a common empirical picture is that factors that account for local production costs such as wages, tax rates, and the exchange rate, to name only a few, are not equalized worldwide. The second approach consequently asks the question whether those cost differences are reflected in local prices or whether goods markets are sufficiently integrated to exclude any room for maneuver in the price-setting schedules of producers. If that is the case, i.e., goods markets are perfectly integrated, a change over time in one of the cost components, say the exchange rate, will leave prices unaltered. To be more specific on definitions, *exchange rate pass-through* is that part of the exchange rate change by which export prices move in the importer's currency. In the extreme case of perfectly integrated world markets with a homogeneous good and an exporting country which is too small to be able to influence world prices, exchange rate pass-through must be zero.

One step further, another refinement can be done in looking at different export markets at one time. The focus is then on how export prices to different countries evolve in relation to each other as a result of relative cost shifts. This third approach is called *pricing to market*.

Figure 1 illustrates these approaches. It shows three countries, *A, B,* and *C*, and their import, export, and domestic production sectors. Studies that have the law of one price as subject generally sample prices of comparable products, one of which is produced and sold in country *A*, and the other is produced and sold in country *B*. However, studies differ according to the definition of the range of products. Some focus on narrowly defined SITC product categories or on goods that are a priori homogeneous, such as gold (see, e.g., Prakash and Taylor 1997). Other approaches use sectoral aggregates, and macroeconomic approaches which include the exchange rate as an endogenous variable use national aggregates such as the producer or consumer price indices. The problem inherent in all these approaches is that, when manufacturing products are included, products from different countries are substitutes rather than completely identical goods, so different prices cannot been taken as a proof for market imperfections.

Figure 1: Various Approaches to International Price Comparisons

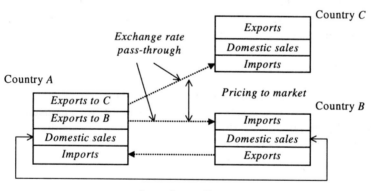

Law of one price

The approach of exchange rate pass-through, on the other hand, looks at transaction prices of trade flows between countries, which do not include nontradable products. However, although the problem of comparing product classification across countries can be avoided, there is still the need to compare price changes with local production cost shifts in order to compute the exact amount of pass-through. The standard empirical pricing-to-market approach is a little more elegant in circumventing this problem of cost measurement because it uses the price of exports from country A to country B and compares it to the export price from country A to country C. With this approach one obtains an implicit measure for the unobservable marginal cost as the common price component to all export regions (see, e.g., Knetter 1993, 1995). Pricing to market can thus be seen as differential pass-through between two different markets.

I.   The Real Exchange Rate and Purchasing Power Parity

The concept of purchasing power parity (PPP) can be defined in its absolute and relative form. The absolute form says that prices in two different countries must be identical when converted by the nominal exchange rate. Another way to express the same idea is that the law of one price holds for all products between countries due to goods market arbitrage. The preconditions for the law of one price to hold are profit maximization and costless transportation, distribution, and resale (see, e.g., Goldberg and Knetter 1997). If p_i^{rs} is defined as the price of product i which is produced in country r and sold in country s, then purchasing power parity requires that all prices p_i^{rs} are identical for all pairs of r and s when all prices are expressed in any arbitrary but identical currency. In particular, for a given export country A and importing countries B and C, it must hold that

(B.1) $p_i^{AA} = p_i^{AB} = p_i^{AC}$.

The price must be identical irrespective of where the product, which originated in country A, is consumed. It must also hold that for a particular importing country B, the prices over all countries of origin, i.e., countries A and D and country B itself, are identical:

(B.2) $p_i^{AB} = p_i^{BB} = p_i^{DB}$.

It is quite obvious that the second condition is less likely to hold in reality if one considers differentiated products which are producer-specific product variants differing in quality and therefore in price.

Suppose the law of one price holds for each good. It must then also hold for a basket of goods. The difficulty in the empirical implementation is that internationally identical baskets of goods have to be constructed, so empirical studies in this direction are rare. One influential contribution in this field is the study of

Summers and Heston (1991), which has revealed noticeable differences in price levels, particularly between low-income and high-income countries. Other theoretically plausible reasons why absolute prices may differ are that costs of transportation and resale are not zero. This is what empirical studies on the law of one price for a single product such as for the magazine *The Economist* (Ghosh and Wolf 1994) show, whereas for Big Mac hamburgers (Cumby 1996) quite a strong reversion to the law of one price with cross-section data has been detected. Another more practical reason that absolute PPP is hard to detect lies in the fact that most of the empirical studies on PPP use consumption or producer (or wholesale) price indices instead of baskets. The problem with indices, however, is that the relevant baskets may differ between countries. Written in terms of price indices, the absolute PPP can be expressed as:

(B.3) $P^A = P^B e^{AB}$,

where P^A and P^B, written in capital letters, denote aggregate country-specific price levels in their respective national currency, and e^{AB} is the nominal exchange rate in terms of currency units of country A which have to be paid for one currency unit of country B.[1] The range of goods covered depends on the use of the specific index. Whereas the producer price index includes only domestically produced goods, the consumption price index includes also imports as part of the basis for price comparison.

The remedy for all those three shortcomings with respect to absolute PPP may be the inclusion of constant price differentials between countries, which leads us to the purchasing power parity in its relative form

(B.4) $P^A = kP^B e^{AB}$,

where k is a nonzero constant. For log-differenced price indices it holds that

(B.5) $\Delta \log(P^A) = \Delta \log(P^B) + \Delta \log(e^{AB})$.

Irrespective of constant price differentials between countries, the idea is that changes in relative price indices lead to exchange rate changes of an equal amount. With the exchange rate being conceived as of being the dependent variable, since prices are generally seen to be substantially persistent, the most often used index is the consumption price index, because it covers a relatively broad spectrum of goods thus being able to have an impact on the exchange rate.

---

[1]   Compare Figure 5.8 in Siebert (1999).

There are numerous advances for testing the relative PPP.[2] The earlier tests on PPP take PPP as the null hypothesis in estimating the relationship between relative price indices and the nominal exchange rate in levels. In addition to the inadequate allowance for possibly nonstationary data, those studies did not model the endogeneity of prices in a simultaneous equation framework.

Tests based on the random walk for the real exchange rate as the null hypothesis are, for example, from Huizinga (1987) and Meese and Rogoff (1988). The real exchange rate based on consumer price indices $RERP^{rs}$ is defined as the nominal exchange rate adjusted by the consumer price indices of the respective countries:

$$(B.6) \quad RERP^{AB} \equiv e^{AB} \frac{P^B}{P^A}.$$

If PPP always holds, and the nominal exchange rate adjusts such that (B.6) holds, the real exchange rate $RERP^{AB}$ then must take the value $1/k$. Tests of stationarity then determine whether the real exchange rate shows a long-run tendency to move toward a constant value which represents $1/k$. The test which has to be implemented is thus whether the log of the real exchange rate is stationary:

$$(B.7) \quad \log\!\left(RERP^{AB}\right) \equiv \log\!\left(e^{AB}\right) + \log\!\left(P^B\right) - \log\!\left(P^A\right).$$

The notion is that if real exchange rates are proven to be stationary, the shocks that move real exchange rates away from equilibrium die out over time, and a tendency toward mean reversion holds. By contrast, the null hypothesis of a random walk poses that shocks change the expected value of a time series permanently one by one (in addition to a probable drift), so that, even after a strong real appreciation has occurred, the real exchange rate is not more likely to depreciate than to further appreciate. However, in view of the high volatility of nominal exchange rates, these approaches have difficulties in distinguishing between mean reversion and the random walk for the real exchange rate, therefore suffering from low power to reject the null of the random walk by means of the Dickey–Fuller or augmented Dickey–Fuller tests (Dickey and Fuller 1979).

Among the successful approaches to discover mean reversion are either those approaches which use very long time series going back at least to the Bretton Woods era or which also use cross-section data in addition to pure time series in order to enhance the level of significance in the mean reversion tests. Concerning the first group of tests, Frankel (1986) is one of the first to use long-horizon time series. By use of the Dickey–Fuller test, he rejects the null hypothesis of a ran-

---

2   A fairly broad overview and classification of the different approaches is given in Froot and Rogoff (1995) and in Rogoff (1996).

dom walk and computed a value for the half-life of deviations from PPP of 4.6 year, implying that an initial deviation from PPP is expected to be cut by one-half after 4.6 years on average. Abuaf and Jorion (1990) and Lothian and Taylor (1996) also rejected the random walk and found a half-life that was somewhat smaller than the one estimated by Frankel. To the second group of tests employ-ing panel data belong the studies of Frankel and Rose (1995) who used quite a large cross section of countries, and Wei and Parsley (1995) who were two of the few to cover only sectors of tradable goods. Interestingly, these panel studies also found half-lives of a bit more than four years, thus being in line with esti-mates using long-horizon data. Quite contrary to expectations, however, the con-centration of Wei and Parsley on only tradable sectors[3] did not lead to smaller half-lives relative to other studies. Still, O'Connell (1998) warns that the enthu-siasm over the easiness to find mean reverting processes in panel data might be unjustified. He points out that one possible problem with panel data may arise if cross-sectional real exchange rates are contemporaneously correlated, so that there is in fact less independent variation in the single series. As a consequence, the actual critical values for rejecting the random walk for the panel are higher than assumed.

Later PPP tests are those which use cointegration techniques (for the founda-tions of cointegration, see Engle and Granger (1987)). Contrary to the tests for stationarity of real exchange rates, cointegration tests also allow a more general linear combination h of relative prices and the nominal exchange rate in their search for stationarity:

$$(B.8) \quad h \equiv \log(e^{AB}) + \vartheta \log(P^B) - \vartheta \log(P^A).$$

Contrary to the definition of the real exchange rate *RERP*, ϑ is not restricted to be one. There have been quite a few studies on simple cointegration tests like this. However, Froot and Rogoff (1995) doubt whether these contributions pro-vide much more insight compared to the restricted stationarity tests.

The very latest group of approaches account for the role of each of the three single variables in the adjustment process from the definition of the real ex-change rate by applying Johansen's (1988) maximum likelihood procedure. Hansen (1998) includes structural equations for money demand in the estimation of cointegrating relations within a vector error correction (VEC) model in order to arrive at sound identifying restrictions. Starting from the null hypothesis of

---

[3]   The criterion for distinction of sectors producing tradables from those producing non-tradables was the trade share of production of 10 percent, following De Gregorio et al. (1994).

PPP, he shows that the relative money demand cointegration relation determines the exchange rate between the German mark and the U.S. dollar.

To conclude, there seems to be little doubt that PPP holds in the long run. However, studies which do not assume the null hypothesis of PPP to hold a priori often find it difficult to prove PPP, especially when they are applied to periods with volatile exchange rates, for example, the post–Bretton Woods era, rather than for fixed exchange rate regimes. Moreover, there is still no consensus as to why the adjustment to PPP takes such a long time. The puzzle seems even to be greater if one acknowledges that nominal exchange rates under flexible exchange rate regimes are commonly quick to adjust, as is evidenced by high empirical exchange rate volatilities. Whereas this study does not attempt to go deeper into nominal exchange rate explanation, the role of the price variables in the adjustment process is highlighted later on. For that purpose, it is of interest to look in greater detail at prices of traded goods because, firstly, they refer to goods which are more or less substitutable in the world goods market, in contrast to nontraded goods where international price differentials are easier to be justified. Secondly, it is international trade and, more specifically, the international trade balance which should play a role in the adjustment process of the real economy. For now, it is sufficient to indicate that imperfect pass-through of domestic cost or exchange rate changes into prices of exported products is crucial for the kind of adjustment process, as is discussed in Chapter F. The literature on pass-through is reviewed briefly in the following Section II.

II.   Cost and Exchange Rate Pass-Through

Pass-through generally refers to the prices of goods which cross the borders. Exchange rate pass-through (ERPT) is defined as the percentage change in local currency import prices when the exchange rate between the exporting and importing country changes one percent (see, e.g., Goldberg and Knetter 1997). The concept of pass-through can be specified to cost changes (cost pass-through) or to specific cost components such as tariffs (tariff pass-through). In some cases, the label *pass-through* is also used for domestic prices, e.g., in Feinberg (1986), who studied the impact of exchange rate changes on German domestic producer prices.

To grasp the pass-through relationship more formally, let export prices of product i from country r to country s in currency of the exporting country r be defined as $p_i^{r*s} = p_i^{rs}e^{rs}$, where the star indicates that contrary to the rule defined above, the price refers to the currency of the exporter's country rather than importer's one.

If one defines the markup factor M as the ratio of prices over marginal costs of production MC, both measured in the currency of the producer, i.e.,

$$\text{(B.9)} \quad M_i^{AB} \equiv \frac{p_i^{A*B}}{MC_i} \equiv \frac{p_i^{AB} e_i^{AB}}{MC_i} \equiv \frac{p_i^{AB}}{MC_i / e_i^{AB}},$$

then the price equation can be written as

$$\text{(B.10)} \quad p_i^{AB} = M_i^{AB} MC_i \frac{1}{e_i^{AB}}.$$

It is evident that a sufficient condition for full pass-through is that both marginal costs and the markup factor do not change in response to exchange rate changes. With constant marginal costs, pass-through is incomplete if importer's prices rise less than proportionately to an appreciation of the exporter's currency because a part of the exchange rate change is absorbed by a cut in the markup factor. It is straightforward to assume that the markup is a function of the nominal exchange rate, the marginal costs of the exporter, and the level of prices (or costs)[4] prevailing in the importing country:

$$\text{(B.11)} \quad M_i^{AB} = f\left(e_i^{AB}, MC_i^A, MC_i^B\right).$$

It is also justified to assume that the markup is a homogeneous function of degree zero in these variables, so that only relative marginal costs matter:

$$\text{(B.12)} \quad M_i^{AB} = f\left(\frac{e^{AB} MC_i^B}{MC_i^A}\right).$$

If only macroeconomic cost aggregates can be observed in the empirical implementation one may combine all three exogenous variables in only one variable, the ratio of domestic and foreign costs, compared in the same currency,

---

[4]   The exact equality of the price and cost level in the importing country only holds if the exporting country is small, so that prices of foreign substitutes in the importing country do not shift relative to foreign costs due to import competition from the exporter. This assumption will be relaxed in Chapter C.

which equals the concept of the real exchange rate based on production costs $(RERC)$:[5]

(B.13) $M_i^{AB} = f\left(RERC^{AB}\right)$.

Interest in the subject of pass-through has grown in recent years when economists have searched for explanations for the remarkable relative inaction of trade balances with respect to exchange rate changes. This puzzle was even greater given the general approval in the empirical literature that the Marshall–Lerner condition is satisfied for most countries (for an overview, see, e.g., Goldstein and Khan 1985), suggesting that export and import elasticities are sufficiently large for the trade balance to react normally to exchange rate changes. That is why estimates of exchange rate pass-through became important. Even when export demand is very elastic with respect to changes in relative prices between countries, reactions of trade flows can be muted if exchange rate changes are incompletely transmitted into import prices in the importer's currency.[6]

Concerning empirical findings, Kreinin (1977) was one of the first to detect incomplete pass-through. He also found that the pass-through into import prices is higher for smaller countries than for relatively large countries. However, he only considered a very small time period with a monodirectional currency alignment. Hooper and Mann (1989) found similar effects for exchange rate and cost pass-through. Depending on the lag structure, they found pass-through coefficients[7] between 60 and 74 percent for aggregate U.S. manufacturing. A disaggregate study for U.S. imports covering particular goods was conducted by Feenstra (1989), with most pass-through coefficients being also in that range. In addition, he found that pass-through is symmetric for tariff and exchange rate changes. Athukorala and Menon (1995) focused on a small exporting country like Sweden and also corroborated the finding of imperfect pass-through. On the other hand, they still came across positive pass-through coefficients even in sectors in which Sweden has a small export share in the world market.[8]

---

5   In the empirical counterpart, the expression *relative unit labor costs* will be used, which is reciprocal to the *real exchange rate based on unit labor costs*.

6   Another explanation for why adjustment of the trade balance takes such a long time are the low short-run quantity elasticities with respect to prices, so that a J-curve of adjustment may result: In the short run, the trade balance may deteriorate as a result of a currency depreciation, whereas in the long run the reaction is positive (Siebert 2000a).

7   The pass-through coefficient is 100 percent if pass-through is complete and zero when there is no pass-through at all.

8   This finding may be attributed to the fact that they covered predominantly sectors producing differentiated products, where even small suppliers have still some monopolistic pricing power and do not take world market prices as given.

What do the results of incomplete pass-through tell about the nature of competition in goods markets? As pointed out by Kreinin (1977) and Goldberg and Knetter (1997), incomplete pass-through may be indicative of incomplete adjustment. On the other hand, incomplete pass-through can be totally in compliance with the law of one price, which is the case if the exporter is able to influence partly the common world market price dominating in the integrated world market. The relationship between market integration and price setting is depicted in Figure 2.

In the benchmark case of perfect competition, the unique price equals marginal costs for all suppliers. The markup factor is then always equal to one, and goods market arbitrage prevents producers to set a higher price. Equally likely, it may hold that price discrimination is not possible because markets are sufficiently integrated, but prices are above marginal costs in order to cover fixed costs. Then imperfect competition applies although the law of one price is still valid. For both cases, pass-through is zero if the producer cannot influence world market prices, otherwise there is some, though incomplete, pass-through if the producer—or the producers of the same country which are all subject to the same

Figure 2: The Classification of Goods According to Integration of Markets and Type of Competition

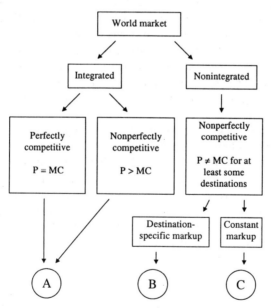

cost or exchange rate disturbance—holds some significant market share in the world market. For later reference in the empirical parts of this study, the class of these goods is named *A*-goods.

Quite the opposite holds for differentiated products belonging to the theoretical framework of imperfect competition, for which some international price differentiation may be possible without causing immediate arbitrage. This may be due to transport costs or other costs of resale or to different national product standards, cultures, or languages. If producer prices are differenced according to export region, then the rule that the price equals marginal costs is necessarily violated for some export destinations.[9] If resale costs between markets are high, but competition within a national market is strong, which is generally the case for local services which are quite homogeneous such as the supply of internet access, then the markups are destination-specific. A currency appreciation or devaluation or cost shifts in the home country of the supplier should therefore leave prices in the currency of the destination countries nearly unaltered. As a consequence, pass-through is incomplete, and in extreme cases can also be zero. These goods are referred to as *B*-goods.

Consider at last the case where competition is extremely imperfect because the differentiation of products is of such a high degree and the substitutability between variants sufficiently low that single producers act nearly as monopolists when they set prices for their respective variant (case of *C*-goods). We can find this scenario in the theoretical literature labelled as *monopolistic competition*. Concerning the particular specification of the demand schedule, one prominent representative is that of Dixit and Stiglitz (1977). In the benchmark case, prices are set as constant markups above marginal costs. The consequence for pass-through is that, as long as the markup is constant, the relative local price change equals the percentage cost or exchange rate change, so pass-through is complete in the benchmark model.

One serious drawback of the empirical pass-through analysis is that marginal costs are difficult to observe and may contain two endogenous elements (see, for example, Goldberg and Knetter 1997). The first is that, if imported inputs are used and the currency depreciates, the observation of imperfect pass-through may be partly due to a reduction in production costs, so pass-through will be underestimated. The second is via the quantity adjustment. Higher product prices in the destination markets have a feedback effect over reduced quantities on marginal costs, which are likely to decline if the supply curve is upward sloping. The

---

[9]   The case that prices are different but marginal costs are equal is termed price discrimination of third degree (Varian 1989). However, this scenario does not apply if differences in destination-specific export prices reflect differences in marginal cost, for example, due to specific transport costs, and do not reflect differences in markups.

actual markup adjustment is less than assumed, and pass-through is again under-estimated. One should therefore be cautious to make inferences from pass-through alone on the kind of competition and market integration. One approach to solving the inherent problem of unobservable marginal costs is to compare prices in different markets, and how they react to exchange rate or cost shifts.

III.   Pricing to Market

The pricing-to-market approach combines the aspect of pass-through with the idea of the law of one price in that it looks at prices in several export markets and compares how they change as a result of changes in relative costs or exchange rates. It is thus of interest to investigate the interrelationship between pass-through and pricing to market, illustrated in Figure 3. Suppose that in addition to the pass-through equation (B.10), indicating the price of exports from country A to country B, one also takes into account the export price to country C as the third country, measured also in the exporter's currency:

$$(B.14) \quad p_i^{A*C} = M_i^{AC} MC_i.$$

The relative export price between both destinations in the exporter's currency is then

$$(B.15) \quad \frac{p_i^{A*B}}{p_i^{A*C}} = \frac{M_i^{AB}}{M_i^{AC}} = f\left(RERC^{AB}, RERC^{AC}\right).$$

If marginal costs are identical over all export regions, the relative export price depends only on the differential change in the markups between the two regions. The problem of measuring marginal costs of the exporter can thus be circumvented. The relative export price is a function of the real exchange rates of the exporter's currency with respect to the two target markets. The interpretation of changes in this relative export price, which depends on both of the exporter's exchange rates with respect to the two export markets, is as follows: If those real exchange rates evolve differently and if pass-through into at least one of the two export markets is imperfect then the relative export price into that market rises where the currency appreciates relative to the other market.[10] Or, to put it sim-

_____

[10]   There may also be pricing to market, if the exchange rates of two destinations appreciate or depreciate by the same proportion, but pass-through differs between markets, for example because market shares are different (Section C.IV.2).

Figure 3: The Link between Cost Competitiveness, Price-Cost Ratios, and Relative Prices

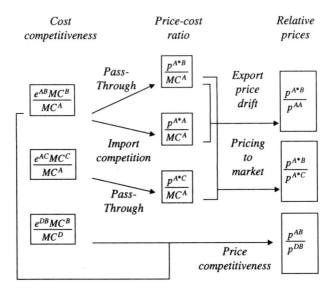

pler, firms set relatively high export prices in markets which have relatively high local prices or costs.

The single rectangular boxes in Figure 3 indicate which variables have to be compared against each other under the different concepts. The notion of cost competitiveness compares (marginal) production costs between countries, measured in the same currency. As already discussed, pass-through is a function of these relative costs and is defined to be complete if the price-cost ratio is constant.

Pricing to market is then determined by comparing the exporter's export prices in different destination markets, in this example countries B and C.

A special case emerges if one of the two destination markets for price comparison is the home market A. The other price, the export price for exports to country B, can be interpreted as being representative for all exports from country A. This change in the export price is then set against the change of the price in the home market A. The difference of both is termed *export price drift*, following the notation of the German Sachverständigenrat zur Begutachtung der gesamtwirtschaftlichen Entwicklung.[11] If the currency of the exporter appreciates,

---

[11]   More specifically, the export price drift is defined as the relative change of the export price index minus the relative change of the domestic consumer price index (Sach-

the relative position of marginal costs and domestic demand is unaffected by the exchange rate change, whereas the foreign demand and marginal cost curves in terms of domestic currency units shift downward relative to domestic marginal costs. If pass-through is complete, implying that the producer considers only the evolution of costs rather than demand conditions for his price setting, then there is no price drift and domestic and export price changes are identical. If, on the other hand, demand conditions play a role, pass-through is incomplete in each single market, and export prices fall whereas domestic prices remain stable, thus leading to a negative export price drift. However, the assumption that domestic prices are unchanged can be rightly questioned with the reasoning that domestic producers are subject to import competition. In the case of an appreciation, import prices fall if the foreign producer passes through at least some part of the exchange rate change to domestic import prices, and if imports compete with domestic products we would also see some downward adjustment in domestic prices. This, in turn, leads to smaller price spreads between the domestic and the export market. The bottom line is thus that a negative export price drift is an indicator of reduced domestic cost competitiveness relative to all other exporters in the world market, but the amount of the export price drift can differ between sectors. Sectors with relatively high pass-through will show relatively small signs of price discrimination between markets. Bearing this result in mind, even a small observed negative price drift of exports in these sectors could mean a serious loss of competitiveness.

If a shock to the exchange rate or to the cost of one of the producers occurs, the law of one price poses certain restrictions on pass-through behavior. Suppose that both producers leave their home market prices unaltered. Either the producer for whom the currency has appreciated keeps his price in the destination market constant, implying that pass-through is zero, or he raises this price by a fraction of the relative appreciation, which results in positive, but incomplete, pass-through, or he even passes through the full amount of the shock. In the first case of zero pass-through, the law of one price across producers holds, but not across countries, since the producer lowers the export price in his own currency. The relation of export to home market price therefore falls. This market-specific price adjustment when prices are compared in the same currency is termed *pricing to market*. At the other extreme with full pass-through, we observe no pricing to market and the law of one price holds across countries, but not across producers.

The questions that arise are: firstly, what factors contribute to high and what factors to low pass-through, and how can the amount of pricing to market be de-

---

verständigenrat zur Begutachtung der gesamtwirtschaftlichen Entwicklung 1996). Since the consumer price index also encompasses nontradable goods, the export price drift thus defined depends also on the intersectoral price relation of tradable versus nontradable goods.

rived from the profit-maximizing behavior of producers? Secondly, given that suppliers from different countries face different production cost shifts when compared in the same currency, how much will this be translated into different prices the various exporters set in the same particular export market?

Another interesting question is whether pricing to market is indicative of a high or low degree of competition. On the one hand, it may be argued that more competition forces producers to adjust their market-specific markups more over marginal cost because the scope for price differentials across producers is smaller. This will lead to more pricing to market, implying a much smoother evolution of prices from the view of the importing country, but at the expense of creating market-specific price gaps for the producer. On the other hand, under the extreme form of perfect competition and with perfect arbitrage it follows that all prices are identical so that the law of one price holds without any scope for pricing to market. For the law of one price to be valid both across producers and across markets, it is necessary that also domestic prices adjust to exchange rate changes, due to import competition. However, the quite restrictive assumptions necessary for perfect market integration are that products are homogeneous and that transportation and resale costs are zero. In practice, these conditions are hardly met.

C. Theoretical Determinants for the Degree of Pass-Through and Pricing to Market

It is a stylized fact that much of the trade between industrial countries is in differentiated products, thus allowing price differences to establish across producers. That is why a model of imperfect competition due to product heterogeneity will be developed in this chapter in order to explain price setting. Another feature is that a substantial amount of value added from the sales of industrial products is from additional services linked to the purchase of those products which are localized in the country of sale and therefore inhibit resale to other countries. This makes pricing to market possible. Picking up the discussion in Chapter B, pass-through and pricing to market will be quantified thoroughly from a profit maximizing framework of the producer. The literature on this subject is quite heterogeneous, with different aspects treated in individual models. In this chapter, all relevant concepts such as pass-through, pricing to market, and relative producer prices are analyzed in a unified framework, and the impact of various demand and product market characteristics will be investigated, so that intersectoral differences in pricing behavior can be accounted for.

Concerning the theoretical framework, different assumptions for market structure and behavior have been used by Dornbusch (1987), who derives the implications for price setting when the exchange rate is incorporated into some standard theoretical frameworks for price determination based on the traditional Cournot model and the modeling framework of Dixit and Stiglitz (1977). Giovannini (1998) draws on a model of monopolistic competition and also allows for uncertainty. Froot and Klemperer (1989) build a two-period model of an international duopoly and distinguish between temporary and permanent exchange rate changes. However, these contributions treat price elasticities of demand as exogenous variables rather than asking what their determinants are. Feenstra et al. (1996) highlight the role of market share for pass-through if utility is a CES function, but they do not allow explicitly for other market characteristics. A recent paper by Bodnar et al. (1997) investigates price and quantity competition allowing for different degrees of substitutability in product space. Their paper focuses on pass-through and exchange rate exposure, but does not cover the aspect of pricing to market since only one market is analyzed.

This chapter generalizes the theoretical approach of Bodnar et al. (1997) to more than two producers in the framework of a general demand system which combines several relevant determinants in a single framework. The degree of substitutability can be varied parametrically, and it thus incorporates the pure case of monopoly when there is no substitution. At the other extreme, one approaches perfect substitution asymptotically. The determinants for pass-through and pricing to market will be accounted for systematically. Of predominant importance is the number of product variants or producers between which the representative consumer can choose, thus determining the shape of the utility and demand functions.

I.   Modeling Framework

The main task which is to be performed by the theoretical model is to explain the stylized fact that there is positive but imperfect exchange rate or cost pass-through. Neither the benchmark case of perfect competition, where pass-through is zero, nor a demand function so defined that demand elasticity is constant and pass-through necessarily one, as argued above, can achieve this. One workable approach is to assume a linear demand function which is characterized by a certain reservation price implying that demand is zero if prices are set too high.[12] The intuition behind this is that when marginal costs increase, leaving the reservation price unaltered, the markup of price over marginal costs is squeezed. Since the markup is an inverse function of the absolute value of the elasticity of demand, this is tantamount to a more elastic demand.

The linear demand schedule for modeling product differentiation is quite common in the industrial organization literature and can be derived from a quadratic utility function. This specification is from Brauer (1999) and similar to that of Shaked and Sutton (1990). In order to cover an arbitrary range of own and cross-price elasticities of demand, not only the reservation price, but a second parameter standing for the degree of substitutability is used as an additional tool to vary price elasticities with a given reservation price.

Consider a representative agent who consumes N varieties of a heterogeneous good and spends the rest of his money R on all other goods, the utility of which is measured in monetary units. x_i denotes the quantity purchased of variety i, with each variety being produced by only one firm. The consumer maximizes his utility function U in each period t, which is quadratic in consumption of each single variety, and all N varieties are treated symmetrically:

---

[12]   The other determinant is the slope coefficient quantifying how much the price has to be changed in order to increase demand by one unit.

(C.1) $U_t(x_{1t}, x_{2t}, ..., x_{Nt}, x_{1,t-1}, x_{2,t-1}, ..., x_{N,t-1}) =$

$$\sum_i (\alpha x_{it} - \beta x_{it}^2 + \gamma x_{it} x_{i,t-1}) - \beta\sigma \sum_i \sum_{j\neq i} x_{it} x_{jt} + R_t, \quad \text{where} \quad 0 \leq \sigma < 2.$$

The marginal utility of R_t is constant, so the optimal quantities of the heterogeneous good only depend on their prices and the number of varieties, provided income is sufficient for an interior solution to exist (i.e., $R_t > 0$). This utility function has been chosen because it incorporates several useful properties:

Utility is increasing in the number of varieties, analogous to the love-of-variety approach of Dixit and Stiglitz (1977). Moreover, as N increases, the term which reflects the cross effects over all varieties gets a larger weight, so utility is rising only less than proportionately in N. This term also implies that each variety's own price elasticity of demand rises with N, reflecting the plausible assumption that demand is becoming more elastic the larger the number of substitutes.

The third term was added to account for intertemporal interdependencies on the consumption side. Specifically, it is assumed that marginal utility of consumption of a certain variety is proportional to the consumption in the period before. This can be due to the fact that consumers get used to that variety or incur switching costs (see, for example, Klemperer 1995). In this framework, hysteretic effects of exchange rate shocks can be handled consistently without relying on the sunk cost hypothesis if N is treated as an endogenous variable, which responds to large and persistent exchange rate misalignments. Producers who are already in the market enjoy an advantage over newcomers due to the positive impact of past quantities on demand. Small and temporary exchange rate changes do not cause exit or entry into a market as opposed to large misalignments, which bring about changes in market structure and have an additional impact on price setting. In this chapter, however, N is exogenous.[13] The following pass-through analysis can thus be interpreted to apply to exchange rate changes which are too small to cause entry or exit.

Utility maximization by consumers yields demand for variety i:[14]

---

[13] This assumption will be relaxed, however, in Chapter F, where the producer's decision to enter the export market will be modeled.

[14] Computations in this chapter have been done with the help of Mathematica 2.0. Since the subsequent analysis of exchange rate and cost changes starts from the symmetry condition of equal costs and thus equal prices of all producers and since prices are only varied marginally, demand for each variety is strictly positive for sufficiently small γ and for σ in the range given above.

$$(C.2) \qquad x_{it} = \frac{\alpha(2-\sigma)+\sigma\sum_{j\neq i}p_{jt} - p_{it}(2+\sigma(N-2))}{\beta(2-\sigma)(2+\sigma(N-1))}$$

$$+ \frac{\gamma(2+\sigma(N-2))x_{i,t-1} - \sigma\gamma\sum_{j\neq i}x_{j,t-1}}{\beta(2-\sigma)(2+\sigma(N-1))}, \qquad \text{where } 0\leq\sigma<2.$$

Consumers and producers are located in two countries, A and B. It is assumed that consumers cannot trade products between national markets, but have to buy them either from domestic producers at the domestic price or from the other country's exporters at their export price. This assumption that reimports are excluded can be justified by national product standards or additional services which are included in the selling price of the product, but consumers can only benefit from them in the country of purchase.

Let there be n^A producers in A and n^B producers in B, and $N = n^A + n^B$. The producer's objective is to maximize his intertemporal value function Π as the sum of all discounted profits of each period, restricted for simplicity to the case of two periods, where λ denotes the discount rate and c denotes variable unit costs. The subscripts 1 and 2 indicate the point of time. The first superscript denotes the country of the producer and the second the country of the buyer:

$$(C.3) \qquad \Pi_i^{rs} = \Pi_{i1}^{rs} + \lambda^r\Pi_{i2}^{rs} = \left(p_{i1}^{r*s} - c_1^r\right)x_{i1}^{rs} + \lambda^r\left[\left(p_{i2}^{r*s} - c_2^r\right)x_{i2}^{rs}\right],$$
$$\lambda^r < 1; \; r = A, B; \; s = A, B; \; i = 1,..., n^r.$$

Remember also that all prices p^{rs} are denoted in the currency of the destination country s and p^{r*s} in the currency of the production country r. Both prices coincide for sales in the respective home market, but have to be transformed, if exports are considered, by the exchange rate e^{AB} which is defined in terms of units of currency of country A needed to buy one unit of currency of country B. Since there are only two countries considered throughout this chapter, the notation of this exchange rate will be shortened to e. For the sake of simplicity, marginal costs are constant and for now are assumed not to depend on prices of imported goods. From the general formula (C.2) some special cases emerge depending on the values selected for n^A and n^B. As a starting point, I discuss the simple case of the monopolist's pricing rule first, and show whether exchange rate shocks exert different effects from cost shocks, and whether reversibility of the shock variable matters. Only later on, the much more sophisticated case of pricing in an oligopolistic market structure will be considered.

II. Nature of the Shock

Assume that there is a single firm located in country A that produces for A and B, implying that $n^A = 1$ and $n^B = 0$. Since there is only one producer the subscript i vanishes. Drawing on (C.2), demand in period t for the representative consumer in country A and B reduces to

$$\text{(C.4)} \quad x_t^{As} = \frac{\alpha - p_t^{As} + \gamma x_{t-1}^{As}}{2\beta}, \quad s = A, B.$$

Now consider the two-period intertemporal profit function defined above. Second-period prices are obtained by static optimization, whereas in the first period the monopolist has to care about demand and profit in the following period when setting his price. It is also assumed for simplicity that demand in the first period does not depend on previous sales, which are thus set to zero in the general utility function.[15] The profit-maximizing prices and corresponding quantities and profits for the two markets in period 2 are:

$$\text{(C.5)} \quad \overline{p}_2^{AA} = \frac{\alpha + c_2^A + \gamma x_1^{AA}}{2}, \qquad \overline{p}_2^{AB} = \frac{\alpha + c_2^A/e_2 + \gamma x_1^{AB}}{2},$$

$$\text{(C.6)} \quad \overline{x}_2^{AA} = \frac{\alpha - c_2^A + \gamma x_1^{AA}}{4\beta}, \qquad \overline{x}_2^{AB} = \frac{\alpha - c_2^A/e_2 + \gamma x_1^{AB}}{4\beta},$$

$$\text{(C.7)} \quad \overline{\Pi}_2^{AA} = \frac{\left(\alpha - c_2^A + \gamma x_1^{AB}\right)^2}{8\beta}, \qquad \overline{\Pi}_2^{AB} = \frac{e_2\left(\alpha - c_2^A/e_2 + \gamma x_1^{AB}\right)^2}{8\beta}.$$

Concerning future values for exchange rates and costs, rational expectations and the absence of uncertainty are assumed when determining first-period prices. Thus, the first-order conditions are:

$$\text{(C.8)} \quad \frac{\partial \Pi^{AA}}{\partial p_i^{AA}} = x_1^{AA} + \left(p_1^{AA} - c_1^A\right)\frac{\partial x_1^{AA}}{\partial p_i^{AA}} + \lambda^A \frac{\partial \overline{\Pi}_2^{AA}}{\partial x_1^{AA}}\frac{\partial x_1^{AA}}{\partial p_i^{AA}} = 0 \quad \text{and}$$

$$\text{(C.9)} \quad \frac{\partial \Pi^{AB}}{\partial p_i^{AB}} = e_1 x_1^{AB} + \left(e_1 p_1^{AB} - c_1^A\right)\frac{\partial x_1^{AB}}{\partial p_i^{AB}} + \lambda^A \frac{\partial \overline{\Pi}_2^{AB}}{\partial x_1^{AB}}\frac{\partial x_1^{AB}}{\partial p_i^{AB}} = 0,$$

---

[15] This assumption is justified since an extension of analysis to more than two periods would not change the qualitative results.

where $\dfrac{\partial \overline{\Pi}_2^{AA}}{\partial x_1^{AA}}, \dfrac{\partial \overline{\Pi}_2^{AB}}{\partial x_1^{AB}} > 0$ according to (C.7).

The last two terms in (C.8) and (C.9) are negative, so quantity is higher and price is lower the larger the direct price elasticity of demand is and the more next period's profit is increasing in the quantity sold in the first period. Equilibrium prices, quantities and profits in period 1 are:

(C.10) $\overline{p}_1^{AA} = \dfrac{8(\alpha + c_1^A)\beta^2 - \lambda \alpha \gamma^2 - 2(\alpha - c_2^A)\lambda \beta \gamma}{16\beta^2 - \lambda \gamma^2}$,

(C.11) $\overline{p}_1^{AB} = \dfrac{8(\alpha e_1 + c_1^A)\beta^2 - \lambda \alpha \gamma^2 e_2 - 2(\alpha e_2 - c_2^A)\lambda \beta \gamma}{16\beta^2 e_1 - \lambda \gamma^2 e_2}$,

(C.12) $\overline{x}_1^{AA} = \dfrac{4(\alpha - c_1^A)\beta - (\alpha - c_2^A)\lambda \gamma}{16\beta^2 - \lambda \gamma^2}$,

(C.13) $\overline{x}_1^{AB} = \dfrac{4(\alpha e_1 - c_1^A)\beta - (\alpha e_2 - c_2^A)\lambda \gamma}{16\beta^2 e_1 - \lambda \gamma^2 e_2}$.

For equilibrium values to be positive, it must hold for the reservation price α that $\alpha \geq c_1^r$ for the home and $\alpha e_t \geq c_1^r$ for the foreign market. Moreover, γ has to be sufficiently small, a necessary condition being that $\gamma^2 < 16\beta^2/\lambda$. This condition can be interpreted that consumers' switching costs are not so great that the producer gives away his products for free in the first period or even charges a negative price. If the condition of positive equilibrium prices is not satisfied then pass-through is also not meaningful implying that these cases are excluded from the pass-through analysis.

1.   Exchange Rate Changes

Since the focus of this analysis is not the level of prices but how they are affected by exchange rate or cost changes, the nature of the shock must be specified. Beginning with exchange rate changes, one has also to define a particular time structure of the exchange rate process. It is assumed that the exchange rate starts from its equilibrium cost-based purchasing-power-parity value. When local currency production costs are normalized to one in either country, the value of this equilibrium exchange rate also equals one. The first exchange rate shock occurs in period 1, and e either remains constant in period 2 or returns to its original value.

a.   *Temporary Shocks*

Assume that the exchange rate shock lasts for only one period, i.e., $e_0 \neq e_1$ and $e_2 = e_0$. Since the discount rate λ^A is constant in the currency of A ($\lambda^A = \lambda$), the relative value of future profit to current profit for a producer in A does not change with the exchange rate. Consequently, the selling price for the home country does not change with e:[16]

(C.14) $\dfrac{\partial p_1^{AA}}{\partial e_1} = 0$ and

(C.15) $E(p_1^{AA}, e_1) = 0$.

All elasticities are evaluated with e and c both being normalized to unity. For the export market B, the absolute and relative movement of the consumption price are:

(C.16) $\dfrac{\partial p_1^{AB}}{\partial e_1} = \dfrac{-8\beta^2 \left[16\beta^2 - \lambda\alpha\gamma^2 - 4(\alpha-1)\lambda\beta\gamma \right]}{\left(16\beta^2 - \lambda\gamma^2 \right)^2}$,

(C.17) $E(p_1^{AB}, e_1) = \dfrac{-8\beta^2 \left[16\beta^2 - \lambda\alpha\gamma^2 - 4(\alpha-1)\lambda\beta\gamma \right]}{\left(16\beta^2 - \lambda\gamma^2 \right)\left[8(\alpha+1)\beta^2 - \lambda\alpha\gamma^2 - 2(\alpha-1)\lambda\beta\gamma \right]}$.

Since the reservation price must be greater than unit costs in internal equilibrium, the range for α is $\alpha > 1$. For $\lambda < 1$ and for positive equilibrium prices and quantities, the denominator must always be positive, whereas the numerator is negative for small γ. If an exchange rate shock occurs, it holds for the change in export prices in the importer's currency that

(C.18) $\dfrac{\partial p_1^{AB}}{\partial e_1} < 0$ and $E(p_1^{AB}, e_1) < 0$.

If the exporter's currency depreciates (e rises), then prices in the destination market B fall, measured in local currency. For a small enough γ, the absolute value of the pass-through elasticity is smaller than one, resulting in incomplete pass-through:

---

[16]   In the following, the bar denoting equilibrium values will be suppressed.

(C.19) $-1 < E(p_1^{AB}, e_1)$.

Figure 4 illustrates this relationship in comparing the magnitude and directions of relative changes of the relevant variables. The horizontal axis measures the relative change of the nominal exchange rate as the underlying exogenous shock variable. As shown here, a movement to the left represents a nominal depreciation of the exporter's currency. Imagine, for example, that the length of the rectangular box represents a one percent depreciation. By definition, this is tantamount to an equiproportionate reduction of domestic costs relative to foreign costs, when domestic costs are transformed into the currency of the target market by dividing through the nominal exchange rate. The ratio of domestic to foreign costs, which is measured on the vertical axis, thus falls one to one with the nominal depreciation (thick arrow). However, if pass-through is imperfect, import prices in the destination market fall only less than proportionately (thin arrow) relative to foreign costs, which are a numeraire for the foreign currency and are unchanged. This arrow is representative of the reaction function of the producer.

Figure 4: The Relationship between Exchange Rate Shocks, Changes in Relative Production Costs, Pass-Through, and Export Price Adjustments

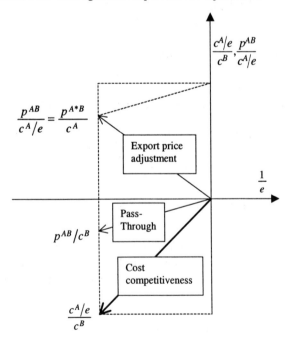

If pass-through is full, the thin arrow coincides with the thick arrow, whereas with zero pass-through, it would lie on the horizontal axis since export prices in the importer's currency would be completely unaffected by the exchange rate change. If this behavior is known, one can also depict pass-through as a comparison of the export price change with the change in the producer's, rather than the importer's, production costs (upper thin arrow). Since the relative change of the producer's production costs relative to the importer's is exogenously given and is assumed to decrease here by the distance of the square, the end of the upper thin arrow is in the positive terrain if pass-through is incomplete. The relative fall in export prices is then less than the relative reduction of domestic costs, both measured in the importer's currency, so the price-cost ratio rises. Of course, one can also compute the price-cost ratio in terms of the exporter's currency by dividing the export price in the exporter's currency by domestic costs. Since domestic costs in the exporter's currency are fixed when only the nominal exchange rate changes, the upper thin arrow then represents the change in the producer's export prices to a nominal depreciation, which is positive if pass-through is incomplete. The steeper this arrow, the larger the absorption of nominal exchange rate changes in the exporter's margin is. If the price for sales in the domestic market is unchanged, this arrow indicates also the export price drift, i.e., the relative change of export prices relative to domestic prices.

A sufficient condition for pass-through to be incomplete is that $\gamma^2 < 8\beta^2/\lambda$.[17] Throughout this chapter, it will always be assumed that the value of γ is small compared to all other parameters when the sign of an expression is computed. In particular, for the special case of no intertemporal spillover term in consumer demand ($\gamma = 0$), one obtains

$$(C.20) \quad \left.\frac{\partial p_1^{AB}}{\partial e_1}\right|_{\gamma=0} = -0.5 \quad \text{and} \quad \left.E\left(p_1^{AB}, e_1\right)\right|_{\gamma=0} = \frac{-1}{\alpha+1}.$$

For $\gamma = 0$, one can easily verify that there is always a certain amount of pass-through for any finite value of α. Since α must be at least one, the limit for pass-through is minus one-half, and the amount of pass-through is decreasing in α:

$$(C.21) \quad -0.5 \leq \left.E\left(p_1^{AB}, e_1\right)\right|_{\gamma=0} < 0,$$

---

[17] The square bracket in the numerator of (C.17) is always smaller than that of the denominator. If the sufficient condition holds, $8\beta^2$ is also smaller than the parentheses of the denominator.

So far, with γ equal to zero, prices are determined only by the movement of costs, evaluated in the currency of the importing country. However, for γ greater than zero the interest rate effect as a second determinant is also working on pass-through. The reason is that the discount rate that relates profits from foreign currency between period 1 and 2 in terms of the importer's currency depends on e_1 as follows:

$$(C.22) \quad \lambda^B = \frac{e_2}{e_1} \lambda^A.$$

Suppose that currency of A depreciates temporarily (e_1 rises), which would reduce the value of expected second-period revenue relative to the first if, as assumed, λ^A is constant, and this induces the monopolist to exploit first-period revenue more by raising p_1 above the price he would set for $\gamma = 0$. When covered interest parity holds, λ^B can also be interpreted as the discount rate in country B (Froot and Klemperer 1989).

Concerning pricing to market, the relationship between pass-through and pricing to market is very simple for the monopoly case, since domestic prices are unaffected by exchange rate changes. Determinants which make pass-through more complete therefore reduce pricing to market, and vice versa.

For the purpose of comparing prices between the export and home market, the price in the export market p^{AB} has to be expressed in currency units of the exporter's country p^{A*B}. The relation between both pass-through elasticities is then

$$(C.23) \quad E(p^{A*B}, e) = E(p^{AB}, e) + 1.$$

This formula holds for both temporary and permanent exchange rate changes. The producer's export price is endogenous to the exchange rate as long as pass-through is incomplete. To show only the example of static price setting with $\gamma = 0$, where pass-through was shown to be incomplete, the producer's export price rises when his currency depreciates according to

$$(C.24) \quad E(p_1^{A*B}, e)\Big|_{\gamma = 0} = \frac{\alpha}{\alpha + 1}.$$

Factors which increase pass-through reduce the adjustment of export prices in the producer's currency, i.e., the producer prices. Pricing to market occurs if the elasticity in terms of producer prices differs between the export and home market. If that is the case, the ratio of the producer's export price relative to that in the home market is affected by the exchange rate. Since the general relationship is

(C.25) $E(p^{A*B}/p^{AA}, e) = E(p^{A*B}, e) - E(p^{AA}, e),$

it is straightforward that pricing to market as a response to exchange rate changes necessarily exists for the monopolist since the sales price for the domestic market is unresponsive to that kind of shocks.

b.   *Permanent Shocks*

Next consider the case $e_0 \neq e_1 = e_2 \equiv e.$

As above, there is no change in the home market price when the exchange rate change is permanent. For the price reaction in the foreign market, one obtains:

(C.26) $\dfrac{\partial p_1^{AB}}{\partial e} = \dfrac{-2\beta(4\beta + \lambda\gamma)}{16\beta^2 - \lambda\gamma^2}$ and

(C.27) $E(p_1^{AB}, e) = \dfrac{-2\beta(4\beta + \lambda\gamma)}{8(\alpha+1)\beta^2 - \lambda\alpha\gamma^2 - 2(\alpha-1)\lambda\beta\gamma}.$

The pass-through elasticity is always negative for the range of parameters as defined above. For $\gamma = 0$, pass-through is again

(C.28) $E(p_1^{AB}, e)\Big|_{\gamma=0} = \dfrac{-1}{\alpha+1}.$

The differential behavior between temporal and permanent exchange rate effects can be seen as the producer's reaction to an expected change in the future exchange rate e_2, as it must be the case that

(C.29) $E(p_1^{rs}, e) = E(p_1^{rs}, e_1) + E(p_1^{rs}, e_2).$

The producer's reaction to a change of only the spot exchange rate e_1 plus the single effect of an expected future exchange rate change e_2 is the same as the impact of an exchange rate change perceived to be permanent (Froot and Klemperer 1989). The role of expectations with regard to the future exchange rate can also be shown separately:

(C.30) $\dfrac{\partial p_1^{AB}}{\partial e_2} = \dfrac{2\lambda\beta\gamma[-16\alpha\beta^2 - 4(\alpha-1)\beta\gamma + \lambda\gamma^2]}{(16\beta^2 - \lambda\gamma^2)^2}$ and

(C.31) $E(p_1^{AB}, e_2) = \dfrac{-2\lambda\beta\gamma[16\alpha\beta^2 + 4(\alpha-1)\beta\gamma - \lambda\gamma^2]}{(16\beta^2 - \lambda\gamma^2)[8(\alpha+1)\beta^2 - \lambda\alpha\gamma^2 - 2(\alpha-1)\lambda\beta\gamma]}.$

For both expressions, the numerator is negative for $\lambda > 0$ and $\gamma > 0$, whereas the denominator is positive, so that current prices always fall to an expected depreciation of the exporter's currency and vice versa. The intuition behind this result is that future sales become more valuable relative to current sales in case of an expected depreciation. Here, there are two effects working into the same direction: the future cost effect and the interest rate effect. The first one makes future profits rise relative to current profits, both evaluated in the currency of the importing country B, whereas the second one makes future profits even higher in the currency of the exporting country A.

2.   Domestic Cost Changes

The above analysis rests on exchange rate changes which in turn cause relative cost movements between countries when costs are measured in the same currency. It was argued that exchange rate changes also alter the discount rate for weighting future against current profits from exporting. To better understand the role of either component it is straightforward to consider the case that changes in relative production costs are not driven by the nominal exchange rate, but by domestic costs. This way, the interest rate effect is not working, and for both the domestic and the export market the discount rate is invariable. Analogously to exchange rate changes, cost changes can be classified into current, permanent, or expected future cost changes. However, it is now necessary to also look at prices for domestic sales and to interpret the different behavior of export and domestic prices.

A temporary current cost change has the same effect in markets A and B and causes prices to move into the same direction as costs, provided the usual assumption of a small γ holds:

$$(C.32) \quad \frac{\partial p_1^{As}}{\partial c_1^A} = \frac{8\beta^2}{16\beta^2 - \lambda\gamma^2} > 0, \quad s = A, B \quad \text{and}$$

$$(C.33) \quad E\left(p_1^{As}, c_1^A\right) = \frac{8\beta^2}{8(\alpha+1)\beta^2 - \lambda\alpha\gamma^2 - 2(\alpha-1)\lambda\beta\gamma} > 0, \quad s = A, B.$$

Compared to the exchange rate elasticity one finds the following relationship, which suggests that the absolute value of the exchange rate elasticity is smaller than or equal to that of the cost elasticity:

(C.34) $\left|E\left(p_1^{AB},e_1\right)\right| = \underbrace{\dfrac{16\beta^2 - \lambda\alpha\gamma^2 - 4(\alpha-1)\lambda\beta\gamma}{16\beta^2 - \lambda\gamma^2}}_{\leq 1} E\left(p_1^{As},c_1^A\right), \quad s = A, B,$

(C.35) $\left|E\left(p_1^{AB},e_1\right)\right| \leq E\left(p_1^{As},c_1^A\right), \quad s = A, B.$

This result is not surprising since the short-run cost elasticity does not comprise any discount rate effect which works against the cost effect.

Figure 5 depicts this relationship. The relationship which matters for pass-through is the relationship between domestic and foreign costs, evaluated in the same currency. Concerning the qualitative impact it is irrelevant for the qualitative effect whether the driving force are costs, as in Figure 5, or the nominal exchange rate from Figure 4. The further effect of the increase in relative production costs is then identical to the mechanism described above. However, a larger amount of pass-through when production costs change is equivalent to a smaller adjustment of export prices in the exporter's currency.

When cost changes are perceived to be permanent, however, there is no difference in pricing behavior compared to exchange rate changes so that

(C.36) $E\left(p_1^{AB},e\right) = -E\left(p_1^{As},c^A\right), \quad s = A, B.$

Figure 5: The Relationship between Domestic Cost Shocks, Pass-Through, and Export Price Adjustments

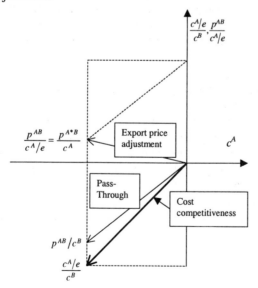

As to the role of future variables, one finds that expected cost changes increase prices in the current period. However, they do not have as much influence on prices as exchange rate changes, again because of the missing discount rate effect in the cost elasticity. Algebraically, it can be shown that:

$$(C.37) \quad E(p_1^{AB}, c_2^A) = \frac{2\lambda\beta\gamma}{[8(\alpha+1)\beta^2 - \lambda\alpha\gamma^2 - 2(\alpha-1)\lambda\beta\gamma]} > 0,$$

$$(C.38) \quad |E(p_1^{AB}, e_2)| = \underbrace{\frac{16\alpha\beta^2 + 4(\alpha-1)\beta\gamma - \lambda\gamma^2}{16\beta^2 - \lambda\gamma^2}}_{>1} E(p_1^{As}, c_2^A), \quad s = A, B, \quad \text{and}$$

$$(C.39) \quad |E(p_1^{AB}, e_2)| > E(p_1^{As}, c_2^A), \quad s = A, B.$$

Concerning pricing to market as a result to cost changes, we face the trivial result that in the monopoly model, there is no mechanism to make a difference between the export market and the home market. If demand is of the same form, pass-through is identical in both markets, and thus there is no justification for pricing to market.[18]

Summarizing the impacts of various kinds of exogenous shocks on the first-period importer's price in his currency (p^{AB}), the first row of Table 1 sketches a comparison of the qualitative results. Both a depreciation of the exporter's currency and a cost reduction in the exporting country A decrease import prices in country B (downward arrow). This reduction is even identical from a quantitative point of view, if the shock is expected to be permanent. Quite contrary, for shocks which are expected to revert completely, the cost effect is stronger than the exchange rate effect, whereas for anticipated shocks an expected exchange rate change has a larger impact than an expected future cost shift. Also note that if you add the impacts of a temporary and an expected shock you will obtain the equivalent of a permanent shock.

Concerning the price measured in the exporter's currency, a strong adjustment of export prices in the importer's currency corresponds per definition to a moderate adjustment of prices in the exporter's currency into the opposite direction, no matter if the currency shock is temporary or permanent. For only expected (future) currency shocks and all kinds of cost shocks, the adjustment of export prices is identical to the adjustment of import prices since the current exchange rate, through which export and import prices are linked by definition, remains unaltered.

---

[18]   Things are different, however, in a Cournot model with two producers, which will be treated in Section C.II.3.

The adjustment of prices for sales in the own domestic market is zero for exchange rate changes, but is identical to export price adjustments if cost changes are the driving force. This trivial result can be accounted for by the nonexistence of foreign competing products, which would constrain domestic producers also in their home market. Since this outcome is certainly unrealistic for general non-monopolistic competition patterns, a second foreign product will be introduced in the next section, and the degree of substitutability with the exporter's product will be treated as a parameter to act on pass-through and pricing to market.

Table 1: The Impact of Various Shocks on Instantaneous Pass-Through, Adjustment of Export and Domestic Prices, and Price Drift for Nonsubstitutable Goods[a]

	Nature of shock											
	Exchange rate depreciation			Exchange rate appreciation			Domestic cost decrease			Domestic cost increase		
Dependent variable	temp.	exp.	perm.	temp.	exp.	perm.	temp.	exp.	perm.	temp.	exp.	perm.
Importer's price	↓	↓↓	↓↓↓	↑	↑↑	↑↑↑	↓↓	↓	↓↓↓	↑↑	↑	↑↑↑
Exporter's price	↑↑↑	↓↓	↑	↓↓↓	↑↑	↓	↓↓	↓	↓↓↓	↑↑	↑	↑↑↑
Domestic price	–	–	–	–	–	–	↓↓	↓	↓↓↓	↑↑	↑	↑↑↑
Price drift	↑↑↑	↓↓	↑	↓↓↓	↑↑	↓	–	–	–	–	–	–

[a]The number of arrows indicates the strength of the adjustment.

III. Demand Characteristics

1. Price Elasticity of Demand

As the reservation price rises relative to unit costs ($\alpha\uparrow$), making demand more inelastic, the monopolist has greater power to set a price above marginal costs:

$$(C.40) \quad \left.\frac{\partial E\left(p_1^{AB}, e_1\right)}{\partial \alpha}\right|_{\gamma=0} = \frac{1}{(\alpha+1)^2} > 0$$

and for $\gamma \neq 0$

(C.41) $\dfrac{\partial E\left(p_1^{AB},e_1\right)}{\partial\alpha} = \dfrac{16\beta^3(4\beta+\lambda\gamma)}{\left[8(\alpha+1)\beta^2 - \lambda\alpha\gamma^2 - 2(\alpha-1)\lambda\beta\gamma\right]^2} > 0$.

An exchange rate depreciation can now be seen as a positive cost shock in terms of the importing country's currency. Due to the declining cost component in price when α rises (C.11), a positive cost shock measured in country B's currency as a result of its own currency depreciation therefore has a relatively smaller impact on price the higher α is (Figure 6). The magnitude of the cost effect is therefore cushioned by a higher markup at the relevant price, or alternatively, a lower price elasticity of demand. Note that the absolute reaction $\partial p_1^{AB}/\partial e_1$ is always minus one-half, so a higher markup (high α) causes a rise in the absolute value of the price elasticity of demand via a higher level of prices.

Figure 6: Pass-Through Elasticities with Increasing α[a]

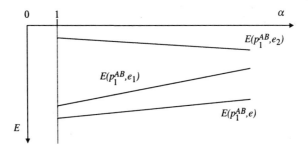

[a]In order to simplify the graphical presentation all curves have been linearized.

Note that the amount of pass-through of future exchange rate changes is increasing in α, i.e., pass-through is more negative (or at least constant):

(C.42) $\dfrac{\partial E\left(p_1^{AB},e_2\right)}{\partial\alpha} = \dfrac{-2\lambda\beta\gamma(2\beta+\gamma)(4\beta+\lambda\gamma)}{\left[8(\alpha+1)\beta^2 - \lambda\alpha\gamma^2 - 2(\alpha-1)\lambda\beta\gamma\right]^2} \le 0$.

This finding is contrary to what was concluded for the pure current exchange rate change. The intuition behind this result is that a larger α makes the cost component of the price smaller in favor of the markup component. Since the markup is variable profit per unit, it is straightforward to conclude that future profits react more to future exchange rate changes and therefore play a greater role in the current pricing decision the larger α is, and thus the smaller the price elasticity of demand (Figure 7).

Figure 7: Cost Pass-Through Elasticities with Increasing α[a]

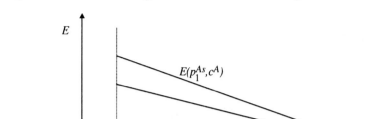

[a]In order to simplify the graphical presentation all curves have been linearized.

For permanent exchange rate changes, the first-period effect is diluted by that of future exchange rate changes, so the impact of α is smaller in the sum.

Next, I turn to the effect of a rising α on cost pass-through. An increasing reservation price and decreasing price elasticity of demand leads to a higher markup, which in turn reduces the producer's price reaction to cost changes. This result holds for temporary, permanent, or expected cost developments:

$$(C.43) \quad \frac{\partial E\left(p_1^{AB},c_1^A\right)}{\partial \alpha} = \frac{-8\beta^2\left[8\beta^2 - \lambda\gamma(2\beta+\gamma)\right]}{\left[8(\alpha+1)\beta^2 - \lambda\alpha\gamma^2 - 2(\alpha-1)\lambda\beta\gamma\right]^2} < 0,$$

$$(C.44) \quad \frac{\partial E\left(p_1^{AB},c^A\right)}{\partial \alpha} = \frac{-2\beta(4\beta + \lambda\gamma)\left[8\beta^2 - \lambda\gamma(2\beta+\gamma)\right]}{\left[8(\alpha+1)\beta^2 - \lambda\alpha\gamma^2 - 2(\alpha-1)\lambda\beta\gamma\right]^2} < 0,$$

$$(C.45) \quad \frac{\partial E\left(p_1^{AB},c_2^A\right)}{\partial \alpha} = \frac{-2\lambda\beta\gamma\left[8\beta^2 - \lambda\gamma(2\beta+\gamma)\right]}{\left[8(\alpha+1)\beta^2 - \lambda\alpha\gamma^2 - 2(\alpha-1)\lambda\beta\gamma\right]^2} < 0.$$

2.   Consumer Switching Costs

The demand schedule has the feature that demand in period t is a positive function of demand in period $t-1$, all other prices being equal. The strength of this intertemporal linkage is rising with γ implying that switching costs of consumers are rising. It has been argued that exchange rate pass-through decreases when γ

rises above zero. This can also be shown algebraically, first for the case of a temporary exchange rate shock:

$$(C.46) \quad \frac{\partial E(p_1^{AB}, e_1)}{\partial \gamma}\bigg|_{\gamma=0} = \frac{\lambda\alpha(\alpha-1)}{4(\alpha+1)^2 \beta} > 0$$

and more generally,

$$(C.47) \quad \frac{\partial E(p_1^{AB}, e_1)}{\partial \gamma} = \frac{16\beta^3(\lambda\gamma + 4\beta)}{\left[8(\alpha+1)\beta^2 - \lambda\alpha\gamma^2 - 2(\alpha-1)\lambda\beta\gamma\right]^2} > 0.$$

This suggests that a rise in γ, i.e., in the intertemporal dependency in consumption due to switching costs, makes pass-through less complete, i.e., less negative (Figure 8). The curve for $E(p_1^{AB}, e_1)$ is thus upward sloping. The producer more strongly smoothes out the effect on export prices of any intermittent movement in the exchange rate.[19] The intuition behind this is that the presence of switching costs leads also future sales to react negatively on current price changes, and the more so, the larger γ is. From the sight of the producer, this has an analogous effect as if the static demand elasticity is increasing. He is therefore less able to pass-through exchange rate changes into the buyer's import prices the larger the switching costs are.

Figure 8: Pass-Through Elasticities with Increasing γ[a]

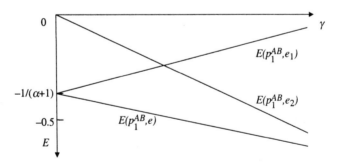

[a]In order to simplify the graphical presentation all curves have been linearized.

---

[19]   If γ, λ, and α are large relative to β, the perverse result of an adverse price reaction to an exchange rate shock might be possible. If this occurs, the discount rate effect overcompensates the first-period cost effect.

Quite contrary, for permanent exchange rate changes, a rise in switching costs increases the negative value of pass-through:

$$\text{(C.48)} \quad \frac{\partial E\left(p_1^{AB}, e\right)}{\partial \gamma} = \frac{-2\lambda\alpha\beta\left(16\beta^2 + 8\beta\gamma + \lambda\gamma^2\right)}{\left[8(\alpha+1)\beta^2 - \lambda\alpha\gamma^2 - 2(\alpha-1)\lambda\beta\gamma\right]^2} < 0,$$

The expression is negative since the numerator is always negative for the restricted domain of parameters. Contrary to the case of a temporary exchange rate shock, pass-through is not decreasing, but increasing in γ, and the curve for $E\left(p_1^{AB}, e\right)$ is downward sloping. This is because the effect of a permanent exchange rate change on λ^B cancels, and the interest rate effect disappears. What is more, the intertemporal link in consumption magnifies the effect of a permanent exchange rate shock. Take again the case of an appreciation, which is now expected to be permanent. Since second-period profit is reduced due to the second-period cost effect, the monopolist raises his price even above the level of static profit maximization, where only the first-period cost effect is effective.

At last, the curve denoting $E\left(p_1^{AB}, e_2\right)$ can be obtained residually as the permanent effect minus the static effect. It is necessarily downward sloping, implying that higher switching costs decrease the export price even more, when a future currency depreciation is expected. This is because a future devaluation increases expected future operating profits per unit sold, and the exporter lowers his price a period before in order to bind customers. He does this even more, the larger the intertemporal linkage effect γ is.

The impact of rising switching costs on cost pass-through can be interpreted analogously to exchange rate pass-through since a domestic cost increase is tantamount to an exchange rate appreciation. Just the same, a rise in switching costs leads the monopolist to charge a lower price, implying a lower markup in the first period. A first-period cost increase, irrespective of its duration, therefore increases the elasticity of first-period prices to cost changes since the cushioning markup component is reduced:

$$\text{(C.49)} \quad \frac{\partial E\left(p_1^{AB}, c_1^A\right)}{\partial \gamma} = \frac{16\lambda\beta^2\left[(\alpha-1)\beta + \alpha\gamma\right]}{\left[8(\alpha+1)\beta^2 - \lambda\alpha\gamma^2 - 2(\alpha-1)\lambda\beta\gamma\right]^2} > 0,$$

$$\text{(C.50)} \quad \frac{\partial E\left(p_1^{AB}, c^A\right)}{\partial \gamma} = \frac{2\lambda\alpha\beta\left[8(2\beta+\gamma)\beta + \lambda\gamma^2\right]}{\left[8(\alpha+1)\beta^2 - \lambda\alpha\gamma^2 - 2(\alpha-1)\lambda\beta\gamma\right]^2} > 0.$$

For expected future cost changes, future profits are reduced relative to current profits, so the producer cares less about intertemporal spillover of demand and rises his first-period price. Expected cost changes therefore lead to price changes before the actual price increase is incurred by the producer.

$$(C.51) \quad \frac{\partial E(p_1^{AB}, c_2^A)}{\partial \gamma} = \frac{2\lambda\alpha\beta[8(\alpha+1)\beta^2 + \lambda\alpha\gamma^2]}{[8(\alpha+1)\beta^2 - \lambda\alpha\gamma^2 - 2(\alpha-1)\lambda\beta\gamma]^2} > 0.$$

The impact of a variation in γ on cost pass-through is also illustrated in Figure 9.

Figure 9: Cost Pass-Through Elasticities with Increasing γ[a]

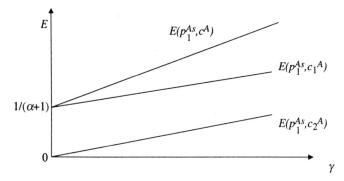

[a]In order to simplify the graphical presentation all curves have been linearized.

3.   **Substitutability between Product Varieties**

Until this point, imperfect pass-through was justified even in a very simple benchmark model like that of a monopolist. One of the mechanisms for imperfect pass-through is the invariability of the consumer's reservation price in a linear demand schedule. But this is not a necessary condition for imperfect pass-through since consumer switching costs can have a second independent effect on reducing the variability of export prices with respect to exchange rate changes. However, concerning pricing to market, the simple monopoly model produced some trivial results. Pricing to market was either tantamount to pass-through when the exchange rate was the driving force, or pricing to market was zero when domestic cost shifts were considered. Those results must be modified if substitution possibilities on the consumption side are taken into account. In order to highlight the role of substitutability in the product space, a two-product model will be analyzed next, of which the monopoly model emerges as a special case if the parameter which stands for substitutability is set to zero.

I turn, thus, to the case of two firms, one firm being located in either country. It is assumed that both firms follow the Bertrand competition model in price setting, taking each other's prices as given. For the second period, the result will be the standard duopoly result with prices, quantities, and profits of either competitor being dependent on costs in both countries, but which is augmented by lagged quantity variables due to the specification of consumer utility as defined above. The demand function for the supplier from country r in country s, which can be derived from the general expression above, is:[20]

$$(C.52) \quad x^{rs} = \frac{\alpha(2-\sigma)+\sigma p^{ss} - 2p^{rs} + 2\gamma x_{-1}^{rs} - \sigma\gamma x_{-1}^{ss}}{\beta(2-\sigma)(2+\sigma)},$$

$$r = A, B; \quad s = A, B; \quad 0 \le \sigma < 2.$$

For setting the first-period price, the rationale is analogous to that of the monopolist, and both firms take into account the effect of first-period sales on second-period profits when maximizing their intertemporal profit function with respect to first-period prices. The resulting equilibrium outcomes are as follows:

$$(C.53) \quad p_1^{AA} = \frac{k_a + k_{aa1}c_1^A + k_{ab1}e_1c_1^B + k_{aa2}c_2^A + k_{ab2}e_2c_2^B}{\left[\beta^2(4-\sigma)^3(4+\sigma)(2+\sigma)^2 - \lambda(8\gamma)^2\right]\left[\beta^2(4-\sigma)(4+\sigma)^3(2-\sigma)^2 - \lambda(8\gamma)^2\right]}$$

with k_a, k_{aa1}, k_{ab1}, $k_{aa2} > 0$ and $k_{ab2} < 0$ for sufficiently small γ (see Chapter C.VI.2 for the ks).

$$(C.54) \quad p_1^{AB} = \frac{k_b + k_{ba1}c_1^A + k_{bb1}e_1c_1^B + k_{ba2}c_2^A + k_{bb2}e_2c_2^B}{\left[\beta^2 e_1(4-\sigma)^3(4+\sigma)(2+\sigma)^2 - \lambda e_2(8\gamma)^2\right]\left[\beta^2 e_1(4-\sigma)(4+\sigma)^3(2-\sigma)^2 - \lambda e_2(8\gamma)^2\right]}$$

with k_b, k_{ba1}, k_{bb1}, $k_{ba2} > 0$ and $k_{bb2} < 0$ for sufficiently small γ (see Chapter C.VI.2 for the ks).

Concerning pass-through elasticities of domestic cost and exchange rate changes for the local price in the export market (p^{AB}), relationships similar to that for the monopolist hold. The expressions for prices (C.53) and (C.54) have been rearranged so that the impact of cost changes can be seen directly. Temporary domestic cost increases ($c^A\uparrow$) raise p^{AB}, since k_{ba1} and the denominator are positive, and p^{AB} rises even more so for permanent increases in c^A, since the second-period effect reinforces the tendency of the first-period impact (k_{ba2} is also posi-

---

[20] If $\sigma = 2$, all varieties are perfect substitutes. Under price competition, only the producer with the lowest marginal costs would survive in the market. In order to have continuous pricing functions, σ is restricted to be lower than two. The case of perfect substitutability is then approached if σ reaches the neighborhood of two.

tive). For permanent effects, it still must hold that there is no difference whether domestic competitiveness is affected by domestic costs or exchange rates. In addition, as in the monopoly case, one sees that the elasticity with regard to temporary movements is greater in absolute value for cost changes because the absolute value of the coefficient on c_i^A is larger than for exchange rate changes than for e_1 (since $|k_{ba1}| > |k_{bb1}|$). Alternatively, this is equivalent of showing that expected exchange rate changes have a larger impact than expected cost changes $(|k_{bb2}| > |k_{ba2}|)$. The reason behind this is still the same and holds for all market forms: the exchange rate movements between period 1 and 2 also affect the effective intertemporal discount rate for foreign exchange and therefore also comprise a valuation effect. The positive price effects of temporary appreciations, for example, are counteracted by the expectation that the value of foreign exchange relative to the domestic currency will be higher in the future, and that dampens the increase in current prices due to market share considerations. This would not be the case if cost changes were the underlying cause of diminishing competitiveness. Insofar, competition between varieties do not change the results qualitatively with respect to the monopolistic outcome.

What is new for the duopoly and what was missing in monopolistic price setting is that the domestic price p^{AA} is also affected by exchange rate movements, namely through the channel of import competition in the exporter's home market. Figure 10 sketches this impact, along with the relative strength of percentage price adjustments due to an exchange rate depreciation. The result that the exchange rate depreciation causes foreign import prices to decline and domestic export prices to rise, which will be shown algebraically in (C.55) and (C.57), corresponds qualitatively to the pass-through behavior of the monopolist. What is different is that the home market price, which the producer sets in its own country of production, also rises (C.56) because competing products from abroad are becoming more expensive. The amount of the exchange rate pass-through in foreign products to domestic import prices is equal to the pass-through of domestic products to foreign import prices, with only the direction of the adjustment being reversed. This symmetric adjustment is clearly due to the symmetric assumptions of production and demand in countries A and B. Concerning the price drift, one may be inclined to argue that it is not relevant for the duopoly model because both home market and export prices increase. However, the calculus of the export price drift reveals that it is still positive for exchange rate depreciations since export prices rise more than domestic prices (C.58). This outcome can be explained by the fact that domestic prices are only increased because foreign production costs in terms of domestic currency units are rising. By contrast, the export price increase is made possible not only because the competitor's costs have gone up, but also because the foreign demand curve as seen by the domestic producer shifts upward, reflecting that a given quantity of foreign demand can be sold at a higher price in terms of domestic currency units. This is the justification for the export price drift when we deal with differentiated products.

Figure 10: The Interrelationship of Different Price Elasticities to an Exchange Rate Depreciation[a]

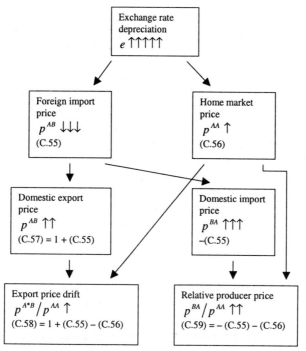

[a]The number of arrows indicates the strength of the relative adjustment of the variable in question in measuring the elasticity of the respective variable to an exchange rate depreciation. For example, the five upward arrows in e and the three downward arrows in the foreign import price mean that the foreign import price falls to an exchange rate depreciation, but this fall is proportionately less than the exchange rate increase.

With at least two countries of production one may be interested in the behavior of the relative producer price, which is the relative price of both producers in the same market and can be measured in terms of the domestic currency as the import price divided by the home market price. The relative producer price is a useful indicator for the degree of competition in a market since it measures how strong the interrelationship between the price setting of different producers is. Starting from the equilibrium condition of equalization of all prices, a given exchange rate change leads to only a small shift in the relative producer price if the substitutability between varieties is high, so that only small price differences are possible. If that outcome is observed, it can be due to either strong adjustment of the home market price, forced by import competition, or due to relative high pricing-to-market behavior.

Another new feature with substitutable products is that costs in country B come into play as a new variable, costs which are now a determinant for prices in the export and home market because the foreign good is a substitute, though an imperfect one, of the domestic good. This can be proved algebraically by realizing that k_{ab1} and k_{bb1} are positive. Moreover, both effects are quantitatively identical when e_2 is set to one. The intuition behind this that there should be no price discrimination between the domestic and foreign market for the domestic producer as long as the discount rate effect is absent due to the symmetry of demand in both countries. Cost changes in general continue to have the same effect for a particular producer in the domestic and foreign market as long as there is no country bias in demand, no transport costs, and equal market shares with respect to the number of firms in both markets. This is because there is no other determinant which makes the market in country A distinct from that in country B. In addition, contrary to exchange rate movements, cost changes do not imply an intertemporal valuation effect for export earnings and are therefore no source for price discrimination between the home and the export market.

Where the cost change takes place does, however, have an impact on elasticities. The impact on prices, both for permanent and temporary cost changes, is larger if costs change in that country where the producer is located ($k_{aa1} > k_{ab1}$ and $k_{aa2} > k_{ab2}$), and equivalently for the export market). Competitor costs have the same qualitative effect, but their impact is smaller. For expected cost changes, on the other hand, even the direction of influence differs. Expected own cost shocks increase both prices of the producer (k_{aa2} and $k_{ba2} > 0$), whereas a positive cost shock in the other country makes the producer cut prices in both markets because his second-period variable profit per unit sold will rise and makes market share more valuable (k_{ab2} and $k_{bb2} < 0$). Another interpretation of these findings is that temporary own cost shocks are smaller in their impact than permanent ones, whereas competitor's cost changes are more important for price setting if they are temporary.

Concerning domestic prices, the effect of foreign cost changes is equivalent to that of exchange rate changes for all time horizons since the valuation effect is absent for domestic sales. Note that for export prices it does matter whether foreign costs or the nominal exchange rate changes. From the values of the elasticities it can be shown that for all time horizons, exchange rates exert a larger influence on prices than competitor costs. A formal derivation is left out in favor of the following intuitive explanation suggesting that exchange rate changes also bring about a shift of foreign demand from the sight of the domestic producer, and this increases the impact relative to competitor cost movements.

Pass-Through Elasticities

In the preceding analysis, both the kind of shock and the time horizon were highlighted as determinants for pass-through. However, the results obtained are very general and do not hinge on particular assumptions for the exact values of the parameters and therefore do not explain differences in pricing behavior between sectors which differ in the degree of substitutability between products, the reservation price relative to marginal costs, or the importance of consumers' switching costs. In order to give an account of either single component, γ is set to zero in order to reduce the complexity of derivatives.

The elasticities are then restricted as follows:[21]

$$(C.55) \quad -E\left(p_1^{AB},e\right)\Big|_{\gamma=0} = E\left(p_1^{AB},c^A\right)\Big|_{\gamma=0} = E\left(p_1^{AA},c^A\right)\Big|_{\gamma=0}$$

$$= \frac{8}{(4+\sigma)[2+\alpha(2-\sigma)]}.$$

Exchange rate pass-through to export prices is again negative and of the same amount as domestic cost pass-through, with absolute values in the interval [0, 2/3]. Whereas in the limit of perfect substitutability, the value of the elasticity is always approaching two-thirds, the monopoly result also depends on α and thus on the elasticity of demand.

For exchange rate pass-through to domestic prices it holds that

$$(C.56) \quad E\left(p_1^{AA},e\right)\Big|_{\gamma=0} = E\left(p_1^{AB},c^B\right)\Big|_{\gamma=0} = E\left(p_1^{AA},c^B\right)\Big|_{\gamma=0} = \frac{2\sigma}{(4+\sigma)[2+\alpha(2-\sigma)]},$$

which is zero for the monopolist and one-third for perfect substitutability.

---

[21] For simplicity, switching costs are assumed to be zero ($\gamma=0$) from this section onward since the functioning of their impact in the duopoly model is not fundamentally different from the monopoly framework (for reference of the equilibrium prices, see Chapter C.VI.3). The impacts of temporal and permanent shocks are thus identical. However, since domestic prices are no longer independent from exchange rate changes, the interested reader who wonders how the elasticities for domestic prices and pass-through must be modified for nonzero switching costs, is requested to refer to Chapter C.VI.3.

Export Price Drift

The significance of price discrimination between the export and home market can be measured in terms of the ratio of export to domestic sales price in the producer's currency. Pricing to market occurs if both prices react differently to exogenous shocks. Since domestic prices are not independent of variations in the exchange rate, contrary to the monopolistic pricing schedule, the conclusions with regard to pricing to market are no longer trivial. It is now required to compare the magnitude of the export price and domestic price elasticities in order to tell if the export price rises, falls, or remains unaltered relative to the domestic price if the exporter's currency depreciates. In order to be able to compare both prices in the same currency units (here the exporter's currency), export price pass-through is recalculated in domestic currency. As the export price elasticity in producer prices is simply the foreign currency export price elasticity of the domestic exporter augmented by one, it holds that

$$(C.57) \quad E\left(p_1^{A*B},e\right)\Big|_{\gamma=0} = \frac{\alpha(4-\sigma)(2-\sigma)+2\sigma}{(4+\sigma)[2+\alpha(2-\sigma)]},$$

which is in the interval $[1/3, 1]$.

For values of σ smaller than 2, one obtains the expression

$$(C.58) \quad E\left(p_1^{A*B}/p_1^{AA},e\right)\Big|_{\gamma=0} = \frac{\alpha(2-\sigma)}{2+\alpha(2-\sigma)}>0$$

for the export price drift which is between zero (perfect substitutability) and one. A depreciation of the exporter's currency thus makes export prices rise more than domestic ones as long as the products are imperfect substitutes.

Relative Producer Price

As already argued, the law of one price can be interpreted either to apply to the prices one and the same producer gets from sales in different markets, or to the prices different producers charge in the same market. The latter concept is here quantified by the price differential of the foreign competitor relative to the domestic producer in the market of country A. An exchange rate depreciation causes the price of imports to increase more than the price the domestic producer sets in his home market. Its elasticity with respect to the exchange rate is:[22]

---

[22] Note that with $\gamma = 0$ the value of the price elasticity with respect to the exchange rate for the foreign supplier is simply minus one times the elasticity for the domestic producer, so that calculation of the relative producer price reaction is straightforward.

(C.59) $E\left(p_1^{BA}/p_1^{AA},e\right)\Big|_{\gamma=0} = \dfrac{2(4-\sigma)}{(4+\sigma)[2+\alpha(2-\sigma)]} > 0$.

The import price in country A relative to the domestic price always rises if country A's currency depreciates. This result can be attributed to the fact that for the domestic producer only foreign costs increase, whereas the relation between demand and his marginal costs is unaltered. For the foreign producer, however, not only his costs increase relative to his competitor's ones, but he is also faced with an upward shift of his costs relative to demand in country A, which will have an additional increasing impact on his prices in terms of the currency of country A. He will thus increase prices in market A more than the local producer in country A.

In the following, it will be investigated how the parameters affect the magnitude of all these elasticities. Starting from the monopolistic model with no substitutability ($\sigma = 0$) between varieties, σ is increased marginally, and the impact on the respective elasticities is computed. Subsequently, it will be asked how the other parameters α and γ will affect the elasticities in the duopoly model with nonzero σ, since it might be possible that the results alter qualitatively when compared to the monopoly benchmark.

Impact of σ

The findings for a monopolist in the last section can now be generalized to values of σ higher than zero. A rise in σ signifies a higher substitutability between products. The derivatives of the elasticities evaluated at $\sigma = 0$ show how pass-through changes when a former monopolist now faces the competition of substitutable products. One cannot tell a priori whether this effect increases or decreases pass-through. On the one hand, more competition could mean that a producer is less able to hand over cost increases to his customers. On the other hand, the markup component of the price, which is reflected in the ratio of price to marginal costs greater than one, is hypothesized to be lower under competition and can therefore to a lesser extent compensate for marginal cost changes in order to limit the effect on prices. In other words, under more competitive price setting, prices would be more closely oriented at marginal cost so that pass-through increases.

In effect, the amount of pass-through of exchange rates and domestic costs to foreign market prices increases in σ, so the second effect dominates. Exchange rate pass-through thus becomes more negative when σ rises:

(C.60) $\dfrac{\partial E\left(p_1^{AB},e\right)}{\partial \sigma}\Bigg|_{\gamma=0} = -\dfrac{16\,[\alpha(1+\sigma)-1]}{(4+\sigma)^2\,[2+\alpha(2-\sigma)]^2} < 0$.

This behavior is equivalent to smaller upward adjustment to the producer's export price in his own currency. Quite contrary, the elasticity relating to the home market rises with σ. A higher substitutability makes import competition more effective and thus increases both the effect of exchange rate changes on domestic prices and the effect foreign costs have on both prices the domestic producer sets in the two markets:

(C.61) $$\left. \frac{\partial E(p_1^{AA},e)}{\partial \sigma} \right|_{\gamma=0} = \frac{2\left[\alpha(8+\sigma^2)+8\right]}{(4+\sigma)^2\left[2+\alpha(2-\sigma)\right]^2} > 0.$$

The ability to price discriminate between markets is reduced to the degree that σ rises, since it holds that

(C.62) $$\left. \frac{\partial E(p_1^{A*B}/p_1^{AA},e)}{\partial \sigma} \right|_{\gamma=0} = \frac{-2\alpha}{\left[2+\alpha(2-\sigma)\right]^2} < 0.$$

In the limit of nearly perfect substitutability ($\sigma \to 2$), the value for the pricing-to-market expression approaches zero in (C.58). The law of one price then holds between the domestic and the export market, and both the export and the domestic price increase by one-third of the relative exchange rate depreciation (Figure 11).

For the relative producer price (i.e., the relative import price) in market A, however, the effect of σ is less straightforward:

(C.63) $$\left. \frac{\partial E(p_1^{BA}/p_1^{AA},e)}{\partial \sigma} \right|_{\gamma=0} =$$

$$\frac{2\left[\alpha\sigma(8-\sigma)-16\right]}{\{(4+\sigma)\left[2+\alpha(2-\sigma)\right]\}^2} \begin{cases} < & 0 & \Leftrightarrow & \alpha & < & 16/[\sigma(8-\sigma)] \\ > & 0 & \Leftrightarrow & \alpha & > & 16/[\sigma(8-\sigma)]. \end{cases}$$

The role of the exchange rate for creating this differential impact on the two producer's prices is more likely to be strengthened the larger are both α and σ. If one starts from a situation with very high monopolistic market power, corresponding to very poor ability of substitution ($\sigma \to 0$) and then makes the two products more similar to each other, the effect of this price differential is always reduced, irrespective of the value of α:

(C.64) $$\left. \frac{\partial E(p_1^{BA}/p_1^{AA},e)}{\partial \sigma} \right|_{\gamma=0,\sigma\to 0} = \frac{-1}{2(\alpha+1)^2} < 0.$$

Figure 11: The Impact of an Increase in σ on Pass-Through, the Export and Home Market Price Adjustments, and the Export Price Drift[a]

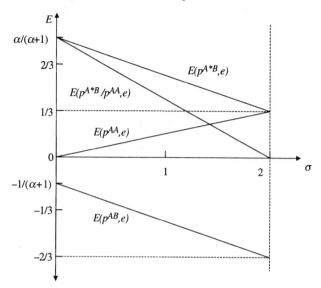

[a]In order to simplify the graphical presentation all curves have been linearized.

The increase in substitutability then causes both producer prices not to deviate so much from each other as a result to exchange rate changes. This is what one would expect a priori. For the monopolist there was no need to adjust home market prices to exchange rate changes, but when competition is emerging, he also adjusts his domestic sales price in the same direction as the import price floats, which thus reduces the price differential between producers. However, with a larger degree of competition, i.e., when σ is strictly positive, there exists a value of α which is large enough to make the relative producer price to increase with a rising σ. This may occur if demand is sufficiently inelastic, brought about by high values of α. Figures 12a and 12b compare two products which differ only in the value of the reservation price α, whereas the range of all possible values of σ can be varied freely.

The first product with a value of α marginally higher than one stands for those sectors where prices are close to marginal costs, markups are low, and fixed costs are relatively unimportant. If such a good is supplied by a monopolist, the pass-through elasticity is one-half, whereas for a value of α which is chosen arbitrarily to equal four, pass-though is only one-fifth of the relative exchange rate change. This pass-through elasticity equally applies to the prices of exports and imports in their respective target markets, implying that import prices in country A increase as a reaction to a depreciation of the domestic currency by one-half and one-fifth, respectively. On the other hand, the maximum value of pass-through is two-thirds when the substitution parameter approaches the value two, irrespective of the realization of α. By comparison, the home market price is completely sticky in the case of zero substitutability, no matter if markups are high or low. At the other extreme of nearly perfect substitutability, domestic prices are adjusted in both cases by one-third of the relative devaluation. If the markup is already sufficiently low (Figure 12a), even if substitutability is poor, the additional impact of rising σ on pass-through into the importer's price can only be small. The rising intensity of import competition, on the other hand, increases the adjustment of home market prices for import competing products when σ increases. As a result, the positive gap between the increase in import prices and the increase in domestic prices will be partly closed when σ rises.

Quite contrary, in the assumed case of a second product with a very large markup due to a high α (Figure 12b), the original impact of exchange rate changes on pass-through is very small since cost shifts can easily be absorbed by markup adjustments. The impact of increased substitutability on the cutting of margins is particularly effective in enhancing pass-through of import prices to exchange rate changes. Since in the end, when σ approaches the value two, import price pass-through must arrive at two-thirds, whereas domestic price adjustment can at best reach only one-third, so the impact of a rising σ on import pass-through may outweigh the increase in domestic price sensitivity.

To conclude, one must certainly consider the relevance of both probabilities. Since, firstly, the maximum values for price adjustment are contingent on particular assumptions concerning the demand structure and Bertrand price-setting competition, other outcomes would probably emerge under alternative settings. Secondly, the impact of a rise in substitutability on the cut in markups can be questioned on the ground that markups are determined in equilibrium at least equally by technological production conditions, such as the ratio of variables to fixed production factors, rather than the substitutability in product space alone. If σ rises, then the competition effect, which brings domestic price adjustment close to import price adjustment, should outperform the "margin" effect.

The explanation for this outcome is that a high reservation price also increases the markup of prices over marginal costs which decreases pass-through into import prices, and likewise the need for the local producer to adjust his domestic price is also less severe. Otherwise, with a moderate reservation price α, a higher degree of substitutability always reduces the price gap caused by an exchange rate change. It is the last case that one intuitively would expect to be the role of σ. To sum up, a higher substitutability reduces the exchange-rate-induced price

Figure 12a: The Impact of Substitutability on Import Price Pass-Through, Domestic Price Adjustment, and Relative Producer Prices when Margins Are Small ($\alpha \rightarrow 1$)

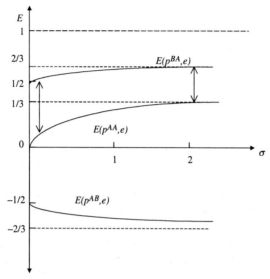

Figure 12b: The Impact of Substitutability on Import Price Pass-Through, Domestic Price Adjustment, and Relative Producer Prices when Margins Are Large ($\alpha = 4$)

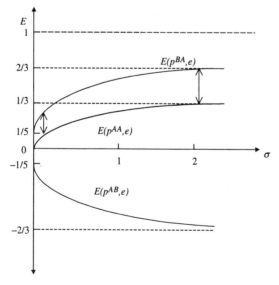

differentials both across export markets and across producers (the latter only if α is small). The general result is ambiguous, however.

The Impact of α in the Duopoly Model

It has been shown in the monopoly model, in which the existence of any substitutable product varieties has not been considered, that a rise in the reservation price α induces the pass-through elasticity of import prices to fall. Because home market prices are not at all affected by exchange rate shifts, the impact of a larger price-cost ratio, brought about by larger values of α, not only increases export price adjustments, but at the same time necessarily increases pricing to market in the form of positive export price drifts in the wake of depreciations.

In the duopoly model, however, the domestic price is not unsheltered from exchange rate changes. The open question thus concerns the behavior of import prices and the price drift when α increases. A priori, a rise in the reservation price can be conjectured to have the same effect on the elasticities as a fall in σ, since both reduce the own price elasticity of demand. This is indeed the case, as the following derivatives show. More inelastic demand, accomplished via a higher reservation price, reduces pass-through to foreign and domestic prices since price setting is mostly demand-determined and therefore more specific to the relevant market. This result is illustrated in Figure 13. Note that (C.65) is just

Figure 13: Exchange Rate Pass-Through and Pricing to Market with Increasing α

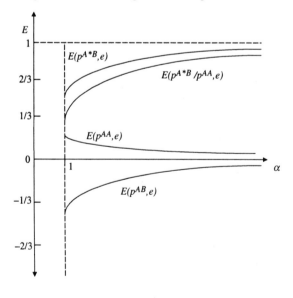

a generalization of the monopoly outcome since the latter can be obtained from the duopoly model by setting $\sigma = 0$, as shown in (C.40):

$$(C.65) \quad \frac{\partial E(p_1^{AB}, e)}{\partial \alpha}\bigg|_{\gamma=0} = \frac{8(2-\sigma)}{(4-\sigma)[2+\alpha(2-\sigma)]^2} > 0$$

$$(C.66) \quad \frac{\partial E(p_1^{AA}, e)}{\partial \alpha}\bigg|_{\gamma=0} = \frac{-2(2-\sigma)\sigma}{(4+\sigma)[2+\alpha(2-\sigma)]^2} < 0.$$

Since the export price in the exporter's currency is then necessarily more elastic to exchange rate changes as opposed to the domestic price, the strategy of pricing to market is increasing in the value of the reservation price:

$$(C.67) \quad \frac{\partial E(p_1^{A*B}/p_1^{AA}, e)}{\partial \alpha}\bigg|_{\gamma=0} = \frac{2(2-\sigma)}{[2+\alpha(2-\sigma)]^2} > 0.$$

It is straightforward to conclude that, just as in the monopolist's specification, an increase in α works toward a diminishing impact of marginal costs on the determination of price, because the proportion of the markup component in equilibrium prices has a larger weight. Consequently, as also shown by Figure 13, pass-through into import prices decreases, and, following the same reasoning, also the domestic price is more immune to exchange rate shocks. The intuition behind this argument can be condensed to the following rule: if the importance of marginal costs in price setting is negligible, then changes in marginal costs, irrespective if they apply to domestic or foreign cost shocks, have a minor impact on local price adjustments. In Figure 13, this result is mirrored by the asymptotic movement of the domestic and import price elasticity curve to the horizontal axis. The adjustment of the relative producer price as the ratio of import to domestic prices therefore declines with rising markups, i.e., with a rising α. Drawing on the algebraic derivation, one obtains:

$$(C.68) \quad \frac{\partial E(p_1^{BA}/p_1^{AA}, e)}{\partial \alpha}\bigg|_{\gamma=0} = \frac{2[\sigma(6-\sigma)-8]}{(4+\sigma)[2+\alpha(2-\sigma)]^2} < 0.$$

The volatility of relative producer prices therefore falls as a result to exchange rate changes when demand conditions play a larger role in price setting, expressed by a larger value of α.

4.   Summary: The Impact of Demand Characteristics on Price Adjustments

Table 2 summarizes the effects of changes in parameters on the absolute value of various elasticities with respect to exchange rate changes. Pass-through to import prices increases with a higher level of substitutability, but declines when the reservation price or switching costs rise. The impact on the export price drift is for all parameters inverse to that of pass-through, implying that the impact on the strength of export price adjustment always dominates that of home market price adjustment. Thus, one only has to investigate how various structural demand conditions influence pass-through in order to obtain their impact on the strength of the export price drift. This relationship holds even though the impact on domestic and export price adjustments might be of the same direction, as in the case of switching costs, which work toward an increase of both export and home market price changes, but, as a net effect, the price drift also increases.

Table 2: The Impact of Various Demand Parameters on the Strength of Adjustment in the Relevant Prices or Price Ratios due to an Exchange Rate Shock[a]

	Reservation price (α)	Substitutability (σ)	Switching costs (γ)
Amount of pass-through	↓	↑	↓
Export price adjustment	↑	↓	↑
Domestic price adjustment	↓	↑	↑
Export price drift	↑	↓	↑
Drift in producer prices	↓	↓	↓

[a]The impact of γ is shown with respect to temporary exchange rate changes. For the other coefficients, it is assumed that γ is set to zero, implying that there is no different impact of temporary and permanent exchange rate changes.

Concerning the change in relative producer prices, defined as the drift of the import price over the domestic one, the significance of this drift of relative producer prices does not necessarily change one to one with that of the export price drift. Only with an increase in substitutability, the incidence of both measures as a result to exchange rate volatility declines because the fact that products are more similar urges all price differentials to come down, and this applies to both the export price drift and the drift in producer prices. By contrast, when it comes to α and γ, things are different: a high reservation price or large consumer switching costs both imply that demand conditions are relatively more important for price setting than the cost side. It is thus no wonder that pass-through decreases so sharply with an increase in either of these parameters that the behavior of domestic prices, which constitute the second component for the price ratios, is negligible. The decrease in pass-through then induces both the export price drift to enlarge and the producer price drift to shrink at the same time.

IV.   Production Characteristics

1.   Number of Firms

It is straightforward to study as a generalization of the previous section the case where the number of domestic and foreign enterprises can also be greater than one. It is also allowed for the possibility that these numbers can differ between both markets. Therefore, n^{rs} indicates the number of enterprises n in country r which are selling to market s. The aim of this generalization is twofold: Firstly, one is able to arrive at statements about the role of market share for pass-through, and, secondly, the impact of the total number of firms can be determined.

Market share is considered first. If one starts from a situation where domestic and foreign firms have equal costs measured in the same currency, sales of each firm would be identical, and the market share s of firms of country r in the market of country s can be represented by the ratio of the number of country r's firms to all firms which sell in that market, i.e., by the ratio

$$(C.69) \quad s^{rs} = \frac{n^{rs}}{n^{rs} + n^{ss}}.$$

In equilibrium, a country's market share in a national market is thus identical to the proportion of its firms in that market.

To begin with, one first has to restate the demand function (C.2) for the particular case where the rest of the firms, the number of which is $N - 1$, is distributed between the home country r and the foreign country s from the point of view of the representative firm in country r. That is, if the focus is on demand in the home market, the relevant figures are $n^{rr} - 1$ for the number of rival firms from the same country as the representative firm and n^{sr} for the number of external competitors. If one turns to the export market, the respective figures are $n^{rs} - 1$ and n^{ss}, respectively. Of course, it must hold that

$$(C.70) \quad n^{sr} + n^{rr} = N^r,$$

which is the total number of firms N which serve market r, and

(C.71) $n^{ss} + n^{rs} = N^s$,

which is the total number of firms N which serve market s.

The demand for the representative firm n from country r in market s depends on its own price p_i^{rs}, the prices of its competitors from the same country p_{-i}^{rs}, and the prices of their foreign competitors p^{ss}. An analogous expression holds for the competitor's price. For simplicity, γ is set to zero since the mechanism behind the dynamics of x_i can be conjectured to work in a similar fashion as in the duopoly model.

(C.72) $x_i^{rs} = \dfrac{\alpha(2-\sigma) + \sigma(n^{rs}-1)p_{-i}^{rs} + \sigma n^{ss}p^{ss} - p_i^{rs}(2+\sigma(N^s-2))}{\beta(2-\sigma)(2+\sigma(N^s-2))}$,

$r = A, B; \quad s \neq r.$

An analogous demand function exists for the representative firm's home sales x_i^{rr}:

(C.73) $x_i^{rr} = \dfrac{\alpha(2-\sigma) + \sigma(n^{rr}-1)p_{-i}^{rr} + \sigma n^{sr}p^{sr} - p_i^{rr}(2+\sigma(N^r-2))}{\beta(2-\sigma)(2+\sigma(N^r-2))}$,

$r = A, B; \quad s \neq r.$

In price equilibrium, the optimality condition for both representative firms of either country must hold, and it is also required that $p_i^{rs} = p_{-i}^{rs}$ for $r = A, B$ and $s = A, B$. Equilibrium prices can be determined from profit maximization for the domestic and foreign producers leading to the respective reaction functions and then computing the reduced form for prices. The resulting prices for the supplier from country A in markets A and B are thus[23]

(C.74) $p^{AA} = \dfrac{[(N^A-2)\sigma+2]\{[(N^A+n^{AA}-3)\sigma+4]c^A + n^{BA}\sigma ec^B\}}{[(N^A-3)\sigma+4][(2N^A-3)\sigma+4]}$

$\qquad + \dfrac{\alpha(2-\sigma)\,[(2N^A-3)\sigma+4]}{[(N^A-3)\sigma+4][(2N^A-3)\sigma+4]}$,

---

[23]   See Appendix C.VI.4.

(C.75) $\quad p^{AB} = \dfrac{\left[(N^B - 2)\sigma + 2\right]\left\{\left[(N^B + n^{AB} - 3)\sigma + 4\right] c^A / e + n^{BB}\sigma c^B\right\}}{\left[(N^B - 3)\sigma + 4\right]\left[(2N^B - 3)\sigma + 4\right]}$

$\quad\quad + \dfrac{\alpha(2 - \sigma)\left[(2N^B - 3)\sigma + 4\right]}{\left[(N^B - 3)\sigma + 4\right]\left[(2N^B - 3)\sigma + 4\right]}.$

The corresponding pass-through elasticities, which are computed in the usual way, are:

(C.76) $\quad E(p^{AA}, e) = E(p^{AA}, c^B)$

$\quad = \dfrac{n^{BA}\sigma\left[(n^{AA} + n^{BA} - 2)\sigma + 2\right]}{\left[4 + (2n^{AA} + 2n^{BA} - 3)\sigma\right]\left[(n^{AA} + n^{BA} - 1)\sigma + (\alpha + 1)(2 - \sigma)\right]} > 0,$

(C.77) $\quad -E(p^{AB}, e) = E(p^{AB}, c^A)$

$\quad = \dfrac{8 + (n^{AB} + n^{BB} - 2)\sigma + (n^{AB} + n^{BB} - 2)(2n^{AB} + n^{BB} - 3)\sigma^2}{\left[4 + (2n^{AB} + 2n^{BB} - 3)\sigma\right]\left[(n^{AB} + n^{BB} - 1)\sigma + (\alpha + 1)(2 - \sigma)\right]} > 0.$

As in the duopoly framework, a foreign cost increase or depreciation of the domestic currency ($e\uparrow$) raises the price in the home market, and the quantitative impact of both shocks is identical. Furthermore, concerning export prices, a domestic cost rise and an exchange rate appreciation both lead to the same upward adjustment of local prices in the target country (p^{AB}). Note that (C.76) and (C.77) are just generalizations of the duopoly pass-through equations (C.55) and (C.55). This can be seen by setting n^{AB}, n^{BB}, n^{BA}, and n^{AA} equal to one in the first two equations, thus obtaining the special case of the duopoly pass-through. The monopoly case is also easily found by setting n^{AB}, and n^{AA} equal to one, and n^{BA} and n^{BB} equal to zero. The analogous relationships also apply for all other elasticities.

For the export price elasticity in the exporter's currency the expression is in the generalized framework:

(C.78) $\quad E(p^{A^*B}, e)$

$\quad = \dfrac{4\alpha(2 - \sigma) - (2 - \sigma)\sigma\left[\alpha(2n^{AB} + n^{BB} - 3) + n^{BB}\right] + n^{BB}(n^{AB} + n^{BB} - 1)\sigma^2}{\left[4 + (2n^{AB} + 2n^{BB} - 3)\sigma\right]\left[(n^{AB} + n^{BB} - 1)\sigma + (\alpha + 1)(2 - \sigma)\right]} \geq 0.$

When (C.78) is compared with (C.76), pricing to market can still be observed. The price drift elasticity is only shown for the particular case when both markets are identical in their structure of suppliers, i.e., when $n^{AA} = n^{AB} = n^A$ and $n^{BA} = n^{BB} = n^B$:

(C.79) $E\left(p^{A*B}/p^{AA},e\right)\Big|_{n^{AA}=n^{AB}\equiv n^{A},\,n^{BA}=n^{BB}\equiv n^{B}}$

$$= \frac{\alpha\,(2-\sigma)}{\left(n^{A}+n^{B}-1\right)\sigma+(\alpha+1)\,(2-\sigma)}\geq 0\,.$$

Note that $n^{A}+n^{B}=N$.

The pricing-to-market elasticity is declining in the total number of suppliers from both countries, again assumed to be identical in both target markets ($N^{A}=N^{B}=N$). This can be seen by realizing that

(C.80) $\dfrac{\partial E\left(p^{A*B}/p^{AA},e\right)}{\partial N}\Bigg|_{n^{AA}=n^{AB}\equiv n^{A},\,n^{BA}=n^{BB}\equiv n^{B}}\leq 0\,.$

Thus, all else equal, a fragmentation of the market in the sense that more firms are competing against each other for the consumers' choice has the effect that the scope for pricing to market is becoming smaller. Again, for $n^{A}=n^{B}=1$ the duopoly case applies, and for $n^{A}=1$, $n^{B}=0$ we have the monopolistic outcome with the export price drift increasing even further.

The impact of an increasing number of total firms in the market on the other elasticities is more difficult to see. In order to isolate the impact of an increase in the total number of firms from that of a change in market share, which will be analyzed later on, it is assumed that the number of domestic firms increases in the same proportion as the number of foreign firms in the relevant market, with market shares thus being kept constant. Concerning the pricing-to-market equation, for which the conditions in both markets are relevant, it is further assumed that the domestic firms' market share is the same in the export and the home market (denoted by s^{A}, s^{B} is the foreign firms' market share) as well as the total number of firms in each market N. These restrictions are implemented by substituting n^{AA} and n^{AB} by $s^{A}N$ and $s^{B}N$ in the elasticities equations and then letting N increase to infinity. The results are:

(C.81) $\displaystyle\lim_{N\to\infty}E\left(p^{AA},e\right)=\lim_{N\to\infty}\frac{s^{B}\sigma\left[\dfrac{N-2}{N}\sigma+\dfrac{2}{N}\right]}{\left[\dfrac{4}{N}+\dfrac{2N-3}{N}\sigma\right]\left[\dfrac{N-1}{N}\sigma+\dfrac{(\alpha+1)(2-\sigma)}{N}\right]}=\dfrac{s^{B}}{2}\,,$

$$(C.82) \quad \lim_{N \to \infty} E(p^{AB}, e) = \lim_{N \to \infty} -\frac{\dfrac{8}{N^2} + \dfrac{N-2}{N^2}\sigma + \dfrac{N-2}{N}\left(1 + s^A - \dfrac{3}{N}\right)\sigma^2}{\left[\dfrac{4}{N} + \dfrac{2N-3}{N}\sigma\right]\left[\dfrac{N-1}{N}\sigma + \dfrac{(\alpha+1)(2-\sigma)}{N}\right]}$$

$$= \frac{-(1+s^A)}{2}.$$

With the number of enterprises approaching infinity, exchange rate pass-through to domestic and foreign prices is independent of demand parameters, with the impact on domestic prices decreasing and the impact on foreign import prices increasing in the value of the domestic firms' market share. The absolute value of both figures is thus neither zero nor one, but somewhere between.

Making use of the relationship that $s^B = 1 - s^A$, for the export price the result is that it fades to zero when fragmentation is nearly perfect:

$$(C.83) \quad \lim_{N \to \infty} E(p^{A*B}, e) = 1 + \lim_{N \to \infty} E(p^{AB}, e) = \frac{(1-s^A)}{2},$$

$$(C.84) \quad \lim_{N \to \infty} E(p^{A*B}/p^{AA}, e) = \frac{(1-s^A)}{2} - \frac{s^B}{2} = 0.$$

The effect of a rise in the number of firms is thus the same on the export price drift as a perfect substitutability (i.e., $\sigma \to 2$), since both work in favor of the law of one price between exports and domestic sales. The foundation for this result lies in the fact that both factors reduce the markup of prices over marginal costs. Thus, both the domestic price and the export price follow the movement of marginal costs one to one, leaving no justification for differential price setting between the export and the home market.

However, when it comes to the relative producer price differential, which was also already shown to approach zero in the limit of perfect substitutability, this differential is not at all minimized with the number of firms increasing. This differential is calculated by using the symmetry condition between markets A and B. As already shown further above, the pass-through elasticity from country B to A is just the negative from A to B, but with s^A substituted by s^B. Subtracting the elasticity with respect to the home market price, one arrives at

$$(C.85) \quad \lim_{N \to \infty} E(p^{BA}/p^{AA}, e) = \frac{(1+s^B)}{2} - \frac{s^B}{2} = \frac{1}{2}.$$

If the exchange rate drives a wedge between foreign and home production costs, this cost wedge is only reflected in the relative prices between imports and domestic production by one-half of the original relative exchange rate change. It is independent of the market share since, when the domestic country is getting smaller relative to the world market, the import price adjustment increases, but also the domestic price adjustment increases due to increasing import competition, leaving the price differential unaffected by the market share of domestic companies, at least in the limit of an infinitely number of enterprises.

2.   Market Share

In the following, the derivatives of pass-through elasticities with respect to the share of domestic firms in the relevant market are calculated. This is done by substituting all n^{rs} by the respective expression for share s and the total number N^s and then deriving, while holding the total number of firms constant. For the home market, the following outcome holds:

$$(C.86) \quad \frac{\partial E(p^{AA},e)}{\partial s^{AA}} = \frac{-\sigma[\sigma(N^A-2)+2]N^A}{\sigma(N^A-2)+\alpha(2-\sigma)+2} < 0.$$

The larger the share of domestic firms in the home market, which is equivalent to saying that import penetration is lower, the smaller the effect of exchange rate changes on domestic prices is.

On the other hand, a larger share of suppliers from country A in the export market, i.e., a larger market share of domestic producers, increases pass-through to export prices in the foreign currency (a depreciation, for example, reduces prices in the export country to a larger extent), therefore limiting the need for the exporter to adjust prices in its own currency:

$$(C.87) \quad \frac{\partial E(p^{AB},e)}{\partial s^{AB}} = \frac{\partial E(p^{A*B},e)}{\partial s^{AB}} = \frac{-\sigma[\sigma(N^B-2)+2]N^B}{\sigma(N^B-2)+\alpha(2-\sigma)+2} < 0.$$

As to pricing to market, in this two-country framework again measured by the export price drift, it is straightforward to conclude from the results for the elasticities with respect to single prices that this drift is larger in amount the smaller the share of domestic exporters in the foreign market and the larger their home market share:

$$(C.88) \quad \frac{E(p^{A*B}/p^{AA},e)}{\partial s^{AB}} = \frac{-\sigma N^B[\sigma(N^B-2)+2]}{[(N^B-2)\sigma+\alpha(2-\sigma)+2][(2N^B-3)\sigma+4]} < 0,$$

(C.89) $\dfrac{E\left(p^{A*B}/p^{AA},e\right)}{\partial s^{AA}}=\dfrac{\sigma N^{A}\left[\sigma\left(N^{A}-2\right)+2\right]}{\left[\left(N^{A}-2\right)\sigma+\alpha\left(2-\sigma\right)+2\right]\left[\left(2N^{A}-3\right)\sigma+4\right]}>0.$

Turning now to the interpretation of these results, it is straightforward to take the duopoly framework of equal market shares (still in terms of the number of firms, not in terms of quantities sold, since the latter depend on the actual realization of costs and the exchange rate) as a benchmark. The question which then arises is: how must the duopoly outcome with a 50 percent market share be modified if this restriction is abandoned in favor of a more generalized framework? In order to increase the correspondence of the theoretical framework with reality, market shares for exporters in foreign markets of significantly less than 50 percent, rather than figures above that level, are realistic. The additional insight from this section is thus that, although incomplete pass-through and pricing to market was already observed in the monopoly and duopoly framework, the importance of these phenomena is even increased with further declining export market shares.

As long as markets are not fully integrated, implying that there exists a home bias for domestic producers which makes their share in the domestic market larger than in the export market, there is an additional justification for pricing to market compared to the assumption of identical market shares across markets.

The consequence is that if the number of national markets increases because more and more distant markets are delivered due to the globalization of product markets, reducing the average exporter's share across destinations, the export price drift becomes more significant. Of course, this reasoning implies the ceteris-paribus assumption of holding the shares in the exporter's home market constant. If, on the other hand, the predominant effect of globalization is an increase in import penetration in the domestic market, implying that s^{AA} is reduced, the export price drift would decline. It is thus an empirical question which effect is the dominant one when the impact of globalization on product markets on the export-domestic price differential is to be predicted. However, concerning price differentials across export markets, i.e., pricing to (export) market effects, the result is unambiguous since an equalization of export market shares in the wake of product market globalization always makes price adjustments more similar across destinations.

3.   Transport Costs

The next focus is on the role of transport costs as a source of asymmetry between domestic and foreign production when sales and market shares are determined. For the algebraic analysis, it is assumed that transport costs t, which are constant in foreign currency, are borne by consumers in addition to the producer price p^{rs} expressed in the local currency s. The modified static demand functions are:

$$(C.90) \quad x^{AA} = \frac{\alpha(2-\sigma)+\sigma(p^{BA}+et)-2p^{AA}}{\beta(2-\sigma)(2+\sigma)},$$

$$x^{AB} = \frac{\alpha(2-\sigma)+\sigma p^{BB}-2(p^{AB}+t)}{\beta(2-\sigma)(2+\sigma)},$$

$$x^{BA} = \frac{\alpha(2-\sigma)+\sigma p^{AA}-2(p^{BA}+et)}{\beta(2-\sigma)(2+\sigma)},$$

$$x^{BB} = \frac{\alpha(2-\sigma)+\sigma(p^{AB}+t)-2p^{BB}}{\beta(2-\sigma)(2+\sigma)}.$$

Equilibrium prices for the domestic supplier as an outcome of the usual Cournot duopoly game are

$$(C.91) \quad p^{AA} = \frac{8c^A+(2-\sigma)(4+\sigma)\alpha+2\sigma e(c^B+t)}{(4-\sigma)(4+\sigma)},$$

$$p^{AB} = \frac{8c^A/e+(2-\sigma)(4+\sigma)\alpha+2\sigma c^B-(8-\sigma^2)t}{(4-\sigma)(4+\sigma)}.$$

As can be seen, the domestic producer is able to raise his price in his home market by a fraction of the transport costs the buyer has to pay when buying from the foreign supplier. That fraction is less than one, since the denominator in price formula p^{AA} is larger than 2σ.

$$(C.92) \quad \frac{\partial p^{AA}}{\partial (te)} = \frac{2\sigma}{(4-\sigma)(4+\sigma)} > 0.$$

In the export market, transport costs are not fully passed through to customers, analogous to the result derived above for domestic cost changes. The exporter therefore lowers his producer price by a fraction of transport costs, with the magnitude of that fraction decreasing in the value of σ, the degree of substitutability of products. Benchmark cases are one-half for the monopolist and one-third for perfect competition.

(C.93) $\dfrac{\partial p^{AB}}{\partial t} = -\dfrac{8-\sigma^2}{16-\sigma^2} < 0.$

Exchange Rate Changes

The next step is to determine in what direction exchange rate pass-through changes when transport costs are involved. In the domestic market, the modified pass-through expression is

(C.94) $E(p^{AA},e) = \dfrac{2\sigma(1+t)}{(4+\sigma)[2+\alpha(2-\sigma)]+2\sigma t}.$

Higher transport costs for the competitor's product increase the price reaction of the domestic enterprise in its own market to a change in relative costs of domestic versus foreign production, as the corresponding partial derivative shows:

(C.95) $\dfrac{\partial E(p^{AA},e)}{\partial t} = \dfrac{2\sigma[\alpha(2-\sigma)(4+\sigma)+4]}{\{(4+\sigma)[2+\alpha(2-\sigma)]+2\sigma t\}^2} > 0$ for $\sigma > 0.$

The result can be interpreted by arguing that the transport costs reduce the markup margin of the foreign competitor, therefore leaving less scope for absorption of relative cost changes in his markup. The result that prices move closer to marginal costs is also transmitted to the domestic firm via Cournot competition as long as there is at least some substitutability in product space, indicated by positive σ.

For the pass-through elasticity for exports from country A to prices in currency of B, the analogous results are the following expressions, the value of pass-through to the foreign currency again being negative:

(C.96) $-E(p^{AB},e) = \dfrac{8}{(4+\sigma)[2+\alpha(2-\sigma)]-(8-\sigma^2)t},$

(C.97) $E(p^{A*B},e) = \dfrac{\alpha(4+\sigma)(2-\sigma)+2\sigma-(8-\sigma^2)t}{(4+\sigma)[2+\alpha(2-\sigma)]-(8-\sigma^2)t} < 1,$

(C.98) $\dfrac{E(p^{AB},e)}{\partial t} = \dfrac{E(p^{A*B},e)}{\partial t} = -\dfrac{8(8-\sigma^2)}{\{(4+\sigma)[2+\alpha(2-\sigma)]-(8-\sigma^2)t\}^2} < 0.$

It can easily been seen that higher transport costs increase the absolute value of pass-through to local prices in the export market and thus reduce the reaction of the home-currency export price to exchange rate changes (since the latter elasticity is positive). The reasoning behind the mechanism has just been given for the foreign enterprise. A rise in transport costs, all other things being equal, means that total costs are nearer to the reservation price α. This has the same qualitative effect for pass-through as a fall in α with constant costs, which has been already investigated for the Cournot duopoly prior to the introduction of transport costs and which has been found to lead to a higher pass-through elasticity.

The next interesting aspect concerns the relative pricing in the two markets from the point of view of the domestic supplier. The ratio of export to home producer prices changes with the exchange rate in the following manner:

$$(C.99) \quad E\left(p^{A*B}/p^{AA},e\right)=1+E\left(p^{AB},e\right)-E\left(p^{AA},e\right)=E\left(p^{A*B},e\right)-E\left(p^{AA},e\right).$$

It was already concluded that the elasticity of that ratio must take a positive value in the absence of transport costs. It is now of interest to see how that value changes if transport costs are introduced. Given the relationship

$$(C.100) \quad \frac{\partial E\left(p^{A*B}/p^{AA},e\right)}{\partial t}=\frac{\partial E\left(p^{A*B},e\right)}{\partial t}-\frac{\partial E\left(p^{AA},e\right)}{\partial t},$$

it is easy to see that

$$(C.101) \quad \frac{\partial E\left(p^{A*B}/p^{AA},e\right)}{\partial t}<0.$$

The existence of positive transport costs reduces the tendency of pricing to market. Conversely, in view of the fact that costs for transportation are generally in the process of decreasing over all broad categories of means of transportation, along with declining costs to transmit information, one would suspect that the phenomenon of pricing to market is becoming more and more prevalent over time.

Faster and cheaper flows of information across borders as a feature of integration of markets might also act on pass-through through the channel of increasing σ, which acts negatively on pricing to market. However, producers have an incentive to seek innovations, which serve temporarily as a shield from competition and reduce σ, and additionally, may even increase α, thus reducing pass-through and increasing pricing to market. For the sum of effects in the aggregate, product market characteristics thus play a predominant role.

Cost Changes

When it comes to the impact of cost changes with the exchange rate held constant, some results have to be modified. For the amount of pass-through into foreign prices, it is irrelevant whether the nominal exchange rate or domestic costs change. With cost changes, however, the elasticity of the exporter's producer price in domestic currency is identical to the pass-through elasticity, and therefore different from the elasticity with respect to exchange rate changes:

$$\text{(C.102)} \quad E(p^{AB},c^A)=E(p^{A*B},c^A)=\frac{8}{(4+\sigma)[2+\alpha(2-\sigma)]-(8-\sigma^2)t}>0\ \dot{\ }$$

For foreign cost changes the analogous expression is

$$\text{(C.103)} \quad E(p^{AB},c^B)=E(p^{A*B},c^B)=\frac{2\sigma}{(4+\sigma)[2+\alpha(2-\sigma)]-(8-\sigma^2)t}>0$$

for $\sigma>0$.

Factors which reduce the elasticity of the export price with respect to the exchange rate, such as an increase in transport costs, now increase the elasticity with respect to costs:

$$\text{(C.104)} \quad \frac{E(p^{AB},c^A)}{\partial t}=\frac{E(p^{A*B},c^A)}{\partial t}=\frac{8(8-\sigma^2)}{\{(4+\sigma)[2+\alpha(2-\sigma)]-(8-\sigma^2)t\}^2}>0$$

and

$$\text{(C.105)} \quad \frac{E(p^{AB},c^B)}{\partial t}=\frac{E(p^{A*B},c^B)}{\partial t}=\frac{2\sigma(8-\sigma^2)}{\{(4+\sigma)[2+\alpha(2-\sigma)]-(8-\sigma^2)t\}^2}>0$$

for $\sigma>0$.

These results can be interpreted by arguing that transport costs reduce the exporter's margins in his export market, so that both domestic and foreign cost changes have a larger influence on prices.

Concerning the home market, transport costs improve the producer's competitive position in his own market relative to the external supplier, leaving him a larger margin for price setting. Home market prices are therefore relatively less responsive to cost changes to the degree that transport costs reduce external competition:

(C.106) $E(p^{AA}, c^A) = \dfrac{8}{(4+\sigma)[2+\alpha(2-\sigma)]+2\sigma t} > 0,$

(C.107) $\dfrac{E(p^{AA}, c^A)}{\partial t} = \dfrac{-16\sigma}{\{(4+\sigma)[2+\alpha(2-\sigma)]+2\sigma t\}^2} < 0$ for $\sigma > 0,$

(C.108) $E(p^{AA}, c^B) = \dfrac{2\sigma}{(4+\sigma)[2+\alpha(2-\sigma)]+2\sigma t} > 0$ for $\sigma > 0.$

(C.109) $\dfrac{E(p^{AA}, c^B)}{\partial t} = \dfrac{-(2\sigma)^2}{\{(4+\sigma)[2+\alpha(2-\sigma)]+2\sigma t\}^2} < 0$ for $\sigma > 0.$

Since it holds that

(C.110) $\dfrac{\partial E(p^{A*B}/p^{AA}, c^r)}{\partial t} = \dfrac{\partial E(p^{AB}, c^r)}{\partial t} - \dfrac{\partial E(p^{AA}, c^r)}{\partial t},$ $r = A, B,$

it must necessarily follow that

(C.111) $\dfrac{\partial E(p^{A*B}/p^{AA}, c^r)}{\partial t} > 0.$

This result is contrary to what was concluded for exchange rate changes. When transport costs are declining, export and domestic prices approach each other and react in a more similar way to both domestic or foreign cost changes. In the limit without any transport costs, there is no reason why there remain price differences across export markets at all, provided that demand characteristics are identical (and other variables of importance, e.g., market share).

4.   Intermediate Inputs

Another feature of the changing conditions of production in the wake of globalization of product markets is the breaking up of the production chain, so that intermediate inputs bought either from other domestic firms or companies from abroad play a more dominant role today than they used to do. The consequence for the representative firm is that its cost structure has to be specified taking into account various forms of inputs into production. Total variable production costs therefore consist of wages and salaries for domestic labor and expenses for intermediates, with h^w being the input coefficient for labor and h^d and h^f the input coefficients for intermediate inputs bought from domestic and foreign firms, respectively. It is assumed for simplicity that the country of foreign production is also the target export country and that it is irrelevant for export, import, and home prices whether the purpose of the good is for production or consumption. Domestic unit costs are thus

(C.112) $\quad c^A = h^w w^A + h^d p^{AA} + h^f p^{BA}$,

where w^A denotes the wage in country A. The units in which the labor input is measured are such that all coefficients sum to unity:

(C.113) $\quad h^w + h^d + h^f = 1$.

Foreign competitors have the same production structure as domestic firms so that

(C.114) $\quad c^B = h^w w^B + h^f p^{AB} + h^d p^{BB}$.

Exchange Rate Pass-Through

Substituting costs into the above expressions for prices and deriving yields

(C.115) $\quad E(p^{AA}, e) = E(p^{AA}, w^B) = E(p^{AB}, w^B)$

$$= \frac{2(\sigma + 4h^f)}{(4+\sigma)(2-\sigma)\alpha + 2(4h^f + 4h^w + \sigma)},$$

(C.116) $\quad -E(p^{AB}, e) = \dfrac{8[a(2-\sigma)h^d + (4-\sigma)h^w]}{(4-\sigma)(4+\sigma)(2-\sigma)\alpha + 2(4h^f + 4h^w + \sigma)},$

(C.117) $\quad E(p^{AA}, w^A) = E(p^{AB}, w^A) = \dfrac{8h^w}{(4+\sigma)(2-\sigma)\alpha + 2(4h^f + 4h^d + \sigma)}.$

In order to isolate the effects of domestic and foreign purchasing of inputs, I start from a situation with labor as the only input and increase the amount of domestic purchases by a margin. This changes the elasticities derived above, which are computed at $h^d = h^f = 0$, in the following way:

(C.118) $\quad \dfrac{\partial E(p^{AA}, e)}{\partial h^d} = \dfrac{2\sigma[4(4-\sigma)+\alpha\sigma^2(2-\sigma)+\alpha^2(2-\sigma)(4+\sigma)]}{(4+\sigma)^2(4-\sigma)[\alpha(2-\sigma)+2]^2} > 0.$

The positive link between the exchange rate and domestic prices is increased because there is also a certain price pressure from the input side in case of a devaluation. Although purchased inputs are sourced exclusively from the home country, input prices are not immune to exchange rate changes because of competition on the consumption side.

One may argue that by the same mechanism, the negative pass-through into export prices is reduced (and the positive impact on export prices in home currency increased). However, this is only the case if the degree of competition σ is high or the reservation price α is low, i.e., when the markup is low, since the last term in the numerator is negative:

(C.119) $\dfrac{\partial E(p^{AB}, e)}{\partial h^d}$

$$= \frac{4[2\sigma(4-\sigma)+\alpha(2-\sigma)(16-3\sigma)-2\alpha^2(2-\sigma)(4+\sigma)]}{(4+\sigma)^2(4-\sigma)[\alpha(2-\sigma)+2]^2} \gtrless 0.$$

There is a countervailing effect at work which increases the weight of domestic demand variables relative to foreign ones when h^d rises. From the view of the importing country B, a rise in the exchange rate e makes α in country A go down together with wages in A, when both terms are measured in the currency of B, so that the partially negative effect on export prices of the relative wage reduction in A is strengthened by the concomitant fall of demand in A. Of course, demand conditions are only dominant for price setting when the markup is high. For a low markup, cost conditions dominate output prices, so the effect that input prices for goods increase relative to wages becomes more influential. In the second case of a low markup, pass-through is reduced since the exporter's cost advantage is diminished, whereas a high markup in the exporter's home country, which is relatively unresponsive to exchange rate movements in terms of the exporter's currency, works into the same direction as the wage effect, since wages in the currency of A do not rise with e, therefore increasing competitiveness.

For each $\sigma < 2$, there exists an α such that both effects cancel. In particular, it holds that

(C.120) $\dfrac{\partial E(p^{AB}, e)}{\partial h^d} \gtrless 0$

$$\Leftrightarrow \alpha \gtrless \frac{(2-\sigma)(16-3\sigma^2)+(2-\sigma)\sqrt{256+16(2-\sigma)\sigma(8+\sigma^2)+9\sigma^4}}{4(2-\sigma)^2(4+\sigma)}.$$

The larger σ the larger has to be α. For perfect competition, α has to be infinitely large so the cost effect of purchased inputs always outweighs the domestic demand effect and pass-through is reduced. In case of pure monopolists, α is required to be larger than one, which is always fulfilled due to the condition that demand is positive when wages are normalized to one. Pass-through is thus increasing in the proportion of inputs purchased at home.

Since domestic inputs increase the price response on the domestic market unambiguously, whereas the effect on export prices is less clear, one might suspect that pricing-to-market effects are smaller. This is indeed the result since the elasticity of the export to domestic price relation with respect to the exchange rate is becoming smaller, indicating less price differentiation with home-purchased inputs for $\alpha > 1$ and $\sigma < 2$:

$$
(C.121) \quad \frac{\partial E\left(p^{A*B}/p^{AA},e\right)}{\partial h^d} = \frac{-2(\alpha-1)\alpha(2-\sigma)^2}{(4-\sigma)[\alpha(2-\sigma)+2]^2} < 0 \quad \text{for } \alpha > 1 \text{ and } \sigma < 2.
$$

A similar reasoning applies to the differential impact of foreign sourced inputs: The effect on pricing to market is precisely identical to the derivative with respect to domestic inputs. However, the single effects on export and home price elasticities are more biased into the positive, with their relative position being unchanged:

$$
(C.122) \quad \frac{\partial E\left(p^{AA},e\right)}{\partial h^f} = \frac{16(4-\sigma)+\alpha(2-\sigma)\left[16(2-\sigma)+\sigma^2(2+\sigma)\right]}{(4+\sigma)^2(4-\sigma)[\alpha(2-\sigma)+2]^2}
$$

$$
+ \frac{\alpha^2\sigma(2-\sigma)(4+\sigma)}{(4+\sigma)^2(4-\sigma)[\alpha(2-\sigma)+2]^2} > 0,
$$

$$
(C.123) \quad \frac{\partial E\left(p^{AB},e\right)}{\partial h^f} = \frac{8\left[4(4-\sigma)+\alpha(2-\sigma)[4+(2-\sigma)(6+\sigma)]-\alpha^2(2-\sigma)^2(4+\sigma)\right]}{(4+\sigma)^2(4-\sigma)[\alpha(2-\sigma)+2]^2} \gtrless 0
$$

$$
\Leftrightarrow \alpha \gtrless \frac{(2-\sigma)[4+(2-\sigma)(6+\sigma)]}{2(2-\sigma)^2(4+\sigma)}
$$

$$
+ \frac{\sqrt{(2-\sigma)[4+(2-\sigma)(6+\sigma)]+16(4-\sigma)(4+\sigma)(2-\sigma)^2}}{2(2-\sigma)^2(4+\sigma)},
$$

$$
(C.124) \quad \frac{\partial E\left(p^{A*B}/p^{AA},e\right)}{\partial h^f} = \frac{-2(\alpha-1)\alpha(2-\sigma)^2}{(4-\sigma)[\alpha(2-\sigma)+2]^2} < 0.
$$

Since foreign inputs enter domestic production directly, input prices are reduced more when there is a depreciation, compared to the less effective channel via competition.

Cost Pass-Through

It has been argued that in the simplest model of the static duopoly, domestic wage and exchange rate shocks are identical for prices in the export market. One may be tempted to conclude that this result can be carried over when the input structure is modified. That this is not the case can be proved quite easily by arguing that the primary effect of domestic wage increases is only a rise in relative costs, whereas an exchange rate appreciation not only affects the ratio of domestic to foreign wages, but also means a rise of the domestic demand curve from the perspective of the partner country, represented by a rise in domestic α when transformed into the foreign currency. This brings about a partially positive effect on pass-through, which is missing when wages rather than the exchange rate are the driving force. The link between wages and prices thus becomes weaker when domestic goods are involved as inputs. Note that contrary to the exchange rate elasticity, this effect is unambiguous:

$$\text{(C.125)} \quad \frac{\partial E\left(p^{AA}, w^A\right)}{\partial h^d} = \frac{\partial E\left(p^{AB}, w^A\right)}{\partial h^d} = \frac{-4[2\sigma + \alpha(2-\sigma)(8+3\sigma)]}{(4+\sigma)^2[\alpha(2-\sigma)+2]^2} < 0.$$

A longer chain of production reduces the impact a wage increase has on prices in both markets. The reason is that one determinant of prices is the demand parameter α, which is unchanged, so goods inputs become proportionately less expensive than the wage rises. The effect on both markets is identical, so relative pricing is unaffected.

A qualitatively identical result applies to foreign inputs:

$$\text{(C.126)} \quad \frac{\partial E\left(p^{AA}, w^A\right)}{\partial h^f} = \frac{\partial E\left(p^{AB}, w^A\right)}{\partial h^f} = \frac{-8[4+(2-\sigma)(6+\sigma)]}{(4+\sigma)^2(4-\sigma)[\alpha(2-\sigma)+2]^2} < 0.$$

Now let me focus on the elasticities with respect to foreign wage changes. The positive link between costs on the one hand and domestic and export prices on the other hand has already been established. The effect of purchased inputs from home is again ambiguous as it is for exchange rate elasticities. In this case, however, the reverse reasoning applies. In a competitive environment (small α and/or high σ) price sensitivity is increased, but is reduced with a high degree of monopoly power. In the former case, prices are set more in line with marginal costs.

(C.127) $\dfrac{\partial E\left(p^{AA},w^{B}\right)}{\partial h^{d}}=\dfrac{\partial E\left(p^{AB},w^{B}\right)}{\partial h^{d}}$

$$=\frac{2\sigma[4-\alpha(2-\sigma)(2+\sigma)]}{(4+\sigma)^{2}(4-\sigma)[\alpha(2-\sigma)+2]^{2}}\gtrless 0 \quad \Leftrightarrow \quad \alpha\gtrless\frac{4}{4-\sigma^{2}}.$$

When inputs are imported the result is unambiguous. Increasing costs in the process of a devaluation support the competition effect for higher prices in the export market, with the latter suggesting that foreign competitors incur higher costs so that the exporter is inclined to raise export prices:

(C.128) $\dfrac{\partial E\left(p^{AA},w^{B}\right)}{\partial h^{f}}=\dfrac{\partial E\left(p^{AB},w^{B}\right)}{\partial h^{f}}=\dfrac{16+\alpha(2-\sigma)\left[4+(2-\sigma)^{2}\right]}{(4+\sigma)^{2}\left[\alpha(2-\sigma)+2\right]^{2}}>0.$

The Impact on Margins

It is also of interest to discuss the differential impact of intermediate inputs for variable profits per output unit, i.e., the difference between price and variable unit costs in the relevant market. With labor as the exclusive input, the price of which is normalized to one, the evolution of variable profit margins is identical to that of producer prices in that market. However, this identity no longer holds if variable unit costs deviate from wages. The consequence is that not only prices, but also variable unit costs are responsive to the exchange rate, or, if wage changes are the driving force, variable unit costs do not necessarily follow the same quantitative path as wages, even though wages are still normalized to one. If one defines the margin of variable unit profits m for the representative producer in country A for market A and B as[24]

(C.129) $m^{AA}=p^{AA}-c^{A}$ and

(C.130) $m^{AB}=p^{A*B}-c^{A}$.

Starting from the situation where h^{d} and h^{f} are equal to zero, the analysis of price determination in the static duopoly setting can be used to determine the relative change of variable profits due to an exogenous shock:

(C.131) $E\left(m^{AA},e\right),\ E\left(m^{AB},e\right),\ E\left(m^{AB}/m^{AA},e\right)>0,$

---

[24] Referring to the markup factor M, defined above as the ratio of prices over marginal costs, it thus holds that $M=1+(m/c)$.

(C.132) $E(m^{AA}, w^A) = E(m^{AB}, w^A) < 0,$ and

(C.133) $E(m^{AA}, w^B) = E(m^{AB}, w^B) > 0.$

To repeat just the qualitative results, exchange rate depreciations increase profit margins in both markets, but in the export market more than in the domestic one. Margins increase if wages are reduced at home or if wages increase in the other country.

I now turn to the problem of determining how these elasticities must be altered if intermediate products are used as inputs. Taking the derivatives with respect to the input coefficient and computing at the point where h^d and h^f equal zero, one obtains

(C.134) $\dfrac{\partial E(m^{AA}, e)}{\partial h^d} = \dfrac{2\sigma[-2(4-\sigma)(2+\sigma)+\alpha(2-\sigma)(4+\sigma)]}{(\alpha-1)(4+\sigma)^2(4-\sigma)(2-\sigma)} \gtrless 0,$

(C.135) $\dfrac{\partial E(m^{AB}, e)}{\partial h^d} = \dfrac{\alpha(2-\sigma)(4+\sigma)(8-\sigma^2)-4(4-\sigma)\sigma(2+\sigma)}{(\alpha-1)(4+\sigma)^2(4-\sigma)(2-\sigma)} \gtrless 0.$

Although price sensitivity to the exchange rate increases unambiguously when domestic goods are used in production, the result for profits depends on whether competition is high or low. In fact, there are two effects working in opposite directions. The first effect works on the input side, where costs increase relatively more to exchange rate depreciations when more domestic goods are used in production since wages are fixed at unity and their weight declines. The second effect affects the output side: it has already been established that the dependency of goods prices on the exchange rate becomes more positive in the home market and perhaps even in the export market, thereby partially increasing profit. In case of a relatively high degree of competition, induced by a low α or a σ close to two, the cost effect dominates, and the exchange rate sensitivity of profits is reduced. If the level of margins is sufficiently high (high α or low σ), the price effect on the output side dominates and the exchange rate sensitivity of profits rises when domestically purchased goods enter the input side.

As was concluded above, a comparison of relative margins between the export and home market shows that depreciations increase profits in the export market relatively more than in the home market. The use of intermediate inputs even strengthens this result since

(C.136) $\dfrac{\partial E(m^{AB}/m^{AA}, e)}{\partial h^d} = \dfrac{\partial E(m^{AB}/m^{AA}, e)}{\partial h^f} = \dfrac{\alpha(2-\sigma)}{(\alpha-1)(4-\sigma)} > 0.$

Note that this finding is contrary to what was found for relative prices, the elasticity of which decreases with the use of intermediate inputs. This has strong implications if one compares two sectors which differ in their share of intermediate inputs, or if one compares two different points in time whereby a smaller part of the value-added chain is allocated to each enterprise at the second point than at the first. From the observation that relative prices are more stable after exchange rate changes one cannot conclude that this also holds for relative profits. The reason is that one also must consider costs, which are more sensitive to the exchange rate the higher the share of intermediate products.

Whether those inputs are imported or are the outcome of domestic production does not matter for relative margins, but only for the strength of each single effect. In fact, the price of imports increases more than the price of domestic production in response to devaluations, the latter price being only affected by competition since the domestic good is a substitute to the foreign one. That is why the cost-pushing impact of a devaluation is higher with imported intermediate goods. In that case it holds that the cost effect always dominates since

(C.137) $\dfrac{\partial E(m^{AA}, e)}{\partial h^f}$

$$= \frac{-\alpha(2-\sigma)(4+\sigma)(16-2\sigma-\sigma^2)-2(4-\sigma)(32+16\sigma+\sigma^2)}{(\alpha-1)(4+\sigma)^2(4-\sigma)(2-\sigma)} < 0,$$

(C.138) $\dfrac{\partial E(m^{AB}, e)}{\partial h^f} = \dfrac{-2[(4-\sigma)(32+16\sigma+\sigma^2)+4\alpha(2-\sigma)(4+\sigma)]}{(\alpha-1)(4+\sigma)^2(4-\sigma)(2-\sigma)} < 0.$

The cost impact also dominates the price side when wage increases at home are the driving force. Although, as was shown above, the upward price sensitivity is reduced with domestic or foreign goods as inputs, the impact on margins is becoming less negative:

(C.139) $\dfrac{\partial E(m^{AA}, w^A)}{\partial h^d} = \dfrac{\partial E(m^{AB}, w^A)}{\partial h^d} = \dfrac{2\sigma(2+\sigma)}{(\alpha-1)(4+\sigma)^2(2-\sigma)} > 0,$

(C.140) $\dfrac{\partial E(m^{AA}, w^A)}{\partial h^f} = \dfrac{\partial E(m^{AB}, w^A)}{\partial h^f} = \dfrac{8(2+\sigma)}{(\alpha-1)(4+\sigma)^2(2-\sigma)} > 0.$

Analogously, intermediate inputs, especially if they are imported, also reduce the sensitivity of profit margins with respect to foreign wage changes, so that an increase in foreign wages makes domestic variable profits go up to a smaller extent:

$$(C.141) \quad \frac{\partial E\left(m^{AA},w^{B}\right)}{\partial h^{d}} = \frac{\partial E\left(m^{AB},w^{B}\right)}{\partial h^{d}} = \frac{-2\sigma(2+\sigma)}{(\alpha-1)(4+\sigma)^{2}(2-\sigma)} < 0,$$

$$(C.142) \quad \frac{\partial E\left(m^{AA},w^{B}\right)}{\partial h^{f}} = \frac{\partial E\left(m^{AB},w^{B}\right)}{\partial h^{f}} = \frac{-8(2+\sigma)}{(\alpha-1)(4+\sigma)^{2}(2-\sigma)} < 0.$$

V.   Summary: What Determines the Link between Relative Costs and Relative Prices?

The objective of the theoretical part is to explain exchange rate and cost pass-through and pricing to market in a theoretical framework that combines various determinants for price setting. Among the most influential factors that are relevant in this respect is the price elasticity of demand which in turn is a function of reservation prices and the substitutability between products if a linear demand schedule is assumed. In addition, switching costs on the consumption side are allowed for, which extend the model to an intertemporal one since the producer takes into account the impact of his current price setting on future profits.

It is shown that a depreciation of the exporter's currency generally leads to a less than proportional increase in export prices in the importer's currency, but also an elasticity greater than one may result if consumers' switching costs are sufficiently high. The expected result that a high degree of substitutability or a reservation price near marginal costs lead to a relatively low amount of pass-through and to less price differentiation across markets is derived. The results for the monopoly and perfect competition emerge as special cases of the general framework. For empirical investigation, this implies that estimates of price responses across sectors should be different between high and low markup sectors. It is also of interest whether the shock is assumed to be temporary or permanent, or if it is only expected for the future. Consumers' switching costs increase the effects of costs on domestic and foreign-currency export prices and also increase exchange rate pass-through to domestic prices, both for temporary and permanent shocks, but decrease the amount of pass-through of temporary exchange rate shocks to export prices in foreign currency, whereas for a permanent shock the impact is again increased.

Imperfect exchange rate pass-through to foreign prices necessarily affects the export price in the exporter's currency. In addition, it has been shown in the duopolistic framework to what extent also domestic prices are affected by exchange rate changes due to import competition. Both effects compared, export prices are shown to rise more than domestic prices when the exporter's currency depreciates, irrespective of the parameters. The differential impact of exchange rate changes on prices the producer gets for sales in different markets is named pricing to market. This phenomenon also applies here where competitive price setting in only two markets is compared, the domestic and the export market. It has been derived that pricing to market plays a great role in sectors where concentration is relatively high and in high markup sectors, since pricing to market is increasing in the reservation price and decreasing in substitutability of products. Switching costs increase pricing to market when the exchange rate change is temporary, but reduce it when the shock is perceived to be permanent. Concerning the differential of prices different producers set in the same market, it does not suffice to know whether markups are low or high, but it is required to look at each single determinant of markups.

For many export products of industrialized countries, it generally holds that prices include substantial markups and that switching costs on the demand side often play a role, so the biggest chunk of an exchange rate change is borne by the producer by means of his markup adjustment. Short-term exchange rate volatility, when compared to long-lasting misalignments, are also conjectured to increase markup adjustment, with a relatively moderate impact on prices in the importer's currency and therefore on trade flows. This is why empirical studies often find a weak role of exchange rates for trade flows relative to other variables explaining demand. Persistent exchange rate misalignments, on the other hand, pose a threat to the international division of labor since they have a relatively large impact on import prices and thus also on trade flows. When a temporary exchange rate and a temporary cost change are compared, the former leads to a larger markup adjustment since the intertemporal discount rate for export earnings is affected, thus reducing pass-through. Cost changes, in turn, are conjectured to lead to a greater quantity adjustment. Concerning the exposure of the exporter, exchange rate changes, especially if their volatility is short-termed, can be hedged more easily across export regions or over time than cost changes, which affect real exchange rates for all destinations in a uniform way.

VI.   Appendix

1.   Derivation of Equation (C.2)

In order to arrive at the demand function (C.2), utility as defined in (C.1) is maximized under the budget constraint

(C.A.129) $Y_t = \sum_i p_{it} x_{it} + R_t,$

where Y_t denotes total income, which can be spent on the variants i of the hetero-geneous good and on all other goods, with this residual expenditure being repre-sented by R_t, which can be interpreted as money left for all other expenses. Since the utility function is specified to be separable in these two broad categories, the marginal utility of R_t does not depend on the amounts of the heterogeneous good consumed and vice versa. Another feature of the utility function is that this con-stant marginal utility of R_t is restricted to be one, thus defining the scale of utility which is generally arbitrary. This is equal to saying that utility is measured in money units. Substituting the budget constraint into the utility function one ob-tains the function

(C.A.2) $U_t(x_{1t}, x_{2t}, \ldots, x_{Nt}, x_{1,t-1}, x_{2,t-1}, \ldots, x_{N,t-1})$

$$= \sum_i \left(\alpha x_{it} - \beta x_{it}^2 + \gamma x_{it} x_{i,t-1} \right) - \beta \sigma \sum_i \sum_{j \neq i} x_{it} x_{jt} + Y_t - \sum_i p_{it} x_{it},$$

from which computing first derivatives leads to

(C.A.3) $\dfrac{\partial U_t}{\partial x_{it}} = \alpha - 2\beta x_{it} + \gamma x_{i,t-1} - \beta \sigma \sum_{j \neq i} x_{jt} - p_{it} \overset{!}{=} 0.$

Solving for x_{it} gives the optimal value for the current-period consumption of variety i:

(C.A.4) $x_{it} = \dfrac{\alpha}{2\beta} + \dfrac{\gamma}{2\beta} x_{i,t-1} - \dfrac{\sigma}{2} \sum_{j \neq i} x_{jt} - \dfrac{p_{it}}{2\beta}.$

However, this equation also contains quantities of the other varieties. For ob-taining the reduced form, the optimal values for all varieties but i have to be de-rived, with the sum of which being

(C.A.5) $\displaystyle\sum_{j \neq i} x_{jt} = (N-1)\dfrac{\alpha}{2\beta} + \dfrac{\gamma}{2\beta} \sum_{j \neq i} x_{j,t-1} - (N-1)\dfrac{\sigma}{2} x_{it}$

$$- \dfrac{\sigma}{2} \underbrace{\sum_{j \neq i} \sum_{k \neq i, j} x_{kt}}_{(N-2)\sum_{j \neq i} x_{jt}} - \dfrac{1}{2\beta} \sum_{j \neq i} p_{jt}.$$

Factorization leads to

$$\text{(C.A.6)}\quad \left[1+\frac{\sigma}{2}(N-2)\right]\sum_{j\neq i}x_{jt}=(N-1)\frac{\alpha}{2\beta}+\frac{\gamma}{2\beta}\sum_{j\neq i}x_{j,t-1}$$

$$-(N-1)\frac{\sigma}{2}x_{it}-\frac{1}{2\beta}\sum_{j\neq i}p_{jt}\;.$$

Solving for the sum of quantities over all varieties but i yields

$$\text{(C.A.7)}\quad \sum_{j\neq i}x_{jt}=\frac{(N-1)\dfrac{\alpha}{2\beta}+\dfrac{\gamma}{2\beta}\displaystyle\sum_{j\neq i}x_{j,t-1}-(N-1)\dfrac{\sigma}{2}x_{it}-\dfrac{1}{2\beta}\displaystyle\sum_{j\neq i}p_{jt}}{\left[1+\dfrac{\sigma}{2}(N-2)\right]}\;,$$

which is then substituted into equation (C.A.4) to obtain

$$\text{(C.A.8)}\quad x_{it}=\frac{\alpha}{2\beta}-\frac{\sigma\left[(N-1)\dfrac{\alpha}{2\beta}+\dfrac{\gamma}{2\beta}\displaystyle\sum_{j\neq i}x_{j,t-1}-(N-1)\dfrac{\sigma}{2}x_{it}-\dfrac{1}{2\beta}\displaystyle\sum_{j\neq i}p_{jt}\right]}{[2+\sigma(N-2)]}$$

$$+\frac{\gamma}{2\beta}x_{i,t-1}\frac{p_{it}}{2\beta}\;.$$

Factorization leads to

$$\text{(C.A.9)}\quad \left[1-\frac{\sigma(N-1)\dfrac{\sigma}{2}}{2+\sigma(N-2)}\right]x_{it}$$

$$=\frac{\alpha}{2\beta}-\frac{\sigma\left[(N-1)\dfrac{\alpha}{2\beta}+\dfrac{\gamma}{2\beta}\displaystyle\sum_{j\neq i}x_{j,t-1}-(N-1)\dfrac{\sigma}{2}x_{it}-\dfrac{1}{2\beta}\displaystyle\sum_{j\neq i}p_{jt}\right]}{[2+\sigma(N-2)]}$$

and division by the term in brackets on the left-hand side finally yields (C.2).

2.   Coefficients in (C.53) and (C.54)

$$k_a = \alpha \big[\beta^2(4-\sigma)^2(4+\sigma)(2-\sigma)(2+\sigma)^2 - 64\lambda\gamma \, (\beta(2+\sigma)+\gamma) \big]$$
$$\times \big[\beta^2(4-\sigma)(4+\sigma)^3(2-\sigma)^2 - \lambda(8\gamma)^2 \big]$$

$$k_{aa1} = 8\beta^2(4-\sigma)(4+\sigma)\big\{ b^2[(4-\sigma)(4+\sigma)(2-\sigma)(2+\sigma)]^2 - \lambda(16\gamma)^2 \big\}$$

$$k_{ab1} = 2\beta^2\sigma(4-\sigma)(4+\sigma)\big\{ \beta^2[(4-\sigma)(4+\sigma)(2-\sigma)(2+\sigma)]^2 - \lambda(8\gamma)^2$$
$$\times(12-\sigma^2)\big\}$$

$$k_{aa2} = 128\lambda\beta\gamma\big[\beta^2(4-\sigma)(4+\sigma)(2-\sigma)(2+\sigma)(16-3\sigma^2) - \lambda(8\gamma)^2 \big]$$

$$k_{ab2} = -64\lambda\beta\gamma\sigma\big[\beta^2\sigma^2(4-\sigma)(4+\sigma)(2-\sigma)(2+\sigma) + \lambda(8\gamma)^2 \big]$$

$$k_b = \alpha\big[\beta^2 e_1(4-\sigma)^2(4+\sigma)(2-\sigma)(2+\sigma)^2 - 64\lambda\gamma(\beta(2+\sigma)+\gamma)e_2 \big]$$
$$\times \big[\beta^2 e_1(4-\sigma)(4+\sigma)^3(2-\sigma)^2 - \lambda e_2(8\gamma)^2 \big]$$

$$k_{ba1} = 8\beta^2(4-\sigma)(4+\sigma)\big\{ b^2 e_1[(4-\sigma)(4+\sigma)(2-\sigma)(2+\sigma)]^2 - e_2\lambda(16\gamma)^2 \big\}$$

$$k_{bb1} = 2\beta^2\sigma(4-\sigma)(4+\sigma)\big\{ \beta^2 e_1[(4-\sigma)(4+\sigma)(2-\sigma)(2+\sigma)]^2 - \lambda e_2(8\gamma)^2$$
$$\times(12-\sigma^2)\big\}$$

$$k_{ba2} = 128\lambda\beta\gamma\big[\beta^2 e_1(4-\sigma)(4+\sigma)(2-\sigma)(2+\sigma)(16-3\sigma^2) - \lambda e_2(8\gamma)^2 \big]$$

$$k_{bb2} = -64\lambda\beta\gamma\sigma\big[\beta^2 e_1\sigma^2(4-\sigma)(4+\sigma)(2-\sigma)(2+\sigma) + \lambda e_2(8\gamma)^2 \big]$$

3.   Role of γ in the Duopoly Model in Chapter C.III.3

One may also turn to the question of how elasticities are affected in the duopoly framework if the consumer's switching costs term gains weight in the utility function, which can be instrumented by a larger γ. As already stated above, the positive impact of lagged period sales on demand in the current period is strengthened by a rise in γ.

Pass-through of permanent exchange rate changes to export prices becomes greater in absolute value with γ, as illustrated in Figure A1. This impact is reversed, however, if the exchange rate shock is perceived to be only temporary.

Figure A1: Pass-Through Elasticities with Increasing γ[a]

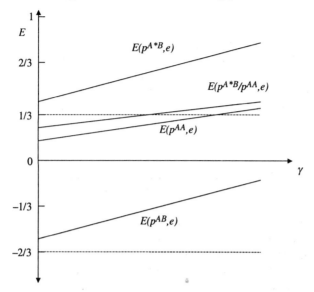

[a]In order to simplify the graphical presentation all curves have been linearized.

Past market share considerations are then more important and dampen the impact of exchange rate changes on prices. In the case of a temporary devaluation, prices are lowered by less if the devaluation is expected to be reversed in the next period. This makes it less valuable for the firm to shift profit to the second period, and the firm is more inclined to increase current profits by means of setting a relatively high current price, so the price fall becomes less marked. The single effect of expected devaluations lowers export prices if γ is strictly positive due to an analogous reasoning. Note that these results hold irrespective of whether export prices are measured in the exporter's or importer's currency since their derivatives are identical:

(C.A.10) $\left.\dfrac{\partial E\left(p_1^{AB},e\right)}{\partial \gamma}\right|_{\gamma=0}$

$$= \dfrac{-128\lambda\left[\alpha\left(16-2\sigma-3\sigma^2\right)+2\sigma\right]}{\beta(2-\sigma)(2+\sigma)(4-\sigma)(4+\sigma)^3\left[2+\alpha(2-\sigma)\right]^2} < 0,$$

(C.A.11) $\left.\dfrac{\partial E\left(p_1^{AB},e_1\right)}{\partial \gamma}\right|_{\gamma=0} = \dfrac{64\lambda(\alpha-1)\left[\alpha\left(8-2\sigma-\sigma^2\right)+2\sigma\right]}{\beta(2+\sigma)(4-\sigma)^2(4+\sigma)\left[2+\alpha(2-\sigma)\right]^2} > 0,$

(C.A.12) $\left. \dfrac{\partial E\left(p_1^{AB},e_2\right)}{\partial \gamma}\right|_{\gamma=0}$

$$= \frac{-64\lambda\left[\alpha(32-6\sigma^2-\sigma^3)+2\sigma\right]}{\beta(2-\sigma)(2+\sigma)(4-\sigma)^2\,(4+\sigma)^3\,[2+\alpha(2-\sigma)]} < 0.$$

Regarding prices of domestic sales, the effect of a rise in γ on pass-through leads to some ambiguous results. Therefore, I start by interpreting the unambiguous effect of γ on first-period exchange rate pass-through to domestic prices, which is

(C.A.13) $\left. \dfrac{\partial E\left(p_1^{AA},e_1\right)}{\partial \gamma}\right|_{\gamma=0} = \dfrac{128\lambda(\alpha-1)\sigma}{\beta(2+\sigma)(4-\sigma)^2\,(4+\sigma)^2\,[2+\alpha(2-\sigma)]^2} > 0.$

It was already concluded for the monopoly that a temporary depreciation leads the domestic enterprise to also raise its price in its own home market. This effect is strengthened by a positive γ. Since the competitive position of the domestic enterprise declines again in the future, past sales are less valuable for the firm, so the current price is raised even more. Note that this fact stands in sharp contrast to what was obtained for export prices, where γ reduced the absolute effect of temporary exchange rate changes due to dynamic considerations.

Concerning future exchange rate changes, which are the new element in Figure A2, a positive γ implies that expected exchange rate or competitor cost

Figure A2: Pricing to Market with Various Natures of Exchange Rate Changes[a]

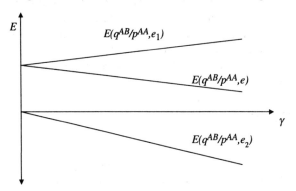

[a]In order to simplify the graphical presentation all curves have been linearized.

changes now affect domestic prices negatively since an established customer base due to past sales is more valuable for the firm in the future:

(C.A.14) $\dfrac{\partial E\left(p_1^{AA},e_2\right)}{\partial \gamma}\bigg|_{\gamma=0}$

$$= \frac{-64\lambda\sigma^2}{\beta(2-\sigma)(2+\sigma)(4-\sigma)^2(4+\sigma)^3[2+\alpha(2-\sigma)]^2} < 0.$$

As opposed to export prices, this mechanism now acts to reduce the absolute value of pass-through to home market prices. If the overall effect of permanent exchange rate changes is split into the pure first-period and second-period effects both counteracting each other, one cannot tell a priori what the total outcome is:

(C.A.15) $\dfrac{\partial E\left(p_1^{AA},e\right)}{\partial \gamma}\bigg|_{\gamma=0}$

$$= \frac{64\lambda\sigma[\alpha(4-\sigma^2)-4]}{\beta(2-\sigma)(2+\sigma)(4-\sigma)(4+\sigma)^3[2+\alpha(2-\sigma)]^2} \gtrless 0.$$

The expression (C.A.15) is positive for $\alpha > 4/(4-\sigma^2)$. The larger σ is and the more we approach the limiting case of perfect substitutability, the larger α has to be in order to make the elasticity positive. For perfect substitutability, α has to be infinite, so for any finite value of α, the influence of past sales via γ decreases pass-through. Since both a low σ and a high α are indicative of high markups, it can be conjectured that the effect of past market share only increases pass-through to domestic prices in high markup sectors.

For the strategy of pricing to market, the result obtained from the monopolist framework also applies here, i.e., that switching costs decrease pricing to market if exchange rate changes are permanent, and increase pricing to market if they are temporary. This is also equivalent to saying that the effect of an expected depreciation leads to negative pricing to market, i.e., the domestic price falls more than the export price. The effects of γ on pricing to market are:

(C.A.16) $\dfrac{\partial E\left(p_1^{A*B}/p_1^{AA},e\right)}{\partial \gamma}\bigg|_{\gamma=0} = \dfrac{-64\lambda\alpha}{\beta(2+\sigma)(4-\sigma)(4+\sigma)[2+\alpha(2-\sigma)]^2} < 0,$

(C.A.17) $\dfrac{\partial E\left(p_1^{A*B}/p_1^{AA},e_1\right)}{\partial \gamma}\bigg|_{\gamma=0} = \dfrac{64\lambda\alpha(\alpha-1)(2-\sigma)}{\beta(2+\sigma)(4-\sigma)^2(4+\sigma)[2+\alpha(2-\sigma)]^2} > 0,$

(C.A.18) $\dfrac{\partial E\left(p_1^{A*B}/p_1^{AA},e_2\right)}{\partial\gamma}\bigg|_{\gamma=0} = \dfrac{-64\lambda\alpha}{\beta(2+\sigma)(4-\sigma)^2(4+\sigma)[2+\alpha(2-\sigma)]} < 0 .$

Concerning the elasticity of intramarket producer price differentials, results hinge upon the assumption governing the discount rate, since they evolve differently for the producers under the assumption of perfect capital mobility. What is sure, however, is that with a temporary exchange rate change, switching costs work toward a stabilization of the local price for the exporter from country A in country B as was just argued, and the effect should lead to lower price spread across producers in the target market.

4.   Derivation of Equations (C.74) and (C.75)

Consider two representative enterprises competing in the market of country s, with the first enterprise producing in a different country r, whereas the second one produces in the country s itself. Maximization of the respective profit functions

(C.A.19) $\Pi_i^{rs} = \left(p_i^{rs}-c^r\right)x_i^{rs} .$

(C.A.20) $\Pi_i^{ss} = \left(p_i^{ss}-c^s\right)x_i^{ss}$

yield, after having replaced quantities by the export and home demand functions according to (C.72) and (C.73),

(C.A.21) $p_i^{rs} = \dfrac{\alpha(2-\sigma)+\sigma(n^{rs}-1)p_{-i}^{rs}+c^r\left(2+\sigma(N^s-2)\right)}{2+\sigma\left(N^s-2\right)},\quad r=A,B;\quad s\neq r,$

(C.A.22) $p_i^{ss} = \dfrac{\alpha(2-\sigma)+\sigma(n^{ss}-1)p_{-i}^{ss}+c^s\left(2+\sigma(N^s-2)\right)}{2+\sigma\left(N^s-2\right)} .$

Since in equilibrium it holds that $p_i^{rs}=p_{-i}^{rs}\equiv\tilde{p}^{rs}$, the reaction functions for the unique export price given the prices of sales from local producers in this market is

(C.A.23) $\tilde{p}^{rs} = \dfrac{\alpha(2-\sigma)+\left[\left(N^s-2\right)\sigma+2\right]c^r+n^{ss}\sigma p^{ss}}{\left[\left(n^{rs}+2n^{ss}-3\right)\sigma+4\right]} .$

Similarly, domestic prices depend on prices of competing imports as follows:

(C.A.24) $\tilde{p}^{ss} = \dfrac{\alpha(2-\sigma)+[(N^s-2)\sigma+2]c^s+n^{rs}\sigma p^{rs}}{[(2n^{rs}+n^{ss}-3)\sigma+4]}.$

Solving this system of equations yields the reduced form for prices in equilibrium, which depends solely on cost measures in the two markets:

(C.A.25) $p^{ss} = \dfrac{[(N^s-2)\sigma+2]\{[(N^s+n^{ss}-3)\sigma+4]c^s+n^{rs}\sigma c^r\}}{[(N^s-3)\sigma+4][(2N^s-3)\sigma+4]}$

$+\dfrac{\alpha(2-\sigma)[(2N^s-3)\sigma+4]}{[(N^s-3)\sigma+4][(2N^s-3)\sigma+4]},$

(C.A.26) $p^{rs} = \dfrac{[(N^s-2)\sigma+2]\{[(N^s+n^{rs}-3)\sigma+4]c^r+n^{ss}\sigma c^s\}}{[(N^s-3)\sigma+4][(2N^s-3)\sigma+4]}$

$+\dfrac{\alpha(2-\sigma)[(2N^s-3)\sigma+4]}{[(N^s-3)\sigma+4][(2N^s-3)\sigma+4]}.$

In order to obtain p^{AA} and p^{AB} in (C.74) and (C.75), one has to be specific about the currency in which prices and costs are measured. As usual, p^{AA} and p^{AB} are in currencies of country A and B, respectively, whereas costs are in terms of currency units of the producing country. Since the nominal exchange rate e is defined in currency units of country A for one unit of B, the substitutions are as follows:

$s = A, \qquad r = B, \qquad c^s = c^A, \qquad c^r = ec^B \qquad$ in (C.74),

$r = A, \qquad s = B, \qquad c^r = c^A/e, \qquad c^s = c^B \qquad$ in (C.75).

5. The Duopoly Prices with $\gamma = 0$ as a Special Case of the General Number-of-Firms Model

If (C.74) and (C.75) are restricted to the case of the duopoly, which is accomplished by setting N^A and N^B equal to two, and n^{AA}, n^{AB}, n^{BA}, and n^{BB} equal to one, one obtains the equilibrium prices for home market A and for imports into market B when intertemporal spillover effects on the demand side are abstracted from, i.e., γ is zero:

(C.A.27) $\quad p^{AA} = \dfrac{\alpha(2-\sigma)(4+\sigma)+8c^A+2\sigma c^B e}{(4-\sigma)(4+\sigma)}$,

(C.A.28) $\quad p^{AB} = \dfrac{\alpha(2-\sigma)(4+\sigma)+8c^A/e+2\sigma c^B}{(4-\sigma)(4+\sigma)}$.

Another possibility to arrive at these solutions is to start from the duopoly model with spillover terms, with equilibrium prices given in (C.53) and (C.54), and then setting γ to zero.

These prices from the simple duopoly framework constitute the basis for the models with transport costs and intermediate inputs. They can also be used to compute directly all the elasticities and their derivatives in Section C.III.3, where γ is restricted to zero, i.e., all equations from (C.55) onward.

D. Empirical Results for the Degree of Pass-Through in Domestic and Export Markets

The previous chapter dealt with theoretical implications for goods prices if production costs, after having been made comparable in the same currency, follow different paths in two countries, with the driving forces being either local price inflation of nontradable factor inputs or exchange rate shifts. One of the main results is that not only prices of exported goods, but also domestically sold goods may follow the cost path of either country, depending on the specific assumptions concerning production and demand patterns, but the most likely outcome is that product prices move somewhere within a range which is delineated by the cost evolutions in both countries.

This chapter constitutes the empirical counterpart of the theoretical reasoning. The approach is both country-specific and sector-specific. Whereas sector-specific export and import price indices are available, this is not the case for bilateral export relations. Thus, a multinational approach is followed here in focusing on sectoral or national import or export price indices and cost indices either of single countries, or of single countries relative to all trading partners. In order to reach consistency, cost and exchange rate data also have to be multilateral. For that purpose, the two-country framework, which has been used so far, has to be transformed into the one-country-versus-the-rest-of-the-world framework, with the rest of the world being all OECD countries. This approach of using cost and trade data only from OECD countries is justified by the intention of this work to only focus on the manufacturing sector rather than to include also price setting of raw materials. Production activities in industrialized countries which result in a higher value added take place predominantly in the finished goods sector.

From the long list of determinants which play a role for price determination two groups can be highlighted. The first one relates to national characteristics, such as openness of the country or world market shares of firms in that country, the second one considers sectoral aspects like the number of firms in the relevant industry. The results will be shown in Section I.

Concerning sectoral aspects, for which the degree of substitutability between product varieties and the relation of prices over marginal costs are most important, sectors are classified empirically in a two-dimensional framework of Section II.

I.   Country-Specific Findings for the OECD

In this section, some empirical evidence will be given for the relationship between prices and relative costs from a sample of national aggregates of OECD
countries. Real exchange rate changes of a country's currency have been shown
to affect the behavior of both export and import prices, so either measure can in
principle be used to determine the degree of pass-through. Unit labor costs
(ULC) are used for the national cost measure, implying that the real exchange
rate is specified as the relative unit labor costs between the country in question
and the reference group. This is done for three reasons: firstly, the cost measure
has to be exogenous and must not depend on prices, since it is the prices which
are to be explained. Secondly, shifts in prices between countries are the result of
differential shifts in input prices of nontradable production factors rather than
those of tradable input factors, which affect producers in all countries indiscrimi-
nately. Thirdly, with wages being country-specific, the impact of a local wage increase or decrease relative to other countries can be accounted for in this framework.

1.   A First Evidence from Charts

Since export or import price indices are not available on a bilateral basis, aggregate indices have been taken. Thus, a multilateral measure of costs is warranted,
so the real effective exchange rates based on unit labor costs on an OECD wide
level has been used for this analysis. Figures 14, 15, and 16 give a visual impression of the evolution of foreign unit labor costs in the manufacturing sector and
import prices for a selection of four OECD countries.

Figure 14 illustrates the incidence of pass-through from the importer's point
of view in displaying time series of the logs in levels of domestic and foreign
unit labor costs and their impact on domestic and import prices in the manufactured goods sector. For the United Kingdom and Japan, it is striking that domestic prices follow domestic unit labor costs, and import prices follow foreign unit
labor costs, which are calculated as the product from the relative unit labor cost
series and domestic unit labor costs, thus being denominated in domestic currency units. For both countries, pass-through seems to be nearly perfect over the
medium run, and domestic prices are barely influenced by foreign unit labor
costs. However, there is a small impact on domestic prices in Japan, where in the
first half of the 1980s, import prices and foreign unit labor costs climbed way
above domestic costs, thus also pulling domestic prices a little higher than domestic unit labor costs. In the 1990s, an analogous relationship holds, but with

Figure 14: Import Prices of Manufactured Goods and Foreign Unit Labor Costs[a]

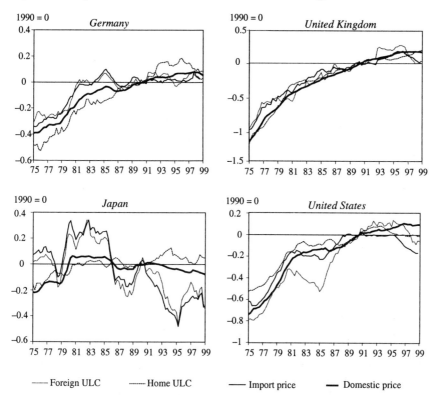

----- Foreign ULC   ------ Home ULC   —— Import price   —— Domestic price

[a]Both series, which are based on indices measured in the importer's currency, have been transformed into natural logarithms. These series *foreign ULC* and *home ULC* are foreign and domestic unit labor costs, the first having been calculated as the ratio of two given OECD series: home unit labor costs/relative unit labor costs. Foreign unit labor costs are thus measured in the importer's currency. The frequency of all series is quarterly. All series apply to the sector of manufacturing goods.

Source: OECD (2000a, 2000b).

the direction being reversed. For Germany, the foreign impact on domestic prices is even more obvious since domestic prices are almost between foreign and domestic unit labor costs. In all three countries, pass-through seems to be nearly complete when a longer interval is considered. In the United Kingdom, though, in the middle of the 1990s, the rise in foreign unit labor costs, which was undoubtedly brought about by the fall in the nominal value of the British pound, could no longer be passed through to U.K. residents. Instead, the import price followed closely the track of domestic prices until the subsequent appreciation of the pound by the end of the 1990s, when there is again a close correspondence between import prices and foreign unit labor costs.

Whereas all those three economies have in common that they are relatively open, this feature does not hold for the United States, where the empirical picture is fundamentally different, too. Foreign unit labor costs seem to be nearly neutral in their impact on the series of domestic and import prices as these are always in the neighborhood of domestic unit labor costs. Only in periods when the U.S. dollar appreciated sharply, e.g., in the first half of the 1980s and in the second half of the 1990s, a certain influence of foreign competition in the form of lower foreign unit labor costs was felt slightly in declining import prices, although import prices could not shake off their ties to domestic unit labor costs over a longer run. Equally remarkable, domestic prices seem to be practically unimpressed by foreign influences.

These results confirm the market share hypothesis which was derived analytical and which states that a large domestic market induces more competition and makes it more difficult for foreign producers to pass through their production costs. A more thorough empirical investigation will follow later on, so other visual evidence on pass-through should be considered first.

What is common for all countries is that a rise in foreign unit labor costs, which can be subscribed mainly to a devaluation of the country's nominal effective exchange rate, is reflected in import prices. However, there is not a one-to-one correspondence which would result if there is full pass-through to importer's prices. Another way of expressing this relationship is by stating that the volatility of import prices is less than the volatility of the unit costs series, for what we can also take Figure 15 as evidence for imperfect pass-through. Figure 15 depicts quarterly changes of the same variables, and reveals that the amount of changes in import prices is less than in foreign unit labor costs, except in Japan, where we again find pass-through to be nearly complete. For the United States, Figure 15, which is particularly suitable for analyzing short-term dependencies, corroborates the general findings of Figure 14 in that import prices have reacted less to changes in foreign unit labor costs in recent years. The decline in import price volatility seems to be a longer process and did not happen discontinuously as some authors pretend (see, for example, Knetter 1994) who attribute the apparently fiercer competition in the U.S. market to the entry of importers into the American market when the U.S. dollar appreciated. Another explanation for the decline in import price volatility, the use of the U.S. dollar as the invoicing currency, fails to explain that evolution either. Since the role of the U.S. dollar in fixing contracts was already great in the first half of the time interval, even an additional increase in invoicing in dollars could not have such a great effect. The most plausible explanation might be the increasing importance of pricing to market, which is reflected particularly in short-term price adjustments, since pricing-to-market strategies aim at reducing volatility in local prices in order to avoid costly adjustments in the customer base.

Figure 15: Volatility of Import Prices of Manufactured Products and Foreign Unit Labor Costs[a]

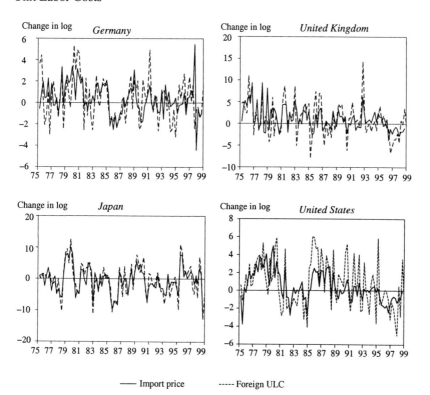

—— Import price   ----- Foreign ULC

[a]Foreign unit labor costs (foreign ULC) are measured in the importer's currency. This series is calculated as the ratio of national unit labor costs to relative unit labor costs. The series have been transformed by computing the natural logarithm and then taking differences. The series represent quarterly changes in logarithms of import prices and foreign unit labor costs in manufacturing, respectively. All series apply to the sector of manufacturing goods.

Source: OECD (2000a).

A more complete picture emerges when the graphical analysis is complemented by a look at the exporter's side. Figure 16 graphs export prices against domestic and foreign unit labor costs. Before looking at price setting, it is important
to realize how cost competitiveness evolved in the individual countries. Particularly in the case of Germany and Japan, we see competitiveness declining over
the last two decades, made visible by a rise of home unit labor costs relative to
foreign ones. Quite contrary, the United States could improve their competitive
position relative to their trade partners. There are three different interpretations
for this evolution of competitiveness.

Figure 16: Export and Domestic Producer Prices, Home and Foreign Unit Labor
Costs[a]

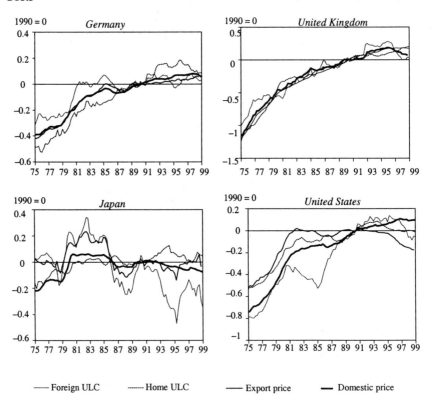

[a]For the definition of foreign ULC and home ULC, see Figure 14. All series apply to
the sector of manufacturing goods.

Source: OECD (2000a, 2000b).

The first interpretation is that for the first two countries, the nominal effective exchange rate appreciated relative to its purchasing power parity based on unit labor costs. The second interpretation focuses on wages in realizing that nominal wages have risen much more than is justified by global conditions. As a third interpretation, one can also state that the increase in productivity has been too slow in these countries to outweigh the impact of differential shifts in wages and the nominal exchange rate relative to trade partners. Before turning to a more elaborate discussion on the possible adjustment mechanisms when imbalances have been built up, the central concern here is to determine the scope for price setting.

If pass-through of domestic costs was zero, the export price series would follow that of foreign unit labor costs, whereas with complete pass-through, export prices would be purely domestically determined and therefore follow domestic unit labor costs, provided that production factors other than labor are excluded, or at least their prices are perfectly correlated with unit labor costs. In addition to export prices, domestic producer prices are also included in order to determine whether both series behave differently. With regard to the theoretical discussion in Chapter C, where it was concluded that exchange rate changes generally have a larger impact on export than domestic prices, one would expect to see export prices move more in line with foreign unit labor costs, and prices for domestic sales more in line with domestic unit labor costs. This is indeed generally the case.

For Germany, the picture for domestic and export prices mirrors that for foreign unit labor costs, but export prices could not climb as much as domestic producer prices in the 1990s, when foreign unit labor costs were below domestic unit labor costs, in line with the expectation one would derive from the theoretical analysis when the domestic real exchange rate appreciates. As was shown, a smaller market share of domestic producers in the world market than in their home country leads to a smaller elasticity for export prices than for home prices. However, this development has come about only since the second half of the 1980s. For Japan, the relative gap in lower export prices has been closed in recent years, but instead we have seen a very high short-term adjustment of export prices to foreign cost developments, i.e., very much pricing to market. It was also derived in Chapter C that short-term and temporary export price adjustments can be subscribed more to exchange rate changes, whereas long-lasting price differentials more to the cost side. From this it may be cautiously concluded that in Japan the exchange rate dominates the appearance of the export price drift, whereas in Germany permanently high wage costs compared to international standards may be the driving force.

Taken altogether, there is quite a good empirical validation of theory when only qualitative effects are considered. The next interesting features concern the

quantitative measurement of relative price stability in the importer's currency
and an investigation of the pattern across countries and sectors.

2.   Evidence from Descriptive Statistics on Price Variability

Figures 14 and 15 reveal that import prices show signs of inertia compared to
foreign unit labor costs in domestic currency units. Pricing to market has been
shown in Chapter C to be a particularly important pricing policy for the short-
time horizon, in which shocks in relative cost competitiveness for a country relative to others are seen to be at least partly reversible. The next step is thus to account quantitatively for this relative stability in import prices. One straightforward concept is measuring the variance of import prices and comparing this to
the variance of unit labor costs in the exporting country. This approach, by which
variances are computed from quarterly changes of logarithms in prices, focuses
on the short-term adjustment since variables have been differenced. The observation that the variance of destination prices in the importer's currency is smaller
than the variance of the exchange rate can be seen as evidence of less than perfect pass-through or pricing to market.

The use of differenced variables is justified if time series are not stationary.
Furthermore, nominal price series often are even of order I(2) (see, for example,
Crowder 1996) which puts an additional constraint on econometric analysis in
order to avoid spurious correlation. The use of relative prices, however, is sound
from both the theoretical point of view and because the degree of integration of
variables might be reduced, provided a cointegration vector corresponding to this
imposed restriction between both variables exists. Indeed, testing for the degree
of integration reveals that for nearly each country the series of relative unit labor
costs, relative import prices, and relative export prices contain a unit root of at
least degree one (Chapter D.III.2). The findings of unit roots necessitate tests for
cointegration in an error-correction framework, which is done in Section D.III. In
that section, it will be discussed that the existence of independent trends for
many variables makes it difficult to establish cointegration relationships for all
countries and to compare them. Another shortcoming of a regression analysis
when applied to the purpose of explaining import prices is that under the hypothesis of complete pricing to market, import prices do not respond at all to
shifts in intercountry cost differentials, so that insignificant coefficients on these
cost variables and a poor fit of the regression as a whole support the hypothesis
of pricing to market. This is contrary to the general procedure in which an alternative hypothesis H_0 is to be rejected in favor of the proposed hypothesis H_1
by proving the significance of some coefficient.

This is why the method of computing variances and comparing their relative strengths will also be applied in order to illustrate the hypothesis of pricing to market. However, a new difficulty arises when variances are interpreted. As long as a fraction of price changes is not caused by shifts in relative price competitiveness but by other factors such as common changes in world commodity prices, a possible spectrum for the import price variance must be allowed for a priori by computing bounds which apply for zero and full pass-through, respectively. Clark and Faruquee (1997) follow this approach, which will be described next before modifying the approach. This modified approach is then used as the basis for interpreting variances empirically in the present study.

a.   *The Relationship between Pass-Through and the Variance of Import Prices*

The data set used for variance computation comprises quarterly series of effective nominal exchange rates, import prices for the aggregate of manufacturing products, and a time series which measures average unit labor costs for each of the countries, the weighting scheme being identical to the construction of the nominal effective exchange rate. In order to develop this approach, first, I bear upon the theoretical result from the reduced-form model that the import price in the importer's currency is a linear combination of domestic and foreign costs, both measured in the importer's currency. Contrary to Chapter C, log-linearized variables will be used in the empirical implementation since this transformation is particularly appropriate for that purpose:

(D.1) $\ln p^{AB} = \phi \ln c^B + \varphi\left(\ln c^A - \ln e\right).$

The further transformation of the series is as follows: After quarterly changes of the logarithms have been calculated, which also serves to detrend the data, the variances based on these series are computed. Equation (D.1) reveals that as long as φ is strictly positive, countries with a large volatility of their exchange rate will also reveal a comparatively large volatility in import prices. A large price volatility thus can be partly caused by a large exchange rate volatility and is not necessarily indicative of a high degree of pass-through. Bearing this in mind, one straightforward way of normalizing the import price variance would be to divide it by the variance of the exchange rate. The ratio $\text{Var}(\hat{p}^{AB})/\text{Var}(\hat{e})$ is thus a measure which is less biased by a country's exchange rate regime but rather reflects price-setting behavior of economic agents. However, the following lines are to show that this measure is still biased and that there do exist better ways to normalize import price variances.

Allowing for the possibility of unequal pass-through of domestic costs and the nominal exchange rate, an assumption which corresponds to the short-term theoretical results in the previous chapter, lagging and subtracting yields

(D.2) $\Delta \ln p^{AB} = \phi \Delta \ln c^B + \varphi_c \Delta \ln c^A - \varphi_e \Delta \ln e$.

Whereas Clark and Faruquee make the implicit assumption that ϕ equals zero and φ_c is equal to one when they derive an upper bound for the variance measure,[25] I propose the more general case that the impact of the importer's costs is not negligible, i.e., $\phi > 0$. The second modification is that the absence of money illusion is supposed to hold, implying that cost and exchange rate pass-through are identical, i.e., $\varphi = \varphi_c = \varphi_e$. Starting from (D.2) one obtains for relative changes:

(D.3) $\hat{p}^{AB} = \phi \hat{c}^B + \varphi(\hat{c}^A - \hat{e})$.

The import price in country B is a linear combination of own costs and costs in the exporter's country. Note that all variables are in terms of the importer's currency. The variances depend on the parameters as follows:

(D.4) $\mathrm{Var}(\hat{p}^{AB}) = \phi^2 \mathrm{Var}(\hat{c}^B) + \varphi^2 \mathrm{Var}(\hat{c}^A - \hat{e}) + 2\phi\varphi \mathrm{Cov}(\hat{c}^B, \hat{c}^A - \hat{e})$,

(D.5) $\dfrac{\mathrm{Var}(\hat{p}^{AB})}{\mathrm{Var}(\hat{c}^A - \hat{e})} = \varphi^2 + \dfrac{\phi^2 \mathrm{Var}(\hat{c}^B) + 2\phi\varphi \mathrm{Cov}(\hat{c}^B, \hat{c}^A - \hat{e})}{\mathrm{Var}(\hat{c}^A - \hat{e})}$.

In the variance ratio defined by (D.5), the variance of import prices is expressed relative to cost variation in the exporter's country, with costs being transformed into the importer's currency. The ratio is an increasing function of the pass-through coefficient φ. In this measurement it is irrelevant whether import prices are affected by changes in the nominal exchange rate or changes in costs. What matters is merely cost competitiveness from the importer's point of view. Suppose the exporter maintains his price-cost margin, so that prices change one to one with costs. Then φ equals one and ϕ equals zero, and the variance ratio is one. However, at the other extreme, if only cost (or price) conditions in the target country matter, the variance ratio may still be positive since the variation of national costs in country B also has an effect. The covariance term contributes to a

---

[25]   In the original formula (6) in Clark and Faruquee (1997), μ corresponds to φ_c and $a - 1$ to φ_e.

second positive bias if both countries use production factors for which the law of one price tends to hold internationally. When prices of production factors which are used to produce competing products in the importing country also move hand in hand with the exchange rate, the incidence of pass-through, indicated by a large ratio, does not only stand for cost-determined price setting, but also for a close comovement of import and home market prices. As a result, one would expect the empirical variance ratio to be slightly higher than implied by φ^2, implying that values higher than one might occur.

b. **The Relationship between Pass-Through and the Variance of Relative Producer Prices**

In a second approach, the price differentials between producers are the basis on which variation measures are built. It has been shown analytically in the duopoly framework that for the prices of two competitors in the same market, cost differentials between the two production locations determine the differential in prices. Another proof of pricing to market can be established if the variation of relative prices is smaller than the variation of relative costs. In order to gain an expression for the price differential between producers, a pricing equation for a second producer, located in country B, can be established analogously to (D.3):

(D.6) $\hat{p}^{BB} = \phi' \hat{c}^B + \varphi' (\hat{c}^A - \hat{e})$.

Combining this equation with (D.6), the variation of the relative producer price is

(D.7) $\hat{p}^{AB} - \hat{p}^{BB} = (\phi - \phi')\hat{c}^B + (\varphi - \varphi')(\hat{c}^A - \hat{e})$.

Under the restrictions that prices are linear homogenous of degree one in all monetary variables it holds that

(D.8) $\phi = 1 - \varphi$ and $\phi' = 1 - \varphi'$ and it follows:

(D.9) $\hat{p}^{AB} - \hat{p}^{BB} = (\varphi - \varphi')(\hat{c}^A - \hat{e} - \hat{c}^B)$.

It has been argued that due to market share considerations it can be taken for granted that $\varphi > \varphi'$. If exports from country A are relatively more expensive in production than competing products in the importing country, the import price in country B rises above the price which domestic producers set. However, under the assumption that all parameters are strictly positive then it must hold that

$0 < \varphi - \varphi' < 1$. If the focus is on variance ratios, it can be deducted that the volatility of relative prices is less than the volatility of relative costs:

(D.10) $\mathrm{Var}(\hat{p}^{AB} - \hat{p}^{BB}) = (\varphi - \varphi')^2 \mathrm{Var}(\hat{c}^A - \hat{e} - \hat{c}^B)$,

(D.11) $\dfrac{\mathrm{Var}(\hat{p}^{AB} - \hat{p}^{BB})}{\mathrm{Var}(\hat{c}^A - \hat{e} - \hat{c}^B)} < 1$.

The limiting cases of the ratio in (D.11) represent complete pass-through for both of the producers on the one end of the spectrum and the prevalence of the law of one price on the other end.

c.   **The Relationship between Pass-Through and the Variance of the Export Price Drift**

The third approach concerns the determinants of the magnitude of the export price drift. Large export price drifts occur if the variation of the exports prices relative to domestic prices is substantial. It is thus necessary to account first for the relative changes of export and domestic prices. The theoretical reasoning on import price changes from Chapter C has already brought forth equation (D.3). By means of the exchange rate the import price is converted into the currency of the exporter and its relative change is compared with that of the domestic price. Assuming linear homogeneity of prices with respect to costs it follows that:

(D.12) $\hat{p}^{A*B} = \phi(\hat{c}^B + \hat{e}) + \varphi \hat{c}^A$ with $\phi = 1 - \varphi$,

(D.13) $\hat{p}^{AA} = \phi''(\hat{c}^B + \hat{e}) + \varphi'' \hat{c}^A$ with $\phi'' = 1 - \varphi''$.

The exporter sets prices in the export and home market depending on costs in the location of his competitors and costs in his own country. Because foreign variables also play a role in the decision on prices, pass-through of domestic costs into either export or home market prices is incomplete. An export price drift establishes when pass-through is different between the export and the home market, i.e., when pass-through to domestic prices is larger than to export prices $(\varphi'' > \varphi)$. The resulting equation for the price drift reveals its negative relation to domestic-foreign costs differential, and the elasticity of the relative price with respect to relative cost changes is smaller than one since $\varphi - \varphi''$ is less than unity:

(D.14) $\hat{p}^{A*B} - \hat{p}^{AA} = \underbrace{(\varphi - \varphi'')}_{<0} (\hat{c}^A - \hat{c}^B - \hat{e}).$

Hence a large variance of relative export prices is indicative of pricing to market, too, and the variance of relative costs serves as a benchmark in order to interpret the scale:

(D.15) $\mathrm{Var}\left(\hat{p}^{AB} - \hat{p}^{AA}\right) = (\varphi - \varphi'')^2 \, \mathrm{Var}\left(\hat{c}^A - \hat{c}^B - \hat{e}\right),$

(D.16) $\dfrac{\mathrm{Var}\left(\hat{p}^{AB} - \hat{p}^{AA}\right)}{\mathrm{Var}\left(\hat{c}^A - \hat{c}^B - \hat{e}\right)} < 1.$

Consequently, the variance of the relative export price, i.e., the ratio of export relative to domestic prices is smaller than the variance of relative costs: In the extreme, pass-through into domestic prices is complete $(\varphi'' = 1)$ and to foreign prices zero $(\varphi = 0)$, such that both variances coincide.

d.   *Empirical Results for Variation Measures*

Table 3 shows for 24 OECD countries the empirical counterpart of the variation measures just derived. In the analytical two-country world, the indicator of relative competitiveness has been the cost ratio between the two countries with the costs being transformed into the same currency by means of the exchange rate. This de facto real exchange rate has its empirical counterpart in the real multi-country world in the real effective exchange rate. Concerning the exact definition of it, there are several alternatives for the choice of the deflator, the most common ones being the consumer price index and the unit labor cost index. For the following empirical analysis, which also includes estimations pooled across countries, the real exchange rate based on relative unit labor costs has been taken here. The quarterly data are from the OECD (2000a) database *International Trade and Competitiveness Indicators* ranging from 1975Q1 to 1999Q1. It contains time series on country-specific import and export prices and unit labor costs as well as relative unit labor costs and relative export prices both being defined on a multilateral basis in terms of relating the values for a particular country to a trade-weighted average of the other 22 OECD countries.[26] The time series *Relative Unit Labor Costs* is in fact a real effective exchange rate index based on nor-

---

[26]   For further details, see OECD (1992).

malized unit labor costs[27] in the manufacturing sector constructed by the OECD on the basis of 21 countries, with the weights being calculated from trade flows in the period 1988–1990. For a country i, this index can be represented as

$$(D.17) \quad E_i = \prod_{i \neq j} \left[\frac{ULC_i \; NER_i}{ULC_j \; NER_j} \right]^{W_{ij}},$$

with j being an index that stands for all direct trade partners or indirect competitors in third markets of country i. W_{ij} is the weight attached by country i to country j. *NER* is the nominal exchange rate in U.S. dollars, and *ULC* is the normalized unit labor cost in the respective country. The weight W_{ij} is constructed as

$$(D.18) \quad W_{ij} = \frac{\sum_k w_i^k s_j^k}{\sum_k w_i^k \left(1 - s_j^k \right)}.$$

The producers in country i and j compete in all markets k, with market share of producers from country i in market k, s_j^k, being calculated on the basis of sales from country j in market k, S_l^k :

$$(D.19) \quad s_j^k = \frac{S_i^k}{\sum_l S_l^k}.$$

The share of country i's output sold in market k is defined by

$$(D.20) \quad w_i^k = \frac{S_i^k}{\sum_n S_i^n}.$$

The weight W_{ij} measures in its numerator how important competitor j is in market k (via its market share), with weighting each market k by the proportion of all exports from country i that go to this market k. This degree of competition between producers i and j is then normalized in the numerator by the degree of competition between country i and all other countries, so that the ratio determines the dominance of competitors from country j for producers in country i relative to all competitor countries.

---

[27]   Normalized unit labor costs are calculated by the OECD in using the trend of output rather than the unrefined figure so that the possible temporary impact of business cycles on this measure has been smoothed out.

Table 3: Variance Pass-Through for Individual Countries[a]

	VARPM	VARPMR	VARULCF	VARULCR	PSHARE	PENE
Australia	9.92	8.23	16.27	22.70	1.34	31.86
Austria	6.57	8.16	2.32	6.54	0.79	49.64
Belgium	4.22	2.66	3.90	4.60	1.36	81.12
Canada	3.44	2.20	4.26	5.66	3.18	49.74
Switzerland	5.42	5.04	9.25	11.71	0.96	.
Germany	2.20	1.53	3.81	7.35	9.71	27.97
Denmark	2.26	1.35	4.49	9.28	0.46	56.71
Spain	10.37	7.58	11.37	11.17	2.88	29.50
Finland	39.18	39.60	7.46	14.36	0.59	34.13
France	3.13	2.28	4.72	5.10	5.53	32.03
United Kingdom	7.09	5.95	15.09	19.38	5.56	36.74
Greece	19.21	18.45	10.74	18.61	0.34	50.07
Ireland	12.95	10.38	7.06	8.44	.	.
Italy	5.49	3.79	7.70	9.42	6.52	27.23
Japan	17.03	13.84	24.64	28.68	17.28	7.73
Korea	18.94	16.03	30.52	43.06	4.79	26.96
Mexico	207.40	123.20	197.97	152.30	3.32	39.15
Netherlands	1.85	2.11	3.21	3.64	1.51	70.69
Norway	5.03	4.62	3.78	11.66	0.39	43.82
New Zealand	12.35	9.70	15.19	14.83	0.29	39.88
Portugal	2.86	9.25	3.56	3.78	0.77	39.78
Sweden	7.19	5.63	10.45	22.23	0.98	43.45
Turkey	78.86	33.07	71.25	88.71	.	.
United States	2.79	2.36	7.19	6.60	32.38	17.91

[a]*VARPM* is the variance of the difference of the log of import prices, and *VARPMR* of the relative import price, i.e., the import price relative to the domestic producer price. *VARULCF* and *VARULCR* are the variances of foreign and domestic relative to foreign unit labor costs, respectively. *PSHARE* are production shares across the OECD. They are calculated as production of manufacturing in the respective country as a percentage of production of manufacturing for the OECD area, being an aggregate of 22 countries (not including Ireland, Luxembourg, Switzerland, Turkey, and Korea). *PENE* is the import penetration calculated as the ratio of imports to total domestic demand, with total domestic demand being calculated from total production plus imports minus exports. The figures for *PSHARE* and *PENE* are computed as means over the period 1988–1990. The time range is restricted for *VARPMR* due to data constraints for the producer price which is only available for Belgium from 1980Q1, for Korea from 1981Q1, for Mexico from 1981Q4, for Sweden from 1982Q1, and for Turkey from 1984Q1. Export and import prices for Austria and Turkey are only available until 1994Q4.

Source: Own calculations. All data for the computation of *PSHARE* and *PENE* are for the manufacturing sector and for the year 1990, the source being OECD (1999), *Main Industrial Indicators*. Producer prices are from OECD (2000b), *Main Economic Indicators*. All other series are from OECD (2000a), *International Trade and Competitiveness Indicators*.

Foreign unit labor costs are constructed from the database by dividing the country's own unit labor costs by the series of relative unit labor costs. The volatility of import prices (*VARPM* in Table 3) can then be compared to the volatility of foreign unit labor costs computed in domestic currency units (*VARULCF*). In addition, ratios of variables such as the import-domestic price relation are also used for computing variances (*VARPMR*), the same with relative unit labor costs in terms of domestic to foreign costs (*VARULCR*). These relative variables have the advantage that they are less influenced by purely local monetary shocks which originate in the importing country and which affect synchronously all nominal prices while having only a limited impact on relative prices. From a comparison of column one and three, it appears that foreign costs and import prices are positively correlated for most countries. Moreover, column two and four suggest that the volatility of relative import prices is less than the volatility of relative unit labor costs. The figures also suggest that countries with a smaller volatility of absolute or relative unit labor costs also show less variation in absolute or relative import prices. These results are clearly indicative of imperfect pass-through implying that cost differentials between countries are imperfectly reflected in output price differentials.

Another issue is whether differences between countries can be explained by characteristics like openness or their share in total OECD production. One crucial result from theoretical reasoning has been that the smaller the country's production share (*PSHARE*) and the larger the import penetration (*PENE*), the greater the extent of pass-through is. Small open countries like Belgium should therefore show a relatively high variance of import prices relative to the variance of foreign unit labor costs in Table 3, whereas the big economies like the United States are expected to have a substantially smaller variation of import prices than of foreign unit labor costs in domestic currency units. Indeed, for Belgium, both variances are roughly identical with values ranging around 4. For the United States, the variance of import prices is 2.79, whereas the variance of foreign unit labor costs amounts to 7.19. For Germany, ranking third according to production shares in the OECD, we also record a significantly lower import price volatility compared to that of foreign unit labor costs (2.20 versus 3.81).

Quite the opposite holds for small economies. If one looks at countries which show a production share smaller than one, the general relationship is that these variances are of an approximately equal order, with only some countries being an exception. It is also possible to rank countries according to import penetration rather than OECD production shares, which gives a somewhat different order, but in general there is a negative correlation between OECD production share and openness.

Concerning the inference from export prices in Table 4, the measurement of imperfect pass-through follows another route. It would be straightforward to take

Table 4: Pricing to Market and Its Determinants across Countries[a]

	VARPXR	VARULCR	CPXRULCR	VRPXPD	XDEP	XSHARE
Australia	10.52	22.70	−0.19	9.65	20.05	0.97
Austria	8.39	6.54	−0.01	2.38	47.64	1.82
Belgium	1.90	4.60	−0.15	1.14	83.66	4.95
Canada	0.90	5.66	−0.43	1.73	49.97	4.92
Switzerland	2.36	11.71	−0.10	6.50	.	2.48
Germany	0.46	7.35	−0.10	1.48	32.93	15.22
Denmark	1.32	9.28	0.16	1.03	58.19	1.39
Spain	4.92	11.17	−0.35	2.00	26.51	2.92
Finland	15.70	14.36	−0.10	11.11	45.00	1.24
France	1.38	5.10	−0.41	1.37	33.68	8.38
United Kingdom	3.04	19.38	−0.54	2.95	34.34	7.59
Greece	35.46	18.61	−0.15	10.41	28.87	0.31
Ireland	7.87	8.44	−0.12	3.70	.	1.41
Italy	5.14	9.42	−0.41	4.58	32.69	7.65
Japan	7.03	28.68	−0.68	6.30	12.70	12.58
Korea	16.87	43.06	−0.38	2.90	28.84	3.72
Mexico	149.26	152.30	−0.80	3.95	39.63	2.52
Netherlands	1.09	3.64	0.15	0.91	72.89	4.78
Norway	13.12	11.66	−0.05	11.89	35.89	0.74
New Zealand	11.36	14.83	−0.45	4.54	35.96	0.38
Portugal	8.36	3.78	−0.40	0.34	33.90	0.76
Sweden	1.63	22.23	−0.19	1.87	50.56	2.52
Turkey	34.29	88.71	−0.49	2.16	.	0.67
United States	1.26	6.60	−0.07	1.62	14.06	16.27

[a]*VARPXR* is the variance of the difference of the log of the relative export price, i.e., the export price relative to the domestic producer price. *VARULCR* is the variance of relative unit labor costs, *CPXRULCR* is the correlation coefficient between the relative export price and relative unit labor costs, *VRPXPD* is the ratio of the variance of relative export prices relative to the variance of domestic producer prices. *XDEP* is the export dependency defined as the share of exports relative to domestic production, and *XSHARE* is the export share of the respective country relative to all OECD countries. The figures for *XDEP* and *XSHARE* are computed as means over the period 1988–1990. As in the tables before, all variables refer to the manufacturing sector. The sources and time ranges are as indicated in Table 3.

Source: See Table 3.

the variance of export prices as evidence for the existence of the export price drift or pricing to market because a large variance of export prices is tantamount to a high degree of adjustment. However, it is reasonable to assume that the bulk of the noise in export prices is due to the volatility of domestic cost factors, and that influences resulting from the external competitive position of that country are only of minor importance. One, thus, has to control for the volatility in economic policy that is reflected in all domestic nominal variables, including export prices. This is accomplished by constructing the relative export price by dividing the nominal export price by the producer price and then looking at the time series behavior of that relative export price.

The main finding is that the variance of the relative export price (*VARPXR*) increases with variation in relative unit labor costs (*VARULCR*) in a cross-country comparison. A look at these variances clearly shows that a volatile real exchange rate in terms of relative unit labor costs transmits the volatility to the relative export price, but it does not actually prove that the relative export price is forced down rather than up if national competitiveness declines with a rise in the real exchange rate, as stated in (D.14). To give an answer to this problem, the coefficient of correlation between both series has also been computed (*CPXRULCR*), and it indeed turns out to be negative for all countries save two exceptions. When relative unit labor costs in a country increase relative to its competitors, the relative decrease in competitiveness is reflected in a lower export price relative to the domestic one. An alternative measure corroborating the prevalence of pricing to market is that the dispersion of export prices relative to the dispersion of domestic prices is greater than one (*VRPXPD*).

Following this idea, the fourth column of Table 4 displays the ratio of the variance of nominal export prices to the variance of domestic producer prices (*VRPXPD*). With only the exception of two countries, these ratios are always much greater than one, thus supporting the hypothesis. It is important to note that these measures are not biased by differences between countries as regards their record of price stability, since high inflation, which in addition is generally also more volatile, causes both variances to increase. To the extent that both increases are equally proportional the ratio is left unaffected.

Whereas export dependency (*XDEP*) does not have any significant impact on ratios, the export share (*XSHARE*) does. Countries with very high *VRPXPD* values such as Finland, Greece, and Norway, which are countries with small world market shares, tend to show more pricing to market, being reflected in the high variability of relative export prices.

The statistical material presented so far generally supports the hypothesis of imperfect pass-through into import prices. These results can be seen complementary to regression results which are still to follow. The advantage to use these variation measures is that so far no structural model specifying the set of explaining variables is needed. The disadvantage, however, lies in the fact that it is not accounted for whether the variables are stationary or integrated or whether any cointegration relationship exists between them. Moreover, the comparison of variances is only justified as long as the time horizon is equal and finite, because with an ever increasing time dimension, variances approach infinity for variables which are integrated. Consequently, in the next section, those properties are investigated before further evidence from regressions is derived.

3. Accounting for the Determinants of Price Setting by Regression Analysis

The following empirical approaches build explicitly on economic relationships which govern the movements of import and export prices. Bearing on theoretical considerations made before, a simple and reasonable way to model empirically testable import and export price equations is to regard these prices as a function of costs and exchange rate variables. For obtaining estimated coefficients which are interpretable by magnitude, a measure for costs has to be chosen which is most comprehensive and which also covers nonlabor input costs. Since a comprehensive cost variable which, in addition, is also comparable across countries is lacking for the sample which is dealt with here, the real exchange rate based on relative consumer prices has been chosen as the empirical counterpart for measuring price competitiveness.

a. *Deriving the Regression Equations*

Starting with import prices, the theoretical rationale behind the empirical approaches can be derived from the simple two-country framework (D.1). Rearranging terms so that an expression in terms of the real exchange rate is the result, one obtains:

$$(D.21) \quad \ln p^{AB} = \varphi \left(\ln c^A - \ln c^B - \ln e \right) + (\phi + \varphi) \ln c^B.$$

Under the assumption that domestic prices follow marginal costs one to one, implying that markups in domestic price setting are constant, and using the definition for the real exchange rate, the expression becomes

$$(D.22) \quad \ln p^{AB} = \varphi \left(- LNRER^{AB} \right) + (\phi + \varphi) \ln c^B.$$

The expectation is that the import price in country B is positively correlated with domestic prices, and, moreover, that it increases ceteris paribus with a decline in the real exchange rate, i.e., a real appreciation of country B's currency.

Under the hypothesis of linear homogeneity, the expression simplifies further to

$$(D.23) \quad \ln p^{AB} = \varphi \left(- LNRER^{AB} \right) + \ln c^B.$$

Turning all bilateral variables into their multilateral counterpart, the error-correction approach for the import price of country i ($LNPM_i$) can be expressed in terms of its real effective exchange rate ($LNREER_i$) and the domestic producer price ($LNPPI_i$), with all variables being transformed into logarithms:

(D.24) $\Delta LNPM_{it}$

$$= (g-1)\left[LNPM_{i,t-1} - aLNREER_{i,t-1} - bLNPPI_{i,t-1} - \sum_{i=1}^{4} e_i \times seas_i \right]$$

$$+ \sum_{j=0}^{q} b_j \Delta LNREER_{i,t-j} + \sum_{j=0}^{q} d_j \Delta LNPPI_{i,t-j} + \sum_{j=1}^{s} d_j \Delta LNPM_{i,t-j} + \varepsilon_t \; .$$

A regression coefficient of g smaller than 1 is significant for a correction of a disequilibrium in the long-term relationship. The lag length q is increased until the error term ε_t becomes stationary. The d_j are the coefficients on the lagged differenced endogenous variable. The variables a and b are long-term coefficients, and $seas_i$ are seasonal dummy variables.

An analogous procedure is applied in modeling export prices. For this purpose, (D.1) can be rewritten to describe import prices in country A in terms of country A's currency units:

(D.25) $\ln p^{BA} = \phi \ln c^A + \varphi \left(\ln c^B + \ln e \right).$

The country which is referred to when export prices are concerned is country B, and in currency units of country B they can be stated as

(D.26) $\ln p^{B*A} = \phi \ln c^A + \varphi(\ln c^B + \ln e) - \ln e,$ or equivalently,

(D.27) $\ln p^{B*A} = \phi \ln c^A + (\varphi - 1)(\ln e + \ln c^B - \ln c^A)$
$$+ (\phi + \varphi - 1)\ln c^A + (\phi + \varphi)\ln c^B \; .$$

Using the real exchange rate and the assumption of linear homogeneity of degree one for the import price function with respect to its arguments from (D.1) one arrives at

(D.28) $\ln p^{B*A} = -\phi \, LNRER^{AB} + \ln c^B \; .$

A rise of the real exchange rate $LNRER^{AB}$, standing for a real appreciation of country B's currency, causes ceteris paribus the export price of country B to fall, measured in this country's currency. The empirical estimation equation for export prices of country i with respect to its trade partners ($LNPX_i$) is analogously:

(D.29) $\Delta LNPX_{i,t}$

$$= (g-1) \left[LNPX_{i,t-1} - aLNREER_{i,t-1} - bLNPPI_{i,t-1} - \sum_{i=1}^{4} e_i \times seas_i \right]$$

$$+ \sum_{j=0}^{q} b_j \Delta LNREER_{i,t-j} + \sum_{j=0}^{q} d_j \Delta LNPPI_{i,t-j} + \sum_{j=1}^{s} d_j \Delta LNPX_{i,t-j} + \varepsilon_t .$$

b.   Estimation Results

The following analysis makes use of the same data set as the empirical studies in Sections D.I.1 and D.I.2, with only the series on real effective exchange rates from OECD (2000b), *Main Economic Indicators*, having been added to the data set. Before turning to the estimations themselves, tests for the degree of integration have been conducted. The results from applying the augmented Dickey–Fuller test for unit root are presented in Table A1. The general picture which emerges is that the logarithms of import, export, and producer prices as well as the logarithms of the real effective exchange rates turn out to be nonstationary for the vast majority of countries since the null hypothesis of nonstationarity nearly always cannot be rejected at the standard 5 percent level of significance. Applying the test to differences in logs, however, generally yields results in favor of stationarity, as shown in Table A2, with a few exceptions for some series like export and import prices for the United States, Portugal, and Korea. These series and others, for which the test has not produced significant evidence for stationarity, are therefore at least I(2), that is, integrated of degree 2, while all others, for which stationarity holds for the differenced transformation but not the levels, are I(1).

Taking account of the incidence of nonstationary time series behavior of variables involved, the search for cointegration relationships between these variables is appropriate. Since for some countries data availability precludes that the full length of the time series is available, the regression period had to be restricted to range only from 1982Q2 to 1999Q2 in order to make the set of countries as large as possible. Nonetheless, some countries still had to be discounted in the analysis due to missing values. All equations are estimated as a system of seemingly unrelated regressions (SUR), which allows for correlation of error terms across equations. This correlation can arise because countries can import similar kinds of manufacturing goods from the same set of exporting countries, with only the exact composition and weights accounting for the difference.

Evidence from Import Prices

As a first step, the system of equations has been estimated without cross-equation restrictions so that all coefficients can vary independently across countries. The purpose of allowing for contemporaneous correlation of error terms across equations by means of applying the SUR method is solely to restore the assumption of independent and identical distributed (iid) errors so that standard critical values for single-equation cointegration frameworks such as those derived by Banerjee et al. (1998) can be applied. The results of this approach for import prices are shown in Table 5.

The first thing to note is that evidence in support of the hypothesis of cointegration is mixed, as the t-statistics for the adjustment coefficients in the first column suggest. Concerning the coefficients in the error-correction term, the long-term regression coefficients on the real exchange rate measure the percentage change of import prices in case of a permanent real appreciation of a country's currency of one percent, provided that domestic producer prices are unchanged, with this ceteris paribus assumption always being implicit when single coefficients are interpreted. The particular source of the real exchange rate appreciation may then be twofold. It may either be a nominal appreciation of the importer's currency or a fall in foreign prices, which both cause the importer's real exchange rate to rise. The implicit assumption is that for the elasticity of the import price it is irrelevant where the cost advantage of foreign goods comes from. It is important to note that the third factor which goes into the real exchange rate, the prices in the importer's country, is restricted to be unchanged. In fact, negative coefficients on the log of the real effective exchange rates have been found, with their magnitude being confined to values between minus one and zero. As (D.23) suggests, full pass-through would hold if the coefficient on the real exchange rate were minus one, and the coefficient on domestic prices one. The failure of the regressions to show this, together with the result that cointegration has often not been found, can be seen as evidence that import prices follow paths which are to a certain degree independent from production costs in the countries of origin.

On the other hand, full pricing-to-market orientation of import prices would have resulted in coefficients on domestic prices around the area of one. This is not always the case either, but for many countries significant values between one-half and one are obtained. The frequent failure of stable long-term relationships of import prices with respect to the explaining variables can be attributed to the fact that in these cases import prices obviously follow independent trends which are separated from movements of aggregate domestic or foreign prices, even in the long run. An explanation for this might be a changing composition of trade partners over time and the fact that the sectoral composition of tradable

Table 5: Country-Specific Error-Correction Regressions for Import Prices[a]

	$g-1$[b]	LNREER	LNPPI	ΔLNREER	ΔLNPPI	SE	DW
Australia	−22.327	−0.842	0.614	−0.595	0.899	1.152	2.22
	(−3.35)	(−11.10)	(10.66**)	(−17.96**)	(4.79**)		
Belgium	−0.015	−38.803	1.563	−0.631	0.798	2.739	1.92
	(−0.002)	(−0.002)	(0.003)	(−2.29*)	(2.59**)		
Canada	−23.632	−0.405	0.113	−0.467	0.337	0.706	1.87
	(−3.73)	(−6.93**)	(2.14)	(−9.91**)	(2.85**)		
Switzerland	−16.562	−0.724	1.515	−0.419	1.235	1.277	2.21
	(−1.75)	(−2.97)	(6.18**)	(−6.11**)	(3.46**)		
Germany	−16.775	−0.663	0.402	−0.249	1.016	1.021	1.76
	(−2.70)	(−3.29)	(2.49)	(−3.01**)	(3.30**)		
Denmark	−7.058	−0.983	0.285	−0.307	0.224	0.780	1.65
	(−1.83)	(−1.63)	(1.20)	(−4.37**)	(2.21*)		
Spain	−28.840	−0.299	0.801	−0.463	0.382	1.252	2.24
	(−4.08+)	(−4.31+)	(14.35**)	(−6.54**)	(1.76+)		
Finland	−47.913	−0.300	1.193	−0.582	0.216	4.791	1.97
	(−3.46)	(−2.69)	(6.65**)	(−2.77**)	(0.27)		
United Kingdom	−24.190	−0.532	0.570	−0.308	1.391	1.105	1.76
	(−3.56)	(−7.46**)	(11.78**)	(−8.95**)	(4.01**)		
Ireland	−58.188	−0.432	0.892	−0.279	1.150	2.500	2.11
	(−4.74*)	(−2.92)	(10.73**)	(−1.50)	(2.16*)		
Italy	−9.526	−0.298	0.702	−0.397	0.427	1.513	1.63
	(−1.71)	(−1.31)	(3.88+)	(−6.27**)	(2.02*)		
Japan	−1.12	−2.883	−2.112	−0.639	0.734	1.543	1.83
	(−0.329)	(−0.458)	(−0.156)	(−16.69**)	(2.15*)		
Mexico	−21.864	−1.189	0.974	−0.967	0.804	3.140	1.37
	(−2.85)	(−7.65**)	(73.22**)	(−25.75**)	(8.79**)		
Netherlands	−3.659	−0.905	0.529	−0.189	0.048	1.177	1.82
	(−1.06)	(−0.554)	(0.390)	(−1.64+)	(0.319)		
Norway	−12.702	−0.308	0.538	−0.302	0.972	2.007	1.95
	(−1.77)	(−0.398)	(2.30)	(−1.97*)	(2.73**)		
New Zealand	−25.477	−0.481	0.574	−0.363	1.267	1.769	1.98
	(−3.29)	(−4.394)	(8.06**)	(−7.23**)	(4.78**)		
Sweden	−13.75	−0.105	0.293	−0.398	0.223	1.343	1.45
	(−2.27**)	(−0.628)	(1.58+)	(−5.78**)	(1.05)		
United States	−11.705	−0.810	−0.529	−0.307	−0.021	0.628	2.03
	(−3.927+)	(−9.51**)	(−3.88+)	(−11.88**)	(−0.21)		

[a]t-statistics in parentheses. **, *, +: significant at a p-value of at least 1, 5, or 10 percent. Concerning the maximum lag length, $s = q = 1$ in (D.24). Coefficients are defined in the text. SE: Standard error of regression. DW: Durbin–Watson test statistic. – [b]Critical values are from Banerjee et al. (1998: 276, Table I) for coefficients in the first three columns when the series of the dependent variable is nonstationary, otherwise the Student's t-distribution is used for testing significance (here only Sweden).

Source: Own calculations based on OECD (2000a, 2000b).

products might be different from domestic sales. The problem aggravates to the extent that sectors behave differently and the sectoral composition of trade varies across trade partners. This difficulty does not only arise when prices of domestic sales are compared to those exported, but also when real exchange rates based on consumer price indices are used which also incorporate prices of nontradable goods.

Leaving the sectoral aspect to a more thorough analysis in the next section, one can turn to the interpretation of the differenced variables. The short-term adjustments that they reflect are not subject to the difficulties one has encountered in finding long-term equilibrium relationships. With the exception of those countries which exhibit differenced variables in Table A2 that are not stationary and therefore might show only spurious correlations, both the significance and magnitude of the coefficients very much corroborate the theoretical propositions. By looking at the pass-through coefficients one gets the rough impression that small economies like Mexico or Finland are attributed a larger degree of pass-through than large economies like the United States or Germany.

As a next step, it is investigated whether countries may be categorized into groups that behave differently. Table 6 presents the results from a system of error-correction equations for import prices simultaneously estimated across countries according to (D.24). At first, a pooled regression covering all countries has been conducted. Then the sample is being reduced to examine the impact which a country-specific attribute has on the values of the parameters. An alternative way to investigate this is to introduce dummy variables reflecting the grouping of countries. Estimations reflecting this heterogeneity between sectors are also given in Table 6. The country groups have been built according to the criteria given in Tables 3 and 4, such as the import penetration ratio, the ratio of shares in OECD production and OECD exports, and the share of exports to domestic production. Country-specific seasonal dummies allowing for the fact that the frequency of the data is quarterly are also included in each of the error-correction terms.

The first sample refers to the general pooled regression without distinguishing between country groups. The coefficient g on the error-correction term is showing a highly negative value and t-statistic. For judging significance in this set of panel data, critical values are calculated on basis of the approach developed by Levin and Lin (1992) for testing unit roots, which incorporates individual-specific intercept terms but no time trends. The rationale is that the finding of stationary error terms in the regression equations is equivalent to a proof of the existence of the cointegration relationship. However, a slight difference might result from the fact that the coefficient in the long-term relationship is also estimated and that there is a fixed effect not only for each individual, but also for each season, but these additional sources of variation should be small when the

Table 6: Pooled Error-Correction Results for the Determinants of Import Price Pass-Through across Countries[a]

Sample[b]	DumReg[c]	Dummy[d]	$g-1$	*LNREER*	*LNPPI*	*ΔLNREER*	*ΔLNPPI*	LR[e]
Full (N = 18)			−4.022 (−5.79)	−0.651 (−5.89)	0.284 (2.63)	−0.506 (−37.29**)	0.456 (10.6**)	
Small countries only (N = 9)			−10.047 (−5.98◊)	−0.811 (−7.22◊)	0.349 (4.68)	−0.513 (−19.00**)	0.545 (7.30**)	
N = 17[f] Dummy for 9 small countries	$g-1$	−6.776 (−4.80)	−3.36 (−6.18)	−0.685 (−8.74◊)	0.396 (7.11◊)	−0.507 (−36.69**)	0.468 (9.88**)	24.05**
	LNREER	−0.546 (−2.58)	−4.238 (−6.07)	−0.538 (−4.91)	0.292 (2.89)	−0.510 (−36.85**)	0.444 (9.29**)	5.30*
	ΔLNREER	−0.063 (−2.39*)	−3.808 (−5.56)	−0.650 (−5.61)	0.238 (2.02)	−0.486 (−29.44**)	0.406 (8.37**)	3.94*
Open countries only (N = 6)			−8.744 (−5.10◊)	−0.343 (−3.46)	0.147 (1.66)	−0.440 (−13.42**)	0.404 (6.26**)	
N = 16[f] Dummy for 6 open countries	$g-1$	−5.105 (−3.87)	−2.910 (−6.69◊)	−0.414 (−4.73◊)	0.184 (2.56)	−0.501 (−35.44**)	0.457 (9.39**)	13.81**
	LNREER	0.361 (1.89*)	−4.232 (−5.57◊)	−0.678 (−5.64◊)	0.363 (3.50)	−0.506 (−35.71**)	0.449 (9.02**)	1.99
	ΔLNREER	0.122 (3.69)	−3.630 (−5.25◊)	−0.624 (−5.06◊)	0.323 (2.88)	−0.541 (−33.90**)	0.507 (10.0**)	8.98**

[a]The definitions of variables and its sources are as indicated in Table 3. t-statistics in parentheses. **, *: Significant at a critical value of at least 1 or 5 percent according to classical Student's t-tests. ◊: Significant at a 5 percent critical value being calculated from Levin and Lin (1992), Theorem 5.2 d. The number of observations is 67. – [b]The specification of alternative regressions is defined in the text. N: Number of countries included in the sample. – [c]Denotes the regressor to which a dummy variable is attached multiplicatively. This term is added to the standard regression, the results of which are presented in the first two lines in this table. – [d]Coefficient on the dummy variable. – [e]The likelihood ratio test statistic is calculated as LR = 2(L$_1$ – L$_0$), with L$_1$ being the value of the likelihood function of the unconstrained model which includes the dummy term, and L$_0$ being the likelihood function of the constrained benchmark model. Critical values are from the χ^2 (1) distribution, but are only valid under the assumption that cointegration relationships exist so as to render the error terms stationary. A value for the empirical test statistic exceeding the critical value signifies that the constraint does not hold and that the two country groups are different with respect to the parameter tested. * and ** denote significance at the 5 and 1 percent level, respectively. – [f]The countries for which data for penetration or production share is missing had to be neglected.

Source: Own calculations based on OECD (2000a, 2000b).

cointegration coefficient is restricted to be identical for all countries, which is done here. Making use of the finding of Levin and Lin (1992) that the term $\sqrt{1.25}t + \sqrt{1.875N}$ follows approximately a standard normal distribution with t standing for the t-statistic of the error-correction adjustment coefficient $g-1$, as long as the time-series dimension T is large in comparison with the cross-section dimension N, or, more accurately, as $\sqrt{N}/T$ converges to zero, and provided that T is not small. With $T = 67$ and N ranging from 6 to 18 according to the sample of countries, these conditions seem to hold to a sufficient degree.

Applying this distribution to the first model shown at the top of Table 6, the adjustment coefficient (column 3) is falling short of significance at a p-value of 0.05 since the empirical t-statistic of –5.79 is of a smaller absolute value than the computed critical value of –6.67. The coefficients on the real exchange rate (*LNREER*) and the domestic price (*LNPPI*) are positive but below the threshold of significance in this pooled regression specification.

The coefficients on the differenced variables are significant, however. For real exchange rate changes, the absolute value of the coefficient on the differenced variable ($\Delta LNREER$) is smaller than for the level coefficient *LNREER*, representing the long-term impact, thus pointing toward an adjustment process which takes more than one period to be completed, which is tantamount to more than a quarter of a year. One disadvantage of pooling all countries together is that the relationships to be estimated by common coefficients may in fact be different. In order to provide a remedy for this shortcoming the sample has been split into two parts. Concerning the classification of countries into one of the two groups, on the basis of which a dummy variable of either one or zero is assigned, the ranking of counties according to their shares in OECD manufacturing production and their import penetration ratios has been used. The division has been made such that the two groups are as homogeneous as possible and any two neighboring countries which show very similar values are not separated into different country groups. In the first group, countries with shares in OECD production smaller than two percent are assigned a dummy variable of one. For the grouping according to penetration ratios the marginal ratio has been fixed at 40 percent, so that countries with larger shares are given a dummy variable of one.

Beginning with the grouping of countries according to the OECD production shares from Table 3, in the second sample, the sample of countries has been restricted to include only small countries in terms of production share. The results for this group of small countries are more or less what one would expect. The co-integration term is significant according to the critical values computed according to Levin and Lin, and the long-term exchange rate coefficient is –0.811, which is remarkably close to the case of full pass-through. Smaller countries thus not only have a long-term relationship for the import price determination which is significant, but also show in their import prices a much closer response to exchange rate changes compared to the analogous coefficient for the full sample. With a coefficient for the differenced exchange rate of –0.513, the instantaneous adjustment in response to a shock is not measurably smaller.

In the third sample, dummy variables have been added on either the adjustment coefficient $g - 1$, the long-term exchange rate coefficient, or the short-term exchange rate coefficient. The outcome is that countries which show a large import penetration ratio display a faster speed of adjustment to the long-run equilibrium relationship because the dummy variable on the adjustment coefficient $g - 1$

(sample 3) is negative (–6.776). When a likelihood ratio test is applied to test the validity of the restricted benchmark model without the dummy variable, the likelihood ratio test statistic exceeds the critical value of 3.84 computed from the χ^2 distribution with one degree of freedom, which corresponds to a level of significance of 5 percent. This test statistic is dependent on the error terms being stationary, which has been shown with a significance of a sufficient degree at least for the subsample of small countries. It can therefore be concluded that the two groups of countries are significantly different so that the model in which all countries are pooled into only one group is an insufficient picture of reality. In the same way, the short-run coefficient is found to be larger in absolute value, suggesting that pass-through is more intense for open economies. This result corroborates the theoretical assertion developed in Chapter C which states that countries with a small market share, being reflected in a large proportion of imported product variants relative to all variants, have a higher level of pass-through because domestic production conditions play only a minor role relative to the global environment.

The market share as the pivotal determining theoretical factor has its empirical counterpart not only in the proportion of total OECD production, but one can also try to measure the determining factor by the import penetration ratio, which is generally larger for smaller economies. In fact, quite similar empirical results are obtained when a distinction is being made along this criterion. More open economies, i.e., those countries with import penetration ratios in excess of 40 percent (sample 4), also display a faster adjustment speed than both the whole sample (sample 1) and the sample of countries which are more oriented toward domestic trade, as indicated by the negative dummy variable in sample 5. Moreover, this group of open economies display a short-term coefficient on the real exchange rate which is larger in absolute value than for the rest.

These results clearly support the hypothesis pointed out in the theoretical part, that for the import prices of small economies pass-through is significantly smaller because the dominance of local producers in the world market constrains foreign producers in their price setting on the domestic market.

Evidence from Export Prices

Up to this point, the analysis has exclusively focused on properties which apply to the characterization of importing countries. It is straightforward to extend the investigation to the case of exporting countries by asking whether the market share or the export-production ratio of the exporting country determines the degree by which export prices respond. To achieve this aim, a system of regression equations analogous to that for the import price has been set up for the export price. Table 7 presents the results of unconstrained single-country estimates within the SUR system.

The difficulty of finding cointegration relationships in the level variables of the import price regressions translates directly to the export side considered now, and is even a more severe problem here. Quite contrary, when first differences are used, the variables have significant explanatory power, at least for the most part of the countries. The evidence of complete pricing to market from the export side would result if the coefficients on the real exchange rate were minus one, and that on the domestic price equal to plus one. In that case, export prices would follow the domestic currency equivalent of the weighted foreign price levels in the export markets. At the other end of the spectrum, if export prices followed domestic producer prices one to one without responding to real exchange rate shifts, then export prices would be either cost-determined or be set with regard to only domestic demand conditions. Two reasons why this second pricing pattern is conceivable are that arbitrage would inhibit producers to price discriminate or that sales into some foreign currency areas are so insignificant that the producer simply does not care what the impact of exchange rate changes that are confined to that particular currency area have on the price competitiveness of his products in that local market. What must be inferred, irrespective of which of the two reasons applies, is that producers operate in a niche of sufficiently differentiated products thus conferring some sort of pricing power on them.

The evidence from Table 7, finally, is supportive of an intermediate position. The response to a real exchange rate appreciation lowers the export price, with the magnitude of that adjustment being on average somewhere around one-half of the real exchange rate shift (column 4). The impact of domestic prices (column 5) varies across countries and is above the value of one as often as it is below one. Taken altogether, adjustments of export prices can obviously be seen as only temporary and serve to dampen fluctuations of prices in local markets. For the long run, however, there is only little evidence that systematic price differentiation between home and export markets can persist permanently, at least when aggregate national price indices are concerned.

Next, the estimations are repeated with cross-equation restrictions imposed upon that part of the coefficients which before were constrained to be common for all countries. The estimation results are presented in Table 8. The first sample in the table reflects the outcome when pooling all countries into one single group. The single coefficients in the long-term relationship of the error-correction term (columns 3–5) are again lacking significance in the full sample of countries. However, the significantly negative coefficient on the contemporaneous differenced real exchange rate (column 6) reveals that a decline in competitiveness, reflected in an increasing real exchange rate, ceteris paribus moves the export price downward as part of a short-term adjustment process. The exact

Table 7: Country-Specific Error-Correction Regressions for Export Prices[a]

	$g - 1$[b]	*LNREER*	*LNPPI*	*ΔLNREER*	*ΔLNPPI*	SE	DW
Australia	2.748	–0.272	1.1487	–0.615	0.631	1.216	2.12
	(1.29)	(–0.376)	(2.85)	(–17.05**)	(3.04**)		
Belgium	5.377	2.817	0.621	–0.425	0.821	2.288	2.14
	(0.593)	(0.602)	(0.404)	(–1.78+)	(2.99**)		
Canada	–0.278	4.583	–0.100	–0.481	0.190	0.766	2.00
	(–0.058)	(0.056)	(–0.008)	(–9.98**)	(1.60)		
Switzerland	–2.058	–0.063	0.312	–0.406	0.639	1.554	3.10
	(–0.422)	(–0.031)	(0.077)	(–4.73**)	(1.55)		
Germany	–14.065	–0.227	0.638	–0.220	1.589	1.150	2.63
	(–1.49)	(–0.929)	(3.09)	(–2.66**)	(5.14**)		
Denmark	–3.71	0.201	0.072	–0.425	0.223	0.785	2.20
	(–0.839)	(0.269)	(0.092)	(–6.10**)	(2.30*)		
Spain	–7.714	0.233	0.824	–0.506	0.491	1.434	2.41
	(–1.69)	(0.787)	(2.62)	(–7.27)	(2.23*)		
Finland	–23.123	–0.079	1.132	–0.741	–1.097	5.776	2.75
	(–1.25)	(–0.274)	(2.32)	(–2.90**)	(–1.14)		
United Kingdom	3.457	0.086	1.194	–0.309	1.060	1.162	2.07
	(0.422)	(0.070)	(1.24)	(–8.84**)	(2.88**)		
Ireland	–16.775	–1.590	0.002	–0.129	1.100	2.861	2.50
	(–2.20)	(–1.99)	(0.006)	(–0.776)	(2.30*)		
Italy	–19.597	–0.107	1.006	–0.340	0.715	1.479	2.07
	(–2.40)	(–0.984)	(15.39**)	(–6.63**)	(3.76**)		
Japan	–3.516	–1.033	–1.871	–0.634	0.374	1.531	2.07
	(–0.640)	(–0.995)	(–0.492)	(–19.40**)	(1.22)		
Mexico	–14.095	–1.238	0.941	–0.993	0.700	2.833	1.91
	(–2.43)	(–5.60**)	(44.98**)	(–27.74**)	(8.19**)		
Netherlands	–7.960	0.363	0.761	–0.247	–0.120	1.178	1.54
	(–1.13)	(0.473)	(1.31)	(–2.26*)	(–0.786)		
Norway	6.398	3.519	1.810	–0.594	0.897	2.12	2.01
	(1.34)	(1.79)	(3.13)	(–4.44**)	(2.61**)		
New Zealand	–7.704	–0.310	0.568	–0.416	1.303	2.106	2.90
	(–1.49)	(–0.703)	(1.85)	(–7.46**)	(4.61**)		
Sweden	–22.84	0.062	0.619	–0.439	0.297	1.508	1.82
	(–2.68)	(0.593)	(6.83**)	(–6.57**)	(1.36)		
United States	–4.871	–0.080	–0.651	–0.356	0.018	0.669	2.10
	(–2.63)	(–0.345)	(–2.26)	(–16.08**)	(0.203)		

[a]t-statistics in parentheses. **, *, +: significant at a p-value of at least 1, 5, or 10 percent. Coefficients are defined in the text. SE: Standard error of regression. DW: Durbin–Watson test statistic. – [b]Critical values are from Banerjee et al. (1998: 276, Table I) for coefficients on λ and α when the series of the dependent variable is nonstationary, otherwise the Student's t-distribution is used for testing significance.

Source: Own calculations based on OECD (2000a, 2000b).

Table 8: Pooled Error-Correction Results for the Determinants of Export Price Setting across Countries[a]

Sample[b]	DumReg[c]	Dummy[d]	g – 1	LNREER	LNPPI	ΔLNREER	ΔLNPPI	LR[e]
Full (N = 18)			–3.277	–0.073	0.201	–0.257	0.372	
			(–5.57)	(–0.652)	(1.35)	(–20.21**)	(10.1**)	
Small countries only (N = 6)			–3.711	–0.330	0.191	–0.275	0.427	
			(–3.370)	(–1.581)	(0.826)	(–12.58**)	(7.40**)	
	g – 1	–3.129	–1.575	–0.146	–0.308	–0.251	0.373	3.91[*]
		(–2.76)	(–2.68)	(–1.26)	(–1.98)	(–19.8**)	(10.1**)	
N = 18 Dummy for 9 small countries	LNREER	–0.529	–3.347	0.154	0.216	–0.256	0.374	5.59[*]
		(–2.63)	(–5.69[◊])	(1.14)	(1.51)	(–20.24**)	(10.4**)	
	ΔLNREER	–0.094	–2.320	–0.217	–0.035	–0.236	0.351	7.76[**]
		(–3.95**)	(–4.24)	(–1.28)	(–0.14)	(–14.69**)	(9.29**)	
Open countries only (N = 12)			–7.529	–0.130	0.429	–0.205	0.441	
			(–4.31)	(–1.24)	(4.32)	(–7.58**)	(8.29**)	
	g – 1	–5.631	–1.335	–0.217	–0.476	–0.252	0.371	12.24[**]
		(–3.96)	(–4.64)	(–2.17)	(–5.16)	(–20.2**)	(10.4**)	
N = 18 Dummy for 6 open countries	LNREER	–0.574	–3.442	0.125	0.209	–0.255	0.376	5.76[*]
		(–2.77)	(–5.85)	(1.01)	(1.49)	(–20.2**)	(10.4**)	
	ΔLNREER	0.032	–2.905	–0.129	0.225	–0.294	0.411	0.80
		(1.24)	(–4.89)	(–1.00)	(1.39)	(–20.1**)	(10.2**)	

[a]The definitions of variables and its sources are as indicated in Table 3. t-statistics in parentheses. **: Significant at a critical value of at least 1 percent according to classical Student's t-tests. [◊]: Significant at a 5 percent critical value being calculated from Levin and Lin (1992), Theorem 5.2 d. The number of observations is 67. – [b]The specification of alternative regressions is defined in the text. N: Number of countries included in the sample. – [c]Denotes the regressor to which a dummy variable is attached multiplicatively. This term is added to the standard regression, the results of which are presented in the first two lines in this table. – [d]Coefficient on the dummy variable. – [e]The likelihood ratio test statistic is calculated as LR = 2(L₁ – L₀), with L₁ being the value of the likelihood function of the unconstrained model which includes the dummy term, and L₀ being the likelihood function of the constrained benchmark model. Critical values are from the χ^2 (1) distribution, but are only valid under the assumption that cointegration relationships exist so as to render the error terms stationary. A value for the empirical test statistic exceeding the critical value signifies that the constraint does not hold and that the two country groups are different with respect to the parameter tested. [*] and [**] denote significance at the 5 and 1 percent level, respectively.

Source: Own calculations based on OECD (2000a, 2000b).

amount of the relative export price decline during the same period is one-fourth the relative change in the real exchange rate. The positive impact of domestic producer price changes (column 7) on the change in export prices comes as no surprise, given the expectation that production for domestic use and production for exports are subject to generally similar cost factors. What is striking, though, is that the interrelationship between domestic and export prices is not of such a degree that the coefficient in column 7 comes close to one. Of course, when one also takes into account the coefficients on the lagged regressors, which are not shown in the table, then it will become evident that they also bear a substantial part of the adjustment. Indeed, the lagged impact of domestic price changes is 0.2444 and that of real exchange rate changes –0.100, both being significant at a p-value of 0.05.

In the next step, dummy variables have been included which take on a value of one for countries with their share in OECD exports being smaller than 5 percent (sample 3). Analogously, the value of one is assigned to the dummy variable for each sample country which shows a ratio of exports to domestic production of more than 40 percent (sample 5). Regressions have also been done with the restricted samples of only small countries (sample 2) and open countries (sample 4). Whereas the error-correction term (column 3) is still not significant, the short-term impact of the real exchange rate is markedly stronger for those countries to which a positive dummy variable is assigned. The obvious interpretation has to be that countries with a small export share relative to the entity of all OECD countries tend to limit cost and exchange rate pass-through as they adapt their export prices to a larger degree to local market conditions.

The finding that the market share of a producer is positively related to pass-through has already been established in Chapter C. The empirical results here complement the findings from the import side, with the market share now being measured in terms of export rather than production share. Taken altogether, the degree of pass-through increases with the exporting country's OECD export share and decreases with the size of the importing country in terms of OECD production share. In addition, there is evidence that relatively open economies show a larger response of both export and import prices to changes in their relative cost competitiveness with respect to the outside world.

Comparing the country-specific evidence from charts, descriptive statistics, and the regression analyses, one can conclude that they unanimously support several hypotheses. The most basic one, which states that pass-through is imperfect, is verified both by a relatively low dispersion of import prices and by a less than proportional reaction of import prices to determining factors, compared to what would be expected with full pass-through. Moreover, this pattern in the prices of tradable products can also be detected from analyzing export prices. The other hypotheses refer to the magnitude of pass-through which has been shown to be determined by country-specific attributes like world market share or openness, with these attributes both referring to importing and exporting countries. Given these country results, the relationships are often not so close as to exclude the possible influence of further factors. One has, thus, to ask whether the unexplained differences in the behavior of prices of tradable goods between countries may be due to differences in the sectoral composition of trade. Moreover, to the extent that there is an international specialization of production so that particular countries specialize in specific sectors of the economy, then we should find export products being overweighted in these sectors compared to the pattern of domestic production. As a result, the sectoral composition of domestic sales and exports would be different, which might explain the often encountered poor results with respect to long-term relationships between trade prices and producer prices. Complementary to the breakdown across countries, a sectoral breakdown next seems to be appropriate in order to shed further light on determining factors for price setting in international trade.

II.   Sector-Specific Results for Western German Manufacturing

It has been shown in Section I that differences in pass-through between countries may be due to country-specific factors like openness, national production, or export share. Other determinants for pass-through are sector-specific since it is appropriate to assume that product characteristics or market structure which have played a crucial role in the theoretical analysis may differ between sectors. This is not only important for accounting for sectoral differences but might also contribute to the explanation of the pattern in the country results.

1.   The Classification of Sectors According to the Type of Good

Before sectors will be grouped into different classifications according to their empirically observable price movements, one has to contemplate a priori what the possible range of outcomes might look like. For that purpose, three different benchmark charts will be developed first by putting a hypothetical exogenous wedge between domestic and foreign unit labor costs in terms of domestic currency units. As to the endogenous price-setting pattern, three extreme benchmark cases emerge, thus creating a framework for classifying sectors empirically. With respect to the theoretical framework in Chapter C, where the producer's cost in equilibrium has been set to one unit of the importer's currency, the parameter α corresponds to the consumer reservation price, also measured in the importer's currency. The import price has been shown to fix somewhere between one and α, and then the impact of a cost shift with the reservation price held constant has been investigated. It is quite straightforward that in the empirical counterpart which is considered here, the reservation price of German consumers is determined by national German price or cost measures. Since reservation prices and their movements are sector-specific, a good approximation of them are sectoral unit labor costs. At the same time, unit labor costs are also representative of production costs of competing German product varieties in the respective sector. In the following empirical analysis the three determining theoretical components foreign unit labor costs, home unit labor costs, and the home reservation price can thus be reduced to just two components: foreign and domestic unit labor costs. It is therefore of interest to see whether import prices follow more closely the German unit labor cost variables or those of the foreign producer.

Figure 17 depicts these scenarios. Starting from a situation where both unit labor costs are equalized in period 0, German costs (thick dotted lines) rise by one percent and foreign costs (thin dotted lines) fall by the same amount in period 1. The real exchange rate based on unit labor costs thus shifts by two percent with Germany's currency appreciating in real terms. In period 2, the initial shock is reversed. Figure 17 also shows the evolution of import prices (thin lines) and compares it to German producer prices (thick lines). The first two figures have in common a close comovement between both series suggesting that prices are set rather competitively.

In the first case, which is arbitrarily given the letter *A* for easier reference later on, the German producers have to adjust their prices on a full scale to changes in world market conditions, which are reflected in import prices. In this case the product can be regarded to be homogenous, there exists a single world market price, and each country is small in the sense that it takes the world market price as given. From the point of view of a single country the domestic producer is constrained in his price setting by world market conditions. These in turn are approximated in the empirical figures by a variable representing unit labor costs of Germany's trading partners, the weight of each trading partner being the share of his exports to Germany in that product category.

In the second case, which is also compatible with comovement of prices, prices are set in order to stabilize prices in the country of destination. This is the pricing-to-market case (case *B*). Here the exporter is constrained in his price setting by conditions in the destination country, which are German unit labor costs. When there are several destinations for sales, those destination-oriented prices may differ when they are made comparable by means of the exchange rate. Therefore the law of one price cannot hold between markets, even though there is a close interdependency between prices in the same market.

The remaining third case (case *C*) is consequently the one with only a loose interdependency in prices, suggesting that prices are mainly determined by costs in the country of production. Import prices follow closely foreign unit labor costs evaluated in German's currency, whereas German producer prices are oriented at German unit labor costs. Import and German goods in this category are particularly imperfectly substitutable (low σ), and both German and foreign suppliers can rely on a substantial degree of monopolistic power within their product variant.

Figure 17: Movement of Import and Domestic Prices by Type of Good

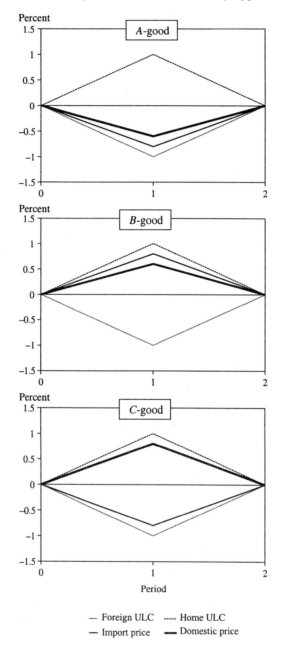

Foreign ULC ----- Home ULC

Import price Domestic price

Figure 18: Unit Labor Costs and Prices in Selected Sectors of German Manufacturing

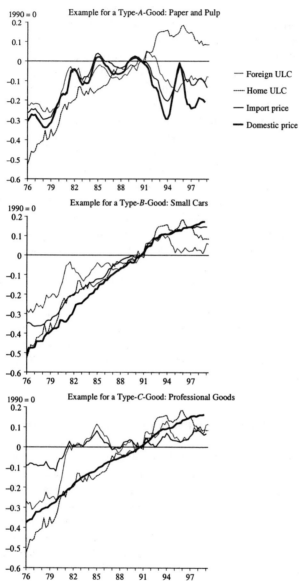

Source: Own calculations based on OECD (2000a, 2000b) and Statistisches Bundesamt, Zeitreihen-service, http://www-zr.destatis.de/dok/sgu3592.htm for import prices, http://www-zr.destatis.de/dok/sgu3596.htm for export prices, http://www-zr.destatis.de/dok/sgu3362.htm for domestic prices, http://www-zr.destatis.de/dok/sgu3363.htm for domestic prices.

Figure 18 shows the empirical counterpart of Figure 17. As a representative of an
A-good, paper and pulp products have been chosen. It is apparent that import
and German prices are determined on the world market, since both follow foreign costs. Especially in the period after 1991, in which Germany has seen a
sharp appreciation of its currency, which corresponds to a fall in foreign unit labor costs relative to German unit labor costs, a substantial discrepancy has been
built up. *A*-goods can thus easily be identified if import prices follow more foreign costs rather than domestic ones. This case exemplifies the benchmark case
of no pass-through of costs and no price discrimination between markets.

However, we see a completely different picture when automobiles with mo-
tors less than 1.5 liters as an example of *B*-goods are taken. There seems to be
enough competition in the German market to ensure that import and German
prices cannot deviate much from each other. Contrary to the case of *A*-goods,
however, both price series are more constrained by German rather than foreign
production costs. There is generally a close correspondence between unit labor
costs, producer prices, and consumer prices, whereas foreign costs show quite a
large volatility relative to each of the other series by the impact of the exchange
rate.

With professional goods as the *C*-case, it can be seen that foreign suppliers are
not forced to price to market, but follow their costs when they determine prices
for their German sales. So their price-setting rationale is similar to that for *A*-
goods. On the other hand, German producers also pursue cost pricing, because
German producer prices follow German costs as in the *B*-case. The new feature
here is that foreign and German prices are set independently and show a low correlation between them.

2.   Evidence from Descriptive Statistics on Time Series of Prices

In this section, the approach taken for analyzing price data across countries is
adapted to the sectoral view. Since the economic analysis produced some conclusions concerning the degree of the response of price data to the underlying
shocks, it is first of interest to investigate whether a corresponding pattern in the
variability of the data series can be found. This approach standardizes the spon-
taneous look at some charts in Section 1 by providing some statistical material
which helps compare the sectors from a descriptive point of view, before some
more rigorous econometric analysis will be applied in Section 3. In doing so,
data from sectoral German import prices will be considered first, and then the
analysis will be extended to cover also export prices.

a. Classifying Sectors from Import Data

The ideas presented so far are summarized in Table 10. Whereas in the case of products with a relatively large degree of homogeneity pass-through generally tends to be substantial, the product groups with more differentiated varieties can show either high or low degrees of pass-through depending on demand, market structure conditions, and the incidence of sunk costs as discussed. Before German manufacturing sectors can be categorized into these groups, some relevant descriptive statistical measures are computed and presented in Table 9. In particular, these include the ratio of the standard deviation of import prices relative to computed foreign export prices (*SDPM/SDPXF*). This ratio is better suited to interpretation than the variance or standard deviation alone because prices may vary due to other determinants such as variations in material input prices. These sources of disturbance should affect both export and import prices, whereas their relative variation compared to each other should be more influenced by structural market features which are the focus here. Measures also included in the table are coefficients of correlations between price series (*CORPMPD* and *CORPXPD*, respectively). The time horizon for computing these statistics is 1976Q1 through 1999Q3.[28]

Figure 19, which illustrates the computed statistical measures from Table 9, gives a more complete picture of how different sectors in German manufacturing can be ranked according to pass-through. Like in the stylized matrix of Table 10, pass-through is measured on the horizontal axis such that products on the right-hand side exhibit more pass-through than products on the left-hand side.

The empirical measure of pass-through is the standard deviation of relative import price changes relative to the standard deviation of foreign export price changes (*SDPM/SDPXF*). The underlying index of foreign export prices itself has been constructed from the series of German import prices divided by a sector-specific nominal effective exchange rate index. The weights used for constructing this index are the same as those applied to the sector-specific relative unit labor cost index, the only difference being that the bilateral nominal exchange rates in terms of domestic currency per foreign currency unit were used instead of foreign unit labor costs. The weights are the sectoral import shares in the product categories specified for 24 OECD countries other than Germany. They are the mean for the years 1989 to 1991 and are shown in Chapter D.III.2. The constructed series *foreign export price index* therefore is from the point of view of Germany's trading partners (country *A*) and is equivalent to the variable p^{A*B} in Chapter C, whereas German (i.e., country *B*) import prices correspond to

---

28 Export prices are only available from 1985 onward for PH, CP, and FU, as well as import prices for EG, TE, and TR, whereas producer price indices are available only since 1980 for CP and FU.

Table 9: A Selection of German Manufacturing Sectors and Sectoral Pricing Behavior[a]

Symbol	Sector	GP89[b]	SDPM/SDPXF	CORPMPD	CORPXPD
CO	Organic chemicals	41	0.94	0.89	0.91
CA	Inorganic chemicals	42	1.02	0.46	0.66
PH	Medicinal & pharmaceutical products	47	1.17	−0.05	0.27
CP	Chemical products	49	1.18	0.11	0.14
RP	Rubber products	59	0.59	0.39	0.55
PP	Paper, paperboard, paper-pulp	55	0.84	0.91	0.93
TX	Textiles	63	0.19	0.70	0.80
PO	Pottery, glassware, nonmetallic mineral manufactures	51	0.43	0.49	0.84
IR	Iron & steel	27	0.68	0.81	0.74
MA	General industrial machinery & equipment	32	0.56	0.53	0.95
OF	Office machines & computers	50	0.89	0.29	0.25
TV	Radio, TV, sound recording app.	366	0.19	0.22	0.40
EL	Electrical machinery	36	0.48	0.61	0.83
FU	Furniture	542	0.32	0.41	0.74
AP	Apparel & clothing accessoires	64	0.12	0.33	0.53
PG	Professional instruments, optical goods, watches	37	0.75	0.20	0.68
NF	Nonferrous metals	28	1.00	0.90	0.88
PL	Plastic goods	58	0.51	0.64	0.86
EG	Electrical goods	363	0.40	0.27	0.31
TE	Telecommunication equipment	365	0.48	0.18	0.38
SH	Shoes	625	0.45	0.49	0.62
CS	Passenger cars < 1.5 l	33111–33112	0.39	0.30	0.18
CL	Passenger cars > 1.5 l	33113–33117	0.42	0.17	0.37
TR	Trucks	3313	0.93	0.27	0.36

[a]*SDPM/SDPXF* is the ratio of the standard deviation of the import price series (in logs and detrended) to the standard deviation of foreign export prices, with foreign export prices being computed as described in the text above. *CORPMPD* and *CORPXPD* are the coefficients of correlation between relative changes of import prices and relative changes of domestic prices, and relative changes of export prices and relative changes of domestic prices, respectively. – [b]For the sectoral classification, see Table A5 in Chapter D.III.2.

Source: Own calculations based on Statistisches Bundesamt, Zeitreihenservice; for details, see Figure 18.

Table 10: Classification of Goods According to Homogeneity and Pass-Through

	Pass-through in import prices low	Pass-through in import prices high
Product homogeneity high	–	A-Goods
Product homogeneity low	B-Goods	C-Goods

Figure 19: Price Correlation (*CORPMPD*) and Pass-Through (*SDPM/SDPXF*) across Sectors[a]

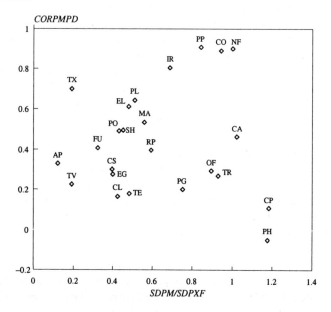

[a]For abbreviations of sectors, see Table 9.

Source: Own calculations based on Statistisches Bundesamt, Zeitreihenservice; for details, see Figure 18.

p^{AB}. Both this newly constructed series and the original German import price series were transformed into logs and then detrended by differentiating.

The reason why not the standard deviation of import price changes alone was used is that the volatility of producer prices and import prices is different across sectors or product categories because input factors differ. Stable import prices do not necessarily mean that pass-through is incomplete and that exporters pursue pricing to market if domestic producer prices and export prices are also relatively stable. On the contrary, goods intensive in certain raw materials with large price fluctuations, for example iron and steel, in general show large volatilities, an observation that should not be confused with high pass-through. If import price volatility is normalized by export price volatility, then this resulting measure can be interpreted in absolute terms. A value smaller than one indicates that import prices are more stable than export prices, which is indicative of imperfect pass-through. In addition to the inherent volatility in prices due to cost changes of production factors, there is a supplementary volatility in export prices in the exporter's currency as a result of the aim of stabilizing import prices in the importer's currency (in this case Germany). As discussed above, *B*-goods should show a low volatility ratio. By contrast, one should expect *A*-goods which are intensive in raw materials to have a volatility ratio near one. If that ratio is one, cost factors totally dominate prices without any trace of pricing to market. At last, *C*-goods have a pricing pattern which is oriented at country-specific determinants like wages or productivity with a high degree of pass-through. Prices in the importer's currency should then be more volatile than export prices since import prices are also affected by exchange rate volatility. As a result, *C*-goods are expected to be situated at the very right on the horizontal axis in Figures 19 and 20.

On the vertical axis, products are sorted according to their degree of product homogeneity so that product groups ranging at the top consist of more substitutable variants. The empirical measure is the coefficient of correlation between growth rates of import and domestic prices. The idea behind this is that import variants are different from domestic ones as was presumed in the theoretical part implying that a higher correlation of prices between those variants stands for a larger σ.

When sectors are allocated along those two dimensions, indeed a triangle emerges. A stylized version of this triangle is given in Figure 20. At the top of the triangle one encounters *A*-sectors like nonferrous metals, organic chemicals, paper and pulp, and iron and steel. It is noticeable that these sectors produce intermediate products with production being intensive in raw materials, a result which is in line with theoretical expectations. Moving down the triangle into the direction of the *B*-corner one realizes that the character of the goods changes. When we stop halfway we find sectors producing capital goods like machinery and electrical machinery, but also those which produce material-intensive consumer goods like plastic goods, shoes, pottery, and rubber products. Finally, at the very left of the triangle the pure consumption goods emerge, specifically wearing apparel, radio and television, electrical goods but also cars and telecommunication equipment, where pass-through is lowest.

Figure 20: The Theoretical Relationship between Substitutability and Pass-Through by Type of Good

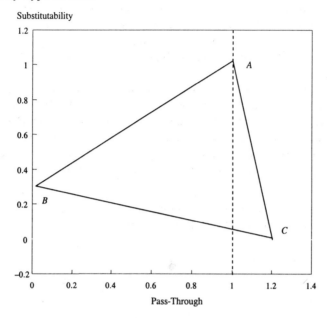

An outlier are textiles with both an extremely low pass-through and a very high degree of homogeneity. One has to note that large cars are found to be less substitutable than small cars, also in line with common sense. The only products which are more homogeneous than large cars are pharmaceutical and chemical goods, which are situated in corner *C*, but also professional goods and trucks are not far apart. On the way back to corner *A*, we lastly hit upon inorganic chemicals which are more homogeneous than organic chemicals and chemical products.

b.   Classifying Sectors from Data on Import and Export Prices

Additional to the interpretation of German import prices, which are also the basis for constructing foreign export prices of Germany's trade partners, one can look at the export prices of Germany itself. These should be driven principally by the same array of exogenous parameters as far as product attributes such as the degree of homogeneity are concerned. So far, one would expect a similar behavior of German export and foreign export prices. However, differences may occur if sector-specific market shares of German exporters are taken into consideration.

If, for example, Germany has a comparative advantage in some sector, thus implying a large share on the world market, some kind of asymmetry between the export and import side would arise because, following the previous theoretical discussion, pass-through on the export side would outperform that on the import side. Another source of asymmetry can be due to different degrees of product homogeneity, which in turn may be attributed to quality differences between imports and exports.

Figure 21 compares the export and import side by setting the correlation between relative export and domestic price changes (*CORPXPD*) against the correlation between relative import and domestic price changes (*CORPMPD*). The first important result is that both measures are positively correlated, with both of them reflecting the degree of homogeneity in product space, which increases along the upper-right direction. Another result is that the correspondence be-

Figure 21: The Correlation of Import Prices (*CORPMPD*) versus the Correlation of Export Prices (*CORPXPD*) with Domestic Prices[a]

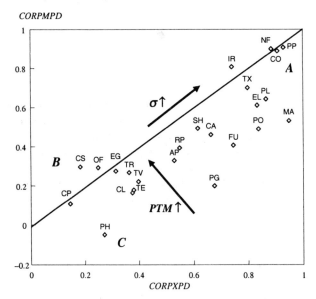

[a]For abbreviations of sectors, see Table 9. *CORPMPD* and *CORPXPD* are the coefficients of correlation between relative changes in import prices and domestic prices, and export prices and domestic prices, respectively.

Source: Own calculations based on Statistisches Bundesamt, Zeitreihenservice; for details, see Figure 18.

tween export and domestic prices is closer than the correspondence between import and domestic prices since the majority of sectors is situated below the diagonal.

This is not an implausible outcome since product varieties sold in the home market should be more similar to those targeted for export than to their imported counterparts. However, there can be some ambiguity because export and domestic prices deviate from each other even in the same product variant, as was shown in the analytical foundation for pricing to market, suggesting that exporters change export prices in order to keep local prices in the importing country constant. Thus, the correlation between domestic and export prices not only gauges homogeneity, but is also biased by factors which engender pricing to market such as strong competition in the respective market and the ability to price discriminate between national markets, which could be due to transport costs or other impediments in general that make reselling costly. The covariance between export and domestic prices therefore is an imperfect measure for product homogeneity. Nonetheless it can be used to determine to what degree German producers can pass through costs to their export markets relative to foreign producers to Germany for a specific product category.

Sectors below or at the right of the diagonal show a high ability to set prices in export markets similarly to domestic markets implying that pricing to market is not an important strategy. Here we encounter typical *C*-goods such as pharmaceutical products or professional goods. Especially the machinery sector exhibits a high comovement of export and domestic prices thus signaling market power for German exporters. Quite contrary, sectors at the upper-left side of the box show a higher correlation of domestic prices with import prices rather than export prices. Producers therefore opt to adjust export prices quite independently from domestic prices in order to comply with market conditions which constrain producers not to deviate too far from prices set by their competitors in the same market. Small cars, office and computing machines, and iron and steel are the most outstanding examples in this category of small price-setting power.

3. Evidence from Real Exchange Rate Effects on Relative Prices

In the last section, the investigation of pricing behavior was based on the use of summary statistics showing that volatility measures of prices can be combined in order to classify sectors into the three groups defined earlier on. The main two advantages of this approach are that a two-dimensional ranking scale could be built up and that no particular assumptions are necessary concerning the exact factors which cause the shock on domestic, export, and import prices. For the measurement of pass-through it was thus irrelevant whether the shock came from exchange rate movements or any shift in domestic or foreign production costs. The relevance of this simplifying procedure is due to the fact that there is only scarce data on unit labor costs and the costs of other input production factors which can be compared both across sectors and across countries.

The other approach, which has also been applied to the country studies in Section I, is to build on relationships based on economic theory which govern the behavior of prices. One particular form of this procedure, which will be applied next, is to regress relative export or import prices on relative unit labor costs, again for Germany as the representative country. These relative prices are the ratios of export or import prices ($LNPX_i$ and $LNPM_i$) over domestic producer prices ($LNPPI_i$). The rationale behind this procedure of using these transformations in terms of price ratios has its justification in the microeconomic approach of Chapter C implying that price ratios and real economic variables as opposed to nominal variables are the crucial objects one has to look at. Moreover, the benefit of using sectoral price ratios is that the problem of nonstationary components as part of driving forces of nominal variables loses its bearing since disaggregated price ratios should tend to equalize in the long run if they are correctly measured and applied to the same category of goods. It is thus assumed that money illusion does not play a role, implying that only relative prices or real variables are important as opposed to nominal series. Nonetheless, even these relative prices often cannot be proved to be stationary at sufficient levels of significance, as Table A6 in Chapter D.III.2 shows. The conservative approach is, therefore, to implement an error correction framework which is particularly warranted in case of nonstationary variables, but which is at the same time not meaningless for those series which pass the test of rejecting the null of nonstationarity.

Suppose that in Germany a relatively high unit labor cost index prevails relative to its trading partners for a certain period of time. Due to increased cost competitiveness of the countries exporting to Germany, a relatively low import price compared to domestic producer prices in Germany would be the result. For German exports, one would also expect that export prices are lower relative to domestic prices. The reason why not levels of import or export prices but their price ratios with respect to domestic producer prices are used is that sectors differ in their dependency on imported inputs. If the export price pertaining to a particular sector is lowered as a response to a domestic currency appreciation, then this might not necessarily be evidence for pricing to market and for the fact that output prices on world markets are seen to be more or less given from the producer's point of view, but it might simply be the result of lowered material input prices which have a dominant impact in a sector heavily dependent on imported inputs. Because not only export but also domestic producer prices would be affected by this appreciation, a suitable way to control for sectoral differences in cost structures concerning the importance of imported components is to look at the ratio of export to domestic prices. Quite analogously, import prices might incorporate material cost components which may also be felt in domestic prices of a comparable product which also uses this input factor. The ratio of import to domestic prices, however, seems to be more or less immune to these kinds of shocks, but reflects a higher amount of nontraded factors inputs and the degree by which producers can pass through these cost components, which is the very focus of interest in this work.

For each sector, a separate series for relative unit labor costs has been constructed in using German sectoral import shares for the relative unit labor cost series in import price regressions (*LNRULCM*), and export shares for computing the relative unit labor cost series in export price regressions (*LNRULCX*).[29] Before turning to the regressions themselves it has to be checked whether each time series is stationary or integrated. Table A6 in Chapter D.III.2 gives the results of the augmented Dickey–Fuller tests for the degree of integration, concluding that for the most part, the series on relative prices are nonstationary, the only exceptions being the sectors of iron and steel, chemical products, and small and large cars for relative import prices, and iron and steel and shoes for relative export prices. For these sectors the finding of stationarity of relative prices can be interpreted as evidence of the long-term tendency for deviations of export prices (or, respectively, import prices) from domestic prices to revert. A further conclusion is that the goods are sufficiently homogeneous in order to prevent divergent paths of both series to occur. Corresponding to the country-specific approach in Section I of this chapter, a suitable approach to account for the fact that time series may be nonstationary is an error-correction specification:

$$(D.30) \quad \Delta \left(LNPM_{it} - LNPPI_{it} \right) =$$
$$(g-1)\left[\left(LNPM_{i,t-1} - LNPPI_{i,t-1}\right) - aLNRULCM_{i,t-1} - v_i\right]$$
$$+ \sum_{j=0}^{q} b_j \Delta LNRULCM_{i,t-j} + \sum_{j=1}^{s} d_j \Delta \left(LNPM_{i,t-j} - LNPPI_{i,t-j}\right) + \varepsilon_t,$$

$$(D.31) \quad \Delta \left(LNPX_{it} - LNPPI_{it} \right) =$$
$$(g-1)\left[\left(LNPX_{i,t-1} - LNPPI_{i,t-1}\right) - aLNRULCX_{i,t-1} - v_i\right]$$
$$+ \sum_{j=0}^{q} b_j \Delta LNRULCX_{i,t-j} + \sum_{j=1}^{s} d_j \Delta \left(LNPX_{i,t-j} - LNPPI_{i,t-j}\right) + \varepsilon_t.$$

---

[29] See Tables A3 and A4 in Chapter D.III.2 for the country weights.

The subscript i stands for the sector, and the v_i are country-specific fixed effects. Equation (D.30) specifies the differential adjustment of import prices versus domestic prices, and (D.31) export versus domestic prices. The coefficient a describes the long-run relationship between the price differentials, which are the import/domestic price ratio in (D.30) and the export/domestic price ration in (D.31), and relative domestic to foreign unit labor costs, b stands for short-term impacts, and d are the coefficients on the lagged differenced endogenous variable. The coefficient on the error-correction term, $g - 1$, can be interpreted as leading toward equilibrium if it turns out to be significantly negative. The current realization of the price drift is thus partly caused by the tendency of long-run disequilibria to be reversed, and is to the other part driven by current innovations in the exogenous variables.

The empirical estimations are for relative export and import prices separately. For each of the two groups, all sectoral equations are estimated jointly by the method of seemingly unrelated regression (SUR). This is done because all sector-specific variables are driven by the same vector of bilateral exchange rates with only the weight of each trading partner being different. Therefore residuals are expected to be correlated between single sectoral equations, a feature that the SUR method uses to enhance efficiency. For the sake of ensuring comparability of results across sectors, the lag length has been restricted to one for all sectors, even though the fact that some figures of the Durbin–Watson statistic are much lower than two points toward a more general lag structure.

a.   *Evidence from Import Prices*

Table 11 depicts the estimation results from the import side, thus generally confirming the findings derived from the variation measures. Pass-through is high if in the import price regression the long-run relationship is prevailing ($g - 1$ is significant) and the long-run coefficient a assumes a substantially negative value. Relative prices and relative unit labor costs are cointegrated, and deviations from this cointegration relationship cause adjustments in the endogenous variable, the relative import price.[30] The long-term coefficient is significantly negative for all sectors which show a stationary time series of relative import prices, i.e., chemical products, iron and steel, and small cars, which for the majority belong to the category of A-goods. This outcome can be explained by the relatively small

---

[30]   It is reasonable to post that relative unit labor costs are strictly exogenous in this long-term relation since exchange rates largely move due to autonomous forces and German wages are negotiated with a periodicity of a year at minimum. Since only wage costs are taken, feedback effects through imported goods are excluded. If strict exogeneity did not hold, a second cointegration vector would exist indicating how relative unit labor costs would adjust to imbalances.

Table 11: Sectoral Error-Correction Results for Import Prices[a]

	$g-1$[b]	a	b	SE	DW
CO	−0.070	0.084	0.003	0.021	1.746
	(−1.969)	(0.359)	(0.033)		
CA	−0.038	−0.889	−0.214	0.024	1.387
	(−2.820)	(−2.172)	(−2.240*)		
CP	−0.049	−0.639	−0.200	0.014	1.744
	(−3.340**)	(−2.478◊)	(−3.685**)		
RP	−0.046	−0.257	−0.090	0.013	1.357
	(−2.173)	(−0.834)	(−1.674+)		
PP	−0.063	0.205	−0.017	0.012	0.914
	(−1.772)	(1.541)	(−0.364)		
TX	−0.032	−0.316	−0.050	0.006	1.338
	(−3.051+)	(−2.227)	(−2.139*)		
PO	−0.053	−0.450	−0.079	0.010	1.195
	(−3.740*)	(−2.857)	(−2.221*)		
IR	−0.065	−0.125	−0.073	0.013	1.008
	(−2.418◊)	(−0.917)	(−1.363)		
MA	−0.071	−0.544	−0.170	0.007	1.382
	(−4.497**)	(−7.323**)	(−7.072**)		
OF	−0.007	−3.896	−0.333	0.014	1.668
	(−0.786)	(−0.684)	(−7.616**)		
TV	−0.032	−0.147	−0.072	0.007	1.642
	(−2.914)	(−0.472)	(−3.499**)		
EL	−0.055	−0.526	−0.136	0.008	1.212
	(−3.163+)	(−4.045**)	(−4.652**)		
AP	−0.031	−0.371	−0.036	0.007	1.279
	(−3.582*)	(−2.325)	(−1.732+)		
PG	−0.035	−0.227	−0.200	0.011	1.246
	(−2.659)	(−0.668)	(−6.140**)		
NF	−0.050	−0.132	−0.173	0.030	1.924
	(−2.000)	(−0.294)	(−1.349)		
PL	−0.040	−0.429	−0.062	0.008	1.411
	(−2.469)	(−2.446)	(−1.825+)		
SH	−0.044	−0.463	−0.219	0.011	2.212
	(−1.510)	(−2.528)	(−5.788**)		
CS	−0.129	−0.250	−0.072	0.009	1.637
	(−5.165**)	(−3.861◊)	(−2.344*)		
CL	−0.139	−0.394	−0.090	0.009	1.948
	(−4.387**)	(−7.337◊)	(−2.618**)		

[a]For the notation of sectors, see Table 9. Some sectors are excluded from regression due to data constraints. t-statistics in parentheses. **, *, +: Significant at a p-value of at least 1, 5, or 10 percent. ◊: Significant at a 5 percent critical value being calculated from Levin and Lin (1992), Theorem 5.2d. Coefficients as defined in the text. SE: Standard error of regression. DW: Durbin–Watson test statistic. The time period covered is from 1976Q1 through 1999Q1 except for PH, CP, and FU, where missing values require a shortening of the time span. – [b]Critical values are from Banerjee et al. (1998: 276, Table I) for coefficients on $g-1$ and a when the series of the dependent variable is nonstationary, otherwise the Student's t-distribution is used for testing significance.

price-cost margins that make it difficult for producers to keep prices in local markets constant or to offer the goods at the same price levels as their local competitors. We thus see at least some pass-through in terms of a change in the relative price of imports to domestic production for these goods.

The working of the error-correction mechanism, together with a significant long-term coefficient, can also be observed for sectors such as machinery, electrical goods, and large cars. Here the property of nonstationarity of the relative import price series is accounted for by the fact that relative unit labor costs are nonstationary for these sectors, and this nonstationary trend of relative unit labor costs is transmitted to relative import prices. Long-term trends in relative unit labor costs therefore explain long-term shifts in relative import prices, but this response is only less than proportional given that the coefficients a are between minus one and zero.

The short-term coefficient b, telling how the ratio between the relative price of imports and domestic sales prices evolves instantaneously as a result to a real exchange rate shock in terms of relative unit labor costs, indicates for the majority of cases significant results. In fact, a real appreciation of the domestic currency (a relative increase of domestic unit labor costs) causes the import price to fall relative to the domestic price. For all sectors, with the exception of the plastic products sector, where none of the coefficients seem to be significant, there is a short-term response of relative import prices to relative unit labor cost changes. The absence of any long-term relationship may either be explained by the lack of pricing power of foreign producers, who are only able to pass through a portion of an exchange rate change in the short run, or because prices may have been agreed upon in the currency of the exporter and are not subject to change when the exchange rate changes and the transaction of the goods trade is effectuated.

b.   *Evidence from Export Prices*

Concerning export prices an analogous reasoning can be made when looking at Table 12. The finding of significantly nonzero coefficients a and b is suggestive for differential price setting between domestic and foreign markets. To begin with the two sectors which exhibit stationary relative export price series, which are according to Table A4 the iron and steel and shoe industries, the outcomes are somewhat heterogeneous. Whereas the short-term dynamics are significant for both sectors, only the shoe industry shows signs of long-term pricing to market. The negative coefficient indicates that an increase in relative unit labor costs of domestic producers over foreign ones leads to a reduction of export prices relative to domestic prices. The finding that such a long-term drift in relative export prices cannot be detected for the iron and steel sector is in line with both previous theoretical arguments and evidence from earlier variance measurements

Table 12: Sectoral Error-Correction Results for Export Prices[a]

	$g-1$[b]	a	b	SE	DW
CO	−0.067	0.546	0.192	0.027	1.361
	(−2.083)	(1.880)	(1.684+)		
CA	−0.073	0.114	0.008	0.011	1.556
	(−1.792)	(0.998)	(0.175)		
RP	−0.032	0.193	0.015	0.009	1.953
	(−2.943+)	(0.646)	(0.402)		
PP	−0.043	0.236	−0.050	0.009	1.646
	(−1.716)	(1.190)	(−1.229)		
TX	−0.032	0.024	−0.013	0.004	1.213
	(−1.709)	(0.189)	(−0.851)		
PO	−0.059	0.210	0.032	0.004	1.938
	(−2.309)	(3.680)	(1.814+)		
IR	−0.120	−0.108	−0.254	0.017	1.247
	(−3.716**)	(−1.042)	(−3.579**)		
MA	−0.088	−0.050	−0.009	0.002	2.478
	(−3.489*)	(−2.946*)	(−1.194)		
OF	−0.090	−0.935	−0.290	0.011	1.923
	(−4.166**)	(−9.776**)	(−5.989**)		
TV	−0.025	−0.155	−0.030	0.005	1.724
	(−0.933)	(−0.770)	(−1.337)		
EL	−0.010	0.062	−0.006	0.003	1.967
	(−0.388)	(0.283)	(−0.558)		
AP	−0.095	0.168	−0.008	0.005	1.571
	(−2.403)	(3.456)	(−0.349)		
PG	0.006	0.628	−0.016	0.004	2.130
	(0.478)	(0.482)	(−1.149)		
NF	−0.223	−0.206	0.024	0.023	1.737
	(−4.363)	(−2.474)	(0.245)		
PL	−0.071	−0.216	−0.024	0.005	1.745
	(−3.751*)	(−4.048**)	(−1.193)		
EG	−0.060	−0.020	−0.038	0.004	1.784
	(−2.619)	(−0.369)	(−2.173*)		
TE	0.000	−751.465	0.085	0.011	1.545
	(0.001)	(−0.001)	(1.797)		
SH	−0.189	−0.267	−0.098	0.006	1.864
	(−4.740**)	(−9.545**)	(−3.484**)		
CS	−0.036	−0.615	−0.109	0.012	2.040
	(−1.954)	(−2.378)	(−2.236*)		
CL	−0.037	−0.415	−0.106	0.008	2.022
	(−1.947)	(−2.493)	(−3.862**)		

[a]Some sectors are excluded from regression due to data constraints. t-statistics in parentheses. **, *, +: significant at a p-value of at least 1, 5, or 10 percent. Coefficients as defined in the text. For abbreviations of sectors, see Table 9. SE: Standard error of regression. DW: Durbin–Watson test statistic. – [b]Critical values are from Banerjee et al. (1998: 276, Table I) for coefficients on λ and α when the series of the dependent variable is nonstationary, otherwise the Student's t-distribution is used for testing significance.

in Section II.1 of this chapter that attribute a larger role of pricing to market to consumption goods sectors such as the shoe industry than to sectors producing relatively homogeneous goods like the steel industry. Other sectors showing significant evidence of pricing to market are machinery, office machines, and plastic goods. The interpretation is that long-term pricing to market is practiced in these sectors with the effect being strongest for office machines and lowest for machinery. A strong long-term pricing-to-market effect is suggestive for the feature that producers are price takers in the export markets, and costs of production do not play a dominant role in price setting.

Turning now to the nonstationary cases, as was already argued for the relative import price, if a price series is nonstationary, a cointegration relationship between relative prices and relative costs may or may not exist. If it does exist then the absence of stationarity in relative export prices is caused by the fact that the nonstationary trend of the relative cost series is transmitted to the relative price series through the long-term relationship.

The next group of sectors comprises those which display only short-term pricing-to-market effects but their relative export price series is nonstationary. Industries, which can be grouped into this category, are those producing electrical goods, radios and televisions, organic chemicals, rubber products, and small and large cars. Products are sufficiently differentiated so that separate long-run pricing trends in the export and home market can be sustained. However, the significant short-term impact of the real exchange rate on relative prices suggests that market share considerations play a crucial role. Thus, the costs that must be incurred to extend the customer base are the main rationale for this price-setting pattern, rather than the producer's anticipation of arbitrage by resale.

Finally, concerning the remaining sectors, neither long-term nor short-term impacts of the real exchange rate can be found. There are two possible explanations for this. The first is that goods are quite homogeneous and price-cost margins are small (A-goods) thus impeding price differentiation across countries. The other possible explanation is that products are differentiated to such a large degree (C-goods) that a nearly monopolistic pricing schedule is applied, which keeps relative price-cost margins both constant and identical across export markets. Indeed, sectors with insignificant coefficients range from homogeneous products such as rubber, pottery, and paper and pulp to professional goods. A judgment on the classification of sectors can therefore only be made when one looks at the import side simultaneously. It then becomes obvious that pricing power with regard to professional goods is indeed noticeable since on the import side, the relative import price varies substantially along with the real exchange rate. Quite contrary, this does not hold for homogeneous goods like pottery or paper and pulp.

To conclude the analysis of exchange rate impacts on prices, it can be stated that the above findings from applying volatility measures in order to classify sectors can be verified by regression analyses as the second approach. The results can be briefly summarized as follows: The table of coefficients for import prices (Table 11) identifies *A*-sectors with highly homogeneous products in those equations with insignificant coefficients. Import, export, and domestic prices cannot deviate sufficiently in order to comply for differences in national production costs. Sectors belonging to this group are inorganic chemicals, rubber products, paper and pulp, iron and steel, and apparel. *B*-goods as pricing-to-market goods, by contrast, are those with medium-sized coefficients in the import price regression and very negative coefficients in the export price regression (Table 12), as it is revealed for office machines, small and large cars, and organic chemicals. *C*-goods with a high level of pass-through show strong negative coefficients in the import price regression and weak coefficients with regard to relative export prices. Sectors which are part of this category are professional goods, chemical products, general and electrical machinery.

4.   Explaining Sectoral Differences

In the last two sections of this chapter, results based on both volatility measures and regressions were generated for each sector. The theoretical considerations in Chapter C provided some explanations for the different pricing pattern between sectors, and the determining factors like price-cost margins or the degree of substitutability of product varieties helped to classify the sectors. However, although the outcomes seem plausible it has not been investigated yet whether these sectors show attributes relating to structural economic fundamentals which account for the price-cost margins or the degree of product homogeneity that cannot be observed, but which are reflected in the pricing behavior in the end. Theoretical considerations from Chapter C lead us to look for quantifiable variables that are related to the elasticity of demand or the market structure in terms of the number of competitors.

The relationship between market structure and markups has been investigated empirically within the field of industrial economics. However, it must be noted that the literature concerning the level of markups is of only indirect relevance insofar as what we are dealing with here is not the *level* of the markup itself, but rather the change in prices which parallels a certain *change* in the markup. Nevertheless, a brief glimpse on the determinants of the markup, the market power, and pricing behavior might be beneficial. One factor is without doubt the level of economies of scale, which determines the number of firms in the market and the average size of the firm. Large economies of scale are generally expected to inhibit market entry of new firms, thus increasing market power of existing firms in the market. A second important determinant influencing entry conditions and market power is the degree of product differentiation (Dixit and Stiglitz 1977) due to sunk costs for research and development (R&D) or advertising. Specifically, Sutton (1991, 1995) developed a discontinuous distribution of firm size as a determinant for the level of profitability. Empirical estimates for that relationship include Blanchard and Melino (1986) and Oliveira-Martins et al. (1996), with the latter study encompassing 14 OECD countries and 36 sectors. In those studies, the profitability variable has been instrumentalized by empirical estimates of the markup ratio. One of the main results of Oliveira-Martins et al. is that markups seem to vary substantially by industry and country, with markups being lower in what the authors denote *segmented* industries rather than in *fragmented* industries. The segmented industries have establishments which are relatively large on average, whereas fragmented ones consist of relatively small firms.

The figures that Oliveira-Martins et al. computed as OECD-wide averages for average establishment size, the R&D intensity by establishment, and the R&D/output intensity are shown in Table 13. They are combined with the sectoral variation ratios of this study which measure pass-through from Table 9.[31] The question whether structural variables play a role for pass-through was only given scarce attention in the literature. Menon (1996) investigated pass-through for Australian imports of manufactures disaggregated across sectors and found that pass-through decreases with the four-firm concentration ratio, the imports/domestic sales ratio, and the degree of product differentiation.

This relationship will next be explored empirically for German sectoral data. As a first step, the statistical volatility measure for relative prices is compared with the average establishment size (*SIZE*) and the average expenses on R&D (*RD*), or alternatively measured, the R&D/output intensity (*RDOUT*). As a result, the general impression one gets when looking at Table 13 is that both R&D activities and the average firm size seem to be positively correlated with the variation ratio *SDPM/SDPXF*. Recall that this ratio is the ratio between the standard deviations of the German import price and the standard deviation of world export prices for exports into Germany, the latter being computed by the use of German import prices and the German nominal effective exchange rate constructed with the relevant sector-specific country weights. This relative volatility of import prices compared to the volatility of export prices is low when exporters stabilize

---

[31] In order to make a comparison possible, for the category of road vehicles a comprehensive variation ratio covering all categories of road vehicles was calculated based on the GP-classification No. 89 and SITC category 78 (symbol in tables: RV). Since the category of industrial chemicals covers both organic and inorganic chemicals for which no combined price series exists, only the variation measure for organic chemicals was used.

Table 13: A Selection of German Manufacturing Sectors and Relative Pass-Through of Import Prices Relative to Export Prices[a]

Symbol	Sector	ISIC	*SDPM/ SDPXF*	*SIZE*	*RD*	*RDOUT*
CO	Industrial chemicals	3510	0.94	268	730	131
PH	Pharmaceutical products	3522	1.17	272	2178	612
CP	Chemical products	3529	1.18	123	212	141
RP	Rubber products	3550	0.59	179	74	66
PP	Paper & pulp	3410	0.84	195	46	12
TX	Textiles	3210	0.19	98	7	11
PO	Pottery & china	3610	0.43	152	33	50
IR	Iron & steel	3710	0.68	336	156	40
MA	Machinery & equipment	3829	0.56	96	84	105
OF	Office & comp. mach.	3825	0.89	271	935	488
TV	Radio & TV	3832	0.19	242	1123	589
EL	Electrical machinery	3839	0.48	151	492	154
RV	Motor vehicles	3843	0.27	255	445	136
FU	Furniture	3320	0.32	62	3	8
AP	Wearing apparel	3220	0.12	72	4	16
PG	Professional goods	3850	0.75	106	197	276
NF	Nonferrous metals	3720	1.00	233	199	54
PL	Plastic products	3560	0.51	75	30	57
SH	Shoes	3240	0.45	109	7	14

[a]*SIZE*: Average employment per establishment normalized by the total manufacturing average in each country. – *RD*: R&D expenses by establishment normalized by the total manufacturing average in each country. – *RDOUT*: R&D expenditure/gross output ratio normalized by the total manufacturing average in each country.

Source: Oliveira-Martins et al. (1996); own calculations.

prices in local markets and the pass-through of cost or exchange rate changes into prices is incomplete.

Moreover, a look at Table 13 reveals that four sectors stand out particularly. These are textiles, furniture, wearing apparel, and shoes. All four industries have in common that they have firm sizes lower than 110, that their R&D expenditures are in the single digits, and that they are also among the sectors with lowest R&D/output ratio. What is striking is that these sectors show a very low import price volatility ratio, which is at maximum 0.45, thus pointing to a high incidence of pricing-to-market strategies within these industries. This shows the importance of price competition and the strain to keep market shares constant especially in low-tech consumer goods sectors, in which products are insufficiently differentiated to allow a monopolistic pricing schedule.

On the other end of the scale we find pharmaceutical products and industrial chemicals, revealing a volatility ratio greater than one. Simultaneously, the pharmaceutical sector is clearly the most R&D intensive one. The high pricing power can therefore be accounted for by the very high entry costs in this sector.

In an intermediate position we encounter as a third group of sectors those with a rather material-intensive input structure, for example rubber products, paper and pulp, iron and steel, pottery, and nonferrous metals. They have in common a large firm size, but only a moderate R&D intensity.

Of course, there are also sectors which do not fit entirely into this picture which has just been drawn. Automobiles and radio and TV, for example, both being part of the consumption good sector, reveal a rather high incidence of pricing to market, notwithstanding the fact that the car and consumer electronics industries have an R&D intensity well above average. Relatively low transport costs and a substitutability in consumption between single variants which is still high in spite of the large technology input might be employed as explanations.

It appears that a large firm size, corresponding generally to a small number of firms in the market and thus a high concentration, enables firms to pass through a higher proportion of their relative cost differentials, which makes import prices in the importer's currency behave relatively volatile. The same applies to a high R&D intensity, which is an indicator of an industry's degree of innovation and can be taken as a rough measure for the degree of product differentiation. Sectors with a high R&D intensity show relatively more pass-through, reflecting higher market power. These results are complementary to those obtained by Oliveira-Martins et al. (1996) who detected relatively substantial markups in sectors with large firms, and in this group even larger markups in sectors with a high degree of product differentiation. As was argued before, if the degree of product differentiation is very high, as it holds for the above-mentioned goods classified as *C*-goods such as professional goods from the above example, pass-through is comparatively high. On the other end of the spectrum, those consumption goods can be arranged which best fit the pricing-to-market schedule, which is indicative of the *B*-goods. Finally, the material-intensive *A*-goods show a mixed picture, with their firm sizes generally being large, but the amount of R&D input relatively small.

Following a procedure analogous to the country analysis in Section 2 of this chapter, the second approach of measuring pass-through and pricing to market is to determine the response of import and export prices to changes in the real exchange rate, here measured in terms of relative unit labor costs. The particular point of interest is how the structural determinants *Size* and *R&D expenditures* affect the regression coefficients. To determine this impact, the regressions (D.21) and (D.22) are now being employed, the only modification being that the coefficients between the single equations in the system of seemingly unrelated regressions (SUR) are constrained to be identical. The cross section of sectors is split into two halves in accordance with the ranking of sectors along these structural criteria, and a dummy variable is introduced into the system of equations in order to account for the intersectoral differences. Concerning the classification of sectors into groups, the marginal values have been chosen such that each resulting subgroup appears to be as homogeneous as possible, and simultaneously, differences between each pair of groups are maximized. That way, the marginal values for *SIZE* have been chosen to be 100, for *RD* 50, and for *RDOUT* 100. The dummy variables have the value of one for figures higher than these numbers, and else zero. For each sector, the equations from the import and export price regression now read as follows:

(D.32) $\Delta\left(LNPM_{it} - LNPPI_{it}\right)=$

$\qquad (g-1)\left[\left(LNPM_{i,t-1} - LNPPI_{i,t-1}\right) - aLNRULCM_{i,t-1} - const_i\right]$

$\qquad + \sum_{j=0}^{q} b_j \Delta LNRULCM_{i,t-j} + \sum_{j=1}^{s} e_j \Delta\left(LNPM_{i,t-j} - LNPPI_{i,t-j}\right)$

$\qquad + dD \times \Delta RULCM_{it} + \varepsilon_t,$

(D.33) $\Delta\left(LNPX_{it} - LNPPI_{it}\right)=$

$\qquad (g-1)\left[\left(LNPX_{i,t-1} - LNPPI_{i,t-1}\right) - aLNRULCX_{i,t-1} - const_i\right]$

$\qquad + \sum_{j=0}^{q} b_j \Delta LNRULCX_{i,t-j} + \sum_{j=1}^{s} e_j \Delta\left(LNPX_{i,t-j} - LNPPI_{i,t-j}\right)$

$\qquad + dD \times \Delta RULCX_{it} + \varepsilon_t.$

As before in the country analysis, the system of equations is estimated simultaneously by applying the SUR method, with implementation of the cross-equation restrictions in terms of identical coefficients. The regressions were run first without the dummy variable D, and then repeated after setting the dummies according to the three different ranking criteria, one after the other. The dummy variables were applied to the differenced contemporaneous real exchange rate variable.

A likelihood ratio test was then conducted by using the likelihood function from the respective model, which incorporates the dummy variable, and from the model without any dummy. This way, the test can be seen as a test of one further restriction, which is that d equals one. If the test statistic, which follows a $\chi^2(1)$-distribution under the condition of stationary residuals, exceeds the critical value, then the specification without this additional restriction can be taken to best describe reality, since the constrained model would imply a significant rise in the residuals. If this turns out to be the case, then it is proved that the two groups of sectors behave differently.

Table 14: The Impact of Structural Determinants on Pass-Through[a]

	$g-1$	*LNRULCM*	Δ*LNRULCM*	Dummy	LR-test[b]
$d=0$	−0.031	−0.276	−0.064		
	(−12.77$^\Diamond$)	(−4.183)	(−6.157**)		
RD	−0.313	−0.272	−0.046	−0.049	7.95••
	(−12.74$^\Diamond$)	(−4.09)	(−3.89**)	(−3.39**)	
RDOUT	−0.031	−0.273	−0.057	−0.026	2.72•
	(−12.71$^\Diamond$)	(−4.12)	(−5.10**)	(−2.02*)	
SIZE	−0.031	−0.277	−0.068	0.007	0.20
	(−12.76$^\Diamond$)	(−4.182)	(−5.22**)	(0.566)	

[a]t-statistics in parentheses. **, *: Significant at a critical value of at least 1 or 5 percent according to classical Student's t-tests. $^\Diamond$: Significant at a 5 percent critical value being calculated from Levin and Lin (1992), Theorem 5.2 d. *RD*: Dummy variable for sectors with a normalized R&D figure higher than 50. *RDOUT*: Dummy variable for sectors with a normalized R&D / output ratio higher than 100. *LNRULCM*: Logarithm of relative unit labor costs, calculated with country weights based on German import shares. *SIZE*: Dummy variable for sectors with a *SIZE* figure greater than 100. For the exact definitions of these structural variables, see Table 12. The number of observations is 91. The table shows the regression results from the system of (D.31) with $q = s = 1$. The sectors included are identical to those listed in Table 11, with the exception of CP, which had to be excluded due to missing values. The number of included sectors is thus 18. The chemical sectors CO and CA from Table 11 have been both linked to CO in Table 13, and CS and CL from Table 11 have been linked to RV from Table 13. – [b]Likelihood ratio test statistic for the significance of the dummy variable. For further details, see Table 6 and the explanations in the text. • and •• denote significance at the 10 and 1 percent level, respectively.

Table 14 displays the results of this regression. The first row shows the estimates without the dummy variable. One obtains the expected result of both the long-term and short-term relationship between relative unit labor costs and relative import prices being negative. A negative coefficient suggests that a rise in domestic unit labor costs relative to the world, thus indicating a deteriorating competitiveness of domestic producers, results in a relative decline of import prices when compared to domestic producer prices. However, the long-term coefficient falls short of significance since the critical value of −6.67 computed according to Levin and Lin (1992) for the 5 percent level of significance has not been reached, but the adjustment coefficient on the error-correction term is negative and significant. This implies that the residuals from the regression are stationary so that the critical values from the $\chi^2(1)$-distribution can be used.

A negative dummy variable signifies that this relationship becomes even more distinct. Indeed, as can be seen from the estimates for the dummy coefficient d, this is the case for the variable *RD* and *RDOUT*. The likelihood ratio test statistic shows values which are significant at the 10 and 1 percent levels, respectively. Sectors which are intensive in R&D input reveal more pass-through, measured as the response of the import price relative to the domestic price when the ratio of domestic to foreign unit labor costs alters. A straightforward way to interpret this outcome is to conclude that the higher the degree of technological sophistication involved in product development, the larger the barrier of entry is, and the less fierce competition from local producers in the export country is. Moreover, taking the customer's perspective, the price elasticity of demand can be assumed to be lower in the case of high-tech products, which are more differentiated and thus less substitutable. The relative price of imports to domestic production is therefore more closely correlated to exchange rate changes in the high-tech sectors. This empirical outcome is a verification of the result from the modeling approach developed in Chapter C. In (C.63), the relative producer price, i.e., the import price relative to the domestic producer price, is shown to decrease with a rising degree of substitutability, provided that the reservation price is within a certain bound. Since higher expenses on R&D are congruent to less substitution, the price gap between imports and domestic production should increase, and this is in fact what is observed here.

The average firm size in a sector, however, does not have any impact on relative producer prices. No other result can be expected, given the fact that the derivative of the relative producer price with respect to the number of firms in Section C.IV.1 has neither yielded a clearly positive nor negative number.

Concerning the export side, negative coefficients on differenced or level variables of relative unit labor costs in Table 15 would be conclusive for a reduction of export prices relative to domestic ones when unit labor costs in the exporter's country rise relative to those in the target country. However, evidence for this seems to be poor. What can be stated, though, is that there are significant differences in pricing-to-market behavior across sectors. Judging from the negative dummy coefficient, which is significant at a level of significance smaller than one percent, this pricing-to-market response is even more pronounced in sectors in which the average firm size is large. Provided that there is a link between a large average firm size and a small number of firms in the market, an increase in pricing to market, which has been shown to hold for a declining number of firms in (C.80), would be observed as well if the average firm size increases. A possible explanation is without doubt that a fragmentation of production to a large number of firms makes the costs of competitors appear more distinctly in the optimal pricing schedule of a representative firm, whereas in the extreme case of a monopolist, only his own (marginal) costs and the demand function are arguments in his optimal price.

Table 15: The Impact of Structural Determinants on Pricing to Market[a]

	$g-1$	*LNRULCX*	*ΔLNRULCX*	Dummy	LR-test[b]
$d=0$	−0.026	0.0018	−0.0098		
	(−5.90)	(0.051)	(−1.91+)		
RD	−0.026	0.199	−0.012	0.275	0.006
	(−5.90)	(0.05)	(−1.33)	(0.29)	
RDOUT	−0.026	0.241	−0.017	0.897	0.69
	(−5.86)	(0.07)	(−1.85+)	(0.98)	
SIZE	−0.025	0.0041	−0.881	−0.040	6.94••
	(−5.68)	(0.10)	(−1.72+)	(−3.17**)	

[a]t-statistics in parentheses. **, +: Significant at a critical value of at least 1 or 10 per-cent according to classical Student's t-tests. The number of observations is 67. *RD*: Dummy variable for sectors with a normalized R&D figure higher than 50. *RDOUT*: Dummy variable for sectors with a normalized R&D/output ratio higher than 100. *LNRULCX*: Logarithm of relative unit labor costs, calculated with country weights based on German export shares. *SIZE*: Dummy variable for sectors with a *SIZE* figure greater than 100. For the exact definitions of these structural variables, see Table 12. The table shows the regression results from the system of (D.31) with $q = s = 1$. The sectors included are identical to those listed in Table 12, with the exception of EG and TE, which had to be excluded due to missing values. The number of included sectors is thus 18. The chemical sectors CO and CA from Table 12 have been both linked to CO in Table 13, and CS and CL from Table 12 have been linked to RV from Table 13. – [b]Likelihood ratio test statistic for the significance of the dummy variable. For further details, see Table 6 and the explanations in the text. •• denotes significance at the 1 percent level.

Following (C.62), an increase in substitutability should also decrease pricing to market because price-cost margins are smaller when products are less differentiated. However, this relationship is not reflected in the empirical results. An explanation might be that there are two forces at work. On the one hand, margins are smaller when there are more possibilities for a substitution. As just discussed, this puts a constraint on pricing to market, since prices should follow more closely the path of marginal costs. On the other hand, the fact that competition is fiercer because consumers can more easily switch to a rival supplier even in the case of small price differentials should set a limit on the impact of exchange rate changes on prices the producer can set in the local markets. Taken altogether, there is no predominance of one of these two forces over the other when one judges by the empirical evidence.

The empirical evidence presented in this chapter has shed some light on several hypotheses concerning the price setting of goods in international trade when there are shifts of costs between the exporting and importing country. Theoretical analysis from Chapter C suggests that the determinants may be both of a micro-economic and aggregate, macroeconomic nature. Consequently, the investigation centered on country features as well as attributes which are characteristic for economic sectors. The focus on countries has revealed that the pricing pattern depends both on the relative size and the openness of both the exporting and importing country. In particular, economies with a large internal market in terms of production shares relative to the entirety of all OECD countries see their import prices less directed by foreign cost or exchange rate factors. This also holds when countries are ranked according to their openness with more open countries showing a larger degree of pass-through than countries which rely more on domestic production. Concerning the features of exporting countries, the large exporters in the OECD area, i.e., those countries with the largest share in the total of all OECD exports, have larger pricing power implying that they are less forced to adjust prices in order to follow conditions in the target country. The same applies to countries with a small share of exports to domestic production, which reveal a smaller response in their price setting relative to changes in external conditions.

Further differences between the price setting of exports between countries can be due to differences in the sectoral composition of traded products. In fact, the sectoral disaggregation applied to German imports and exports has revealed sectoral differences in price setting. Whereas sectors producing goods with a rather large degree of homogeneity between product varieties generally reveal a relatively large degree of pass-through into their import prices, the incidence of this outcome in the other sectors depends on further determinants like the importance of sunk costs and the market in the particular sector. Overall, the evidence from export prices is less clear than the evidence from the import side.

III.   Appendix

1.   Figures

Figure A3: Pass-Through into Import Prices for Further Selected Sectors

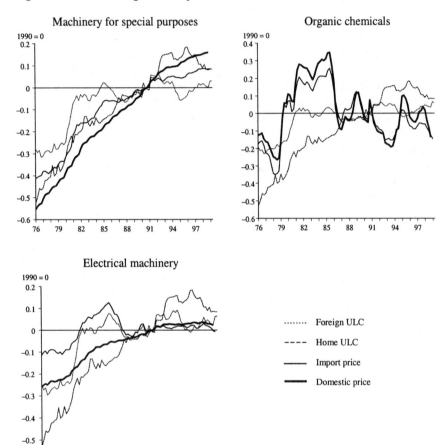

Figure A3: continued

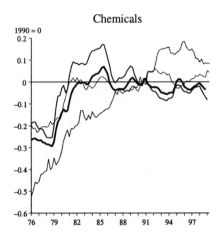

Chemicals

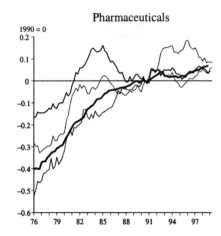

Pharmaceuticals

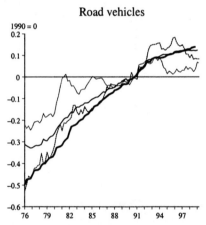

Road vehicles

········ Foreign ULC

---- Home ULC

——— Import price

——— Domestic price

Source: OECD (2000a, 2000b).

2.   Tables

Table A1: Augmented Dickey–Fuller Test for Unit Roots Applied to the Price and Real Exchange Rate Series across Countries[a]

	LNPM		LNPX		LNPPI		LNREER	
	P(DF)[b]	Lag[c]	P(DF)[b]	Lag[c]	P(DF)[b]	Lag[c]	P(DF)[b]	Lag[c]
Australia	0.896	2	0.731	3	0.989	3	0.016	7
Austria	0.948	4	0.963	3	0.641	5	0.240	3
Belgium	0.618	4	0.075	3	0.032	3	0.088	3
Canada	0.164	10	0.090	6	0.114	5	0.246	7
Switzerland	0.911	10	0.917	2	0.945	4	0.020	5
Germany	0.186	10	0.534	3	0.799	5	0.482	5
Denmark	0.726	3	0.825	3	0.768	4	0.230	5
Spain	0.731	4	0.929	2	0.816	9	0.421	10
Finland	0.409	3	0.810	10	0.754	3	0.565	3
France	0.435	9	0.955	4	0.871	4	0.229	7
United Kingdom	0.995	8	0.755	2	0.224	3	0.048	8
Greece	0.996	2	0.996	3	0.997	7	0.763	2
Ireland	0.416	7	0.355	2	0.282	3	0.948	8
Italy	0.368	3	0.285	4	0.147	3	0.473	3
Japan	0.190	3	0.507	5	0.513	3	0.271	5
Korea	0.178	8	0.204	9	0.264	5	0.203	3
Mexico	0.981	5	0.961	5	0.806	3	0.401	5
Netherlands	0.635	3	0.659	3	0.470	3	0.180	4
Norway	0.961	7	0.919	4	0.940	7	0.382	3
New Zealand	0.939	6	0.904	2	0.548	7	0.052	8
Portugal	0.411	2	0.426	4	0.909	9	0.526	3
Sweden	0.002	2	0.920	7	0.763	3	0.475	8
Turkey	0.919	2	0.941	2	0.891	2	0.256	3
United States	0.675	10	0.561	3	0.094	5	0.570	6

[a]The definitions of variables and its sources are as follows: *LNPM*, *LNPX*, and *LNPPI* are the logarithms of import, export, and producer price, respectively, all applying to the manufacturing sector. *LNREER* is the logarithm of the real effective exchange rate, the source being OECD (2000b), *Main Economic Indicators*. The sources of all other variables are as indicated in Table 3. The sample range is from 1975Q1 through 1999Q2. The regressions include time series trends and seasonal dummy variables. P(DF) is the marginal level of significance for the augmented Dickey–Fuller test. – [b]p-values are computed by the TSP regression software as interpolations from Osterwald–Lenum (1992, Table 2). – [c]Optimal lag length according to the Akaike Information Criterion AIC2 described in Pantula et al. (1994).

Table A2: Augmented Dickey–Fuller Test for Unit Roots Applied to the Differenced Series of Prices and Real Exchange Rates across Countries[a]

	ΔLNPM		ΔLNPX		ΔLNPPI		ΔLNREER	
	P(DF)[b]	Lag[c]	P(DF)[b]	Lag[c]	P(DF)[b]	Lag[c]	P(DF)[b]	Lag[c]
Australia	0.000	2	0.001	2	0.068	6	0.007	2
Austria	0.001	3	0.000	2	0.006	2	0.234	2
Belgium	0.509	3	0.044	2	0.011	2	0.176	2
Canada	0.491	8	0.169	3	0.284	6	0.130	4
Switzerland	0.020	9	0.000	2	0.001	10	0.193	3
Germany	0.035	9	0.106	2	0.018	2	0.019	4
Denmark	0.027	2	0.002	2	0.012	5	0.087	3
Spain	0.001	3	0.260	6	0.249	9	0.683	8
Finland	0.000	2	0.001	6	0.016	2	0.042	2
France	0.257	7	0.100	3	0.021	6	0.132	3
United Kingdom	0.013	5	0.000	2	0.000	2	0.014	2
Greece	0.000	2	0.000	2	0.000	2	0.241	6
Ireland	0.009	6	0.001	2	0.005	7	0.032	2
Italy	0.025	5	0.002	3	0.010	2	0.090	2
Japan	0.006	5	0.003	2	0.002	2	0.012	2
Korea	0.717	5	0.123	8	0.004	3	0.288	4
Mexico	0.002	4	0.119	3	0.009	2	0.235	2
Netherlands	0.000	2	0.004	2	0.002	2	0.003	2
Norway	0.007	6	0.000	2	0.000	3	0.004	9
New Zealand	0.026	5	0.002	8	0.161	8	0.008	2
Portugal	0.323	2	0.996	10	0.374	2	0.816	5
Sweden	0.001	2	0.244	6	0.205	7	0.008	10
Turkey	0.113	2	0.066	2	0.033	2	0.118	2
United States	0.305	9	0.223	2	0.168	5	0.313	4

[a]The definitions of variables and its sources are as follows: ΔLNPM, ΔLNPX, and ΔLNPPI are first differences in the logarithms of import, export, and producer prices, respectively, all applying to the manufacturing sector. ΔLNREER is the first difference of the logarithm of the real effective exchange rate, the source being OECD (2000b), *Main Economic Indicators*. The sources of all other variables are as indicated in Table 3. The sample range is from 1975Q1 through 1999Q2. The regressions include time series trends and seasonal dummy variables. P(DF) is the marginal level of significance for the augmented Dickey–Fuller test. – [b]p-values are computed by the TSP regression software as interpolations from Osterwald–Lenum (1992, Table 2). – [c]Optimal lag length according to the Akaike Information Criterion AIC2 described in Pantula et al. (1994).

Table A3: Germany's Country-Specific Import Share with Respect to Total Imports in the Respective Sector (in Percent)

	Sector												
	CP	PP	TX	IR	MA	OF	TV	EL	RV	FU	AP	PG	CO
Australia	0.1	0.0	0.0	0.0	0.1	0.0	0.0	0.0	0.0	0.0	0.0	0.2	0.0
Austria	3.5	11.0	7.1	7.9	8.5	0.5	8.1	8.4	3.6	8.3	3.8	3.6	1.5
Belgium	15.4	6.6	15.7	24.4	4.2	2.1	8.3	4.6	23.6	8.4	3.3	4.8	14.6
Canada	0.3	1.7	0.1	0.3	0.9	0.3	0.1	0.7	0.1	0.2	0.0	0.3	0.1
Switzerland	9.2	3.6	6.9	3.5	10.4	0.9	0.6	6.8	1.4	5.3	2.5	14.0	8.8
Denmark	1.3	1.3	1.8	1.2	4.8	0.6	1.5	1.2	0.8	13.6	2.6	2.2	0.7
Spain	1.5	0.7	1.7	3.3	2.6	2.1	1.9	3.0	7.4	1.8	0.4	1.0	1.6
Finland	0.6	14.9	0.3	2.1	1.1	0.3	1.7	0.6	0.4	1.0	0.4	0.4	0.3
France	15.9	12.8	11.8	16.0	13.9	9.2	8.8	11.8	17.4	8.0	5.9	10.1	14.2
United Kingdom	9.9	4.4	5.0	9.2	8.1	17.4	12.5	9.2	6.2	3.2	3.6	9.5	11.8
Greece	0.1	0.0	1.7	0.7	0.1	0.0	0.0	0.3	0.0	0.1	9.3	0.0	0.0
Ireland	1.1	0.0	0.5	0.1	0.8	4.9	0.4	2.3	0.1	0.1	0.4	1.1	0.9
Iceland	0.0	0.0	0.0	0.0	0.0	0.0	0.0	0.0	0.0	0.0	0.0	0.0	0.0
Italy	7.5	8.0	24.9	11.4	16.3	4.6	4.4	9.8	11.2	32.4	28.5	5.9	7.2
Japan	2.9	0.8	2.2	1.0	6.8	19.5	30.6	15.0	16.1	0.2	0.8	18.1	4.1
South Korea	0.1	0.1	1.1	0.2	0.2	0.8	9.8	2.4	0.0	0.1	6.1	0.7	0.2
Mexico	0.1	0.0	0.1	0.1	0.1	0.1	0.2	0.1	0.2	0.0	0.0	0.1	0.2
Netherlands	19.9	10.7	10.7	8.5	7.4	12.4	4.2	7.9	6.7	9.0	7.4	8.0	23.7
Norway	1.0	2.9	0.1	1.8	0.4	0.4	0.1	0.4	0.2	0.5	0.0	0.2	1.0
New Zealand	0.1	0.0	0.0	0.0	0.0	0.0	0.0	0.0	0.0	0.0	0.0	0.0	0.0
Portugal	0.2	0.3	1.9	0.1	0.5	0.1	3.1	2.3	0.2	0.7	7.0	0.6	0.2
Sweden	2.1	17.1	0.9	7.1	4.8	2.4	0.4	1.6	1.3	5.3	0.2	1.9	0.7
Turkey	0.1	0.0	3.4	0.4	0.1	0.0	1.5	0.4	0.1	0.6	16.9	0.1	0.1
United States	7.3	2.9	2.2	0.6	8.3	21.1	1.8	11.0	3.1	1.3	0.7	17.3	7.9

Table A3: continued

	Sector												
	EG	PH	RP	CP	PL	PO	NF	CS	TE	SH	CA	CL	TR
Australia	0.0	0.0	0.0	0.0	0.0	0.0	1.8	0.0	0.1	0.0	0.8	0.0	0.0
Austria	8.1	5.0	6.1	2.1	7.6	1.0	5.9	0.1	2.8	7.5	3.5	1.0	9.6
Belgium	4.5	7.8	9.3	13.4	17.3	10.7	14.8	19.2	5.3	0.6	12.6	40.1	19.1
Canada	0.5	0.7	0.2	0.4	0.1	0.0	1.7	0.0	0.3	0.0	0.9	0.1	0.0
Switzerland	8.8	22.7	2.4	7.5	7.9	1.3	5.9	0.0	2.1	1.4	2.1	0.2	4.1
Denmark	7.2	3.1	0.7	1.7	1.9	3.3	1.1	0.4	2.5	1.2	0.3	0.4	1.7
Spain	2.1	2.0	4.7	0.8	0.9	1.9	1.5	23.1	1.5	9.1	0.9	1.1	0.1
Finland	0.7	0.5	0.2	0.6	1.0	0.3	1.7	0.0	1.0	0.1	0.7	0.7	0.2
France	13.5	14.1	24.9	19.7	10.9	6.4	14.8	19.6	7.9	6.3	17.7	12.0	8.0
United Kingdom	5.1	10.1	10.9	12.8	6.6	16.0	11.2	0.2	9.7	1.0	12.9	3.5	1.1
Greece	0.1	0.1	0.2	0.0	0.2	1.0	1.0	0.0	0.2	0.5	0.1	0.0	0.0
Ireland	1.4	1.8	2.5	1.5	1.1	0.0	0.1	0.0	1.2	0.0	0.3	0.0	0.0
Iceland	0.0	0.0	0.0	0.1	0.0	0.0	0.9	0.0	0.0	0.0	0.0	0.0	0.0
Italy	21.7	6.2	13.0	3.9	14.5	23.3	5.1	12.2	3.0	51.4	6.3	6.7	11.0
Japan	6.1	2.5	8.4	3.0	6.0	5.8	0.7	21.1	41.1	0.1	1.5	22.3	1.1
South Korea	0.2	0.1	1.5	0.1	0.4	2.4	0.0	0.1	2.9	4.4	0.1	0.0	0.0
Mexico	0.1	0.1	0.0	0.0	0.0	0.1	0.1	0.0	0.1	0.3	0.1	0.0	0.0
Netherlands	5.8	6.6	8.4	17.3	16.5	10.2	16.1	4.0	6.1	3.7	18.7	5.0	39.3
Norway	0.4	0.1	0.5	0.5	0.2	0.0	9.5	0.0	0.7	0.0	3.3	0.0	0.1
New Zealand	0.0	0.0	0.0	1.0	0.0	0.0	0.0	0.0	0.0	0.0	0.0	0.0	0.0
Portugal	0.6	0.2	0.1	0.5	0.1	14.6	0.0	0.0	0.9	11.6	0.0	0.2	0.0
Sweden	3.8	5.7	1.7	1.9	1.8	0.5	2.6	0.0	1.0	0.1	3.4	1.4	4.4
Turkey	0.1	0.1	0.3	0.0	0.0	0.3	0.4	0.0	0.1	0.3	0.3	0.0	0.0
United States	9.2	10.2	4.1	11.1	4.9	0.6	3.2	0.0	9.6	0.6	13.6	5.4	0.1

Source: Own calculations based on Eurostat (2000).

Table A4: Germany's Country-Specific Export Share with Respect to Total Exports in the Respective Sector (in Percent)

	Sector												
	CH	PP	TX	IR	MA	OF	TV	EL	RV	FU	AP	PG	CO
Australia	0.9	1.3	0.5	0.4	1.2	0.5	0.6	0.9	0.6	0.3	0.2	1.2	0.6
Austria	5.8	6.6	8.8	5.4	7.8	5.9	5.6	7.8	5.2	13.8	15.3	6.8	2.5
Belgium	8.5	9.1	7.8	10.4	7.0	5.4	7.4	6.3	13.3	11.8	10.3	5.0	10.0
Canada	0.9	0.6	0.6	1.0	1.1	0.9	0.1	1.0	1.2	0.4	1.2	0.9	1.0
Switzerland	7.3	6.7	6.2	6.0	7.4	4.9	4.8	6.3	4.9	14.7	14.1	7.7	8.1
Denmark	2.2	2.7	2.6	2.9	2.5	2.3	3.1	2.3	1.1	1.4	2.0	2.3	0.9
Spain	4.2	3.8	2.7	4.8	4.5	5.3	6.6	5.3	5.7	1.9	1.6	4.7	4.1
Finland	1.4	0.9	1.5	1.2	1.9	1.1	0.8	1.7	1.1	0.6	0.9	1.5	0.6
France	14.5	20.6	14.4	14.9	15.0	15.9	18.6	14.3	11.4	12.3	8.8	13.9	11.5
United Kingdom	9.3	14.0	9.7	11.0	9.3	14.1	10.9	9.6	13.3	8.2	9.6	9.1	7.9
Greece	1.1	1.1	4.1	0.9	0.9	0.5	2.0	1.0	1.0	0.5	1.5	0.8	0.5
Ireland	0.7	0.6	0.7	0.2	0.5	2.3	0.5	1.0	0.3	0.3	1.2	0.3	0.6
Iceland	0.0	0.1	0.0	0.0	0.1	0.0	0.0	0.1	0.0	0.1	0.2	0.1	0.0
Italy	12.0	9.1	12.8	10.0	10.0	9.3	18.9	12.8	12.9	3.1	3.9	11.2	10.5
Japan	4.9	0.6	1.6	0.3	2.1	1.5	0.3	2.3	6.3	1.5	1.2	3.9	5.3
South Korea	1.2	0.2	0.5	0.6	2.0	0.2	0.1	0.6	0.2	0.1	0.1	1.3	1.2
Mexico	0.6	0.1	0.2	1.1	0.9	0.4	0.3	0.6	0.5	0.4	0.1	0.7	1.0
Netherlands	10.8	15.0	12.9	13.5	8.6	15.6	9.9	8.8	5.1	20.4	20.8	7.8	17.4
Norway	0.9	0.6	0.7	1.6	1.4	1.0	0.9	1.3	0.6	0.5	1.3	1.1	0.5
New Zealand	0.2	0.2	0.1	0.0	0.1	0.1	0.1	0.1	0.1	0.0	0.0	0.2	0.1
Portugal	1.1	0.5	3.7	1.3	0.8	1.2	2.3	1.4	0.9	0.4	1.1	1.0	0.8
Sweden	2.8	2.0	2.2	3.7	4.5	2.4	2.8	4.2	3.0	2.5	2.0	4.6	1.6
Turkey	1.2	0.4	2.0	1.2	1.2	0.6	1.2	1.4	0.6	0.2	0.2	1.0	1.1
United States	7.6	3.4	3.6	7.5	9.1	8.5	2.2	9.0	10.9	4.6	2.7	13.0	12.2

Table A4: continued

	Sector												
	EG	PH	RP	CP	PL	PO	NF	CS	TE	SH	CA	CL	TR
Australia	1.1	2.3	0.8	0.9	0.6	0.8	0.3	0.0	1.0	0.3	0.5	0.7	0.4
Austria	7.5	8.3	7.3	5.6	6.8	8.1	8.7	4.9	10.4	17.0	5.3	3.7	6.6
Belgium	6.4	6.5	10.7	7.8	7.9	5.9	7.0	27.4	8.5	8.4	7.9	9.5	8.7
Canada	0.6	1.2	0.6	0.8	0.8	0.9	0.5	0.0	0.2	1.1	0.5	1.8	0.0
Switzerland	7.0	11.1	5.5	5.4	7.4	8.6	8.4	2.4	8.1	12.3	3.4	6.1	7.1
Denmark	2.7	1.8	2.3	2.6	3.2	1.9	2.8	1.5	3.0	3.9	2.3	0.5	1.8
Spain	4.3	4.1	5.0	4.9	4.0	3.2	3.6	1.0	5.3	1.0	2.4	4.9	9.2
Finland	1.7	1.1	1.4	1.6	1.4	0.8	1.4	1.1	1.9	2.2	2.1	0.7	1.5
France	15.3	7.4	17.0	20.9	17.7	10.0	17.1	9.4	13.7	14.5	14.2	6.5	19.7
United Kingdom	9.3	8.7	9.9	8.8	12.4	3.4	11.9	13.4	7.1	5.5	10.2	15.0	12.9
Greece	1.3	1.6	1.1	1.3	0.9	1.4	0.7	2.2	3.2	0.3	0.5	0.7	1.9
Ireland	0.5	1.3	0.5	0.4	0.9	0.2	0.5	0.8	0.4	0.7	0.4	0.2	0.4
Iceland	0.1	0.0	0.1	0.0	0.1	0.2	0.0	0.0	0.1	0.2	0.0	0.0	0.1
Italy	10.8	10.3	10.1	11.7	10.4	24.1	11.9	24.8	8.6	3.7	6.9	12.0	16.8
Japan	2.1	14.7	2.3	4.1	1.0	3.5	1.5	0.2	0.4	1.0	5.3	11.8	0.1
South Korea	2.4	0.5	0.3	1.5	0.5	0.1	0.7	0.0	0.4	0.2	3.9	0.1	0.0
Mexico	0.7	0.8	1.2	0.6	0.3	0.1	0.2	0.0	1.0	0.0	0.4	0.0	0.1
Netherlands	8.8	5.0	11.0	8.5	12.7	8.4	10.3	6.7	10.2	15.1	11.2	3.0	7.9
Norway	1.4	0.8	1.2	1.1	0.8	1.5	0.9	0.5	1.1	1.5	0.8	0.6	0.8
New Zealand	0.1	0.3	0.1	0.2	0.1	0.1	0.0	0.0	0.1	0.0	0.1	0.1	0.0
Portugal	1.0	1.2	1.0	1.3	1.1	0.5	1.0	2.3	5.5	4.1	0.6	0.5	1.3
Sweden	5.1	2.7	4.0	3.0	3.1	4.3	3.5	1.3	2.2	2.9	4.4	2.9	1.1
Turkey	1.1	1.0	0.5	1.2	0.6	0.5	1.0	0.1	2.4	0.2	0.8	0.4	1.6
United States	8.8	7.2	6.3	5.8	5.2	11.5	6.1	0.0	5.2	3.9	15.8	18.3	0.1

Source: Own calculations based on Eurostat (2000).

Table A5: The Correspondence between Sector Classifications and SITC Trade Categories used in Chapter D

Sector	GP89[a]	SITC
CO	41	51
CA	42	52
PH	47	54
CP	49	59
RP	59	62
PP	55	64
TX	63	65
PO	51	66
IR	27	67
MA	32	74
OF	50	75
TV	366	761–763
EL	36	77
FU	542	82
AP	64	84
PG	37	87
NF	28	68
PL	58	58
EG	363	8413–8419
TE	365	764
SH	625	85
CS	33111–33112	87032110; 87032219
CL	33113–33117	87032319; 87032400
TR	3313	870422

[a]For the sectors CS, CL, and TR, the combined classification has been used.

Table A6: Tests for Integration Applied to the Sectoral Relative Import and Export Prices and Relative Unit Labor Costs[a]

	LNPMR		LNRULCM		LNPXR		LNRULCX	
	DF	Lag	DF	Lag	DF	Lag	DF	Lag
CO	−2.469 (0.344)	4	−1.938 (0.635)	2	−2.469 (0.344)	3	−2.870 (0.172)	5
CA	−1.793 (0.708)	3	−2.918 (0.156)	5	−2.549 (0.304)	3	−2.820 (0.190)	5
CP	−3.225 (0.080+)	5	−2.804 (0.195)	5				
RP	−3.05 (0.119)	3	−2.621 (0.270)	3	−1.185 (0.914)	7	−3.124 (0.101)	6
PP	−1.988 (0.608)	6	−3.040 (0.121)	6	−1.934 (0.637)	3	−3.132 (0.099)	6
TX	−1.786 (0.711)	3	−4.103 (0.006**)	10	−2.209 (0.485)	2	−3.407 (0.050*)	10
PO	−3.033 (0.123)	3	−3.301 (0.066+)	6	−1.974 (0.615)	2	−2.778 (0.205)	5
IR	−3.542 (0.035*)	3	−3.652 (0.026*)	10	−3.561 (0.033*)	5	−3.202 (0.084+)	4
MA	−2.111 (0.540)	7	−2.498 (0.329)	3	−1.573 (0.803)	10	−3.010 (0.130)	5
OF	−1.109 (0.928)	3	−2.646 (0.259)	3	−2.605 (0.277)	5	−3.017 (0.127)	6
TV	−3.052 (0.118)	3	−3.646 (0.026*)	3	−1.489 (0.833)	2	−3.612 (0.029*)	10
EL	−2.374 (0.393)	3	−2.662 (0.252)	3	−2.026 (0.587)	6	−3.022 (0.126)	5
AP	−1.733 (0.736)	3	−4.487 (0.002**)	10	−2.562 (0.298)	3	−1.745 (0.731)	2
PG	−2.866 (0.174)	3	−2.611 (0.275)	3	−1.054 (0.936)	8	−2.856 (0.178)	5
NF	−2.128 (0.530)	2	−2.890 (0.165)	10	−2.811 (0.193)	2	−3.022 (0.126)	6
PL	−1.646 (0.774)	5	−2.105 (0.543)	2	−2.048 (0.575)	6	−3.108 (0.104)	6
EG					−2.123 (0.561)	2	−3.021 (0.126)	5
TE					−1.591 (0.796)	6	−3.499 (0.040*)	10
SH	−2.281 (0.445)	6	−3.085 (0.110)	5	−3.172 (0.090+)	4	−2.011 (0.595)	2
CS	−3.894 (0.012*)	3	−3.200 (0.084+)	2	−1.837 (0.687)	2	−3.729 (0.021*)	10
CL	−3.126 (0.100*)	2	−2.891 (0.165)	3	−2.145 (0.521)	2	−2.580 (0.289)	5

[a]DF is the coefficient on the laged variable in an augmented Dickey–Fuller test. p-values in parentheses. **, *, +: significant at a p-value of at least 1, 5, or 10 percent. Coefficients as defined in the text. *LNPMR* is the logarithm of the relative import price, i.e., the import price relative to the domestic producer price. *LNPXR* is the equivalent for the export price. *LNRULCM* and *LNRULCX* are the logarithms of the relative unit labor cost, computed on the basis of trade weights on the import and export side, respectively. For the abbreviations of the sectors, see Table 9.

E. The Impact of Cost Competitiveness on Relative Export Prices and World Market Shares

So far, various pieces of empirical evidence on pass-through and pricing to market have been given in Chapter D. One of the main conclusions was that world market conditions constrain national producers in their price adjustment as a response to local cost shocks in their home country. To the extent that local cost or exchange rate shifts are not passed through but are absorbed in operating profits of producers, these shifts have only a minor impact on relative export prices and demand shifts between countries. The consequence is that exchange rate or wage policies become less effective in their impact on the real sector, at least in the short term. It is therefore next of interest to tackle the interrelationship between pass-through analysis and the topic of international competitiveness. Whereas Chapter D already dealt with pass-through from the point of view of a particular country, the focus now is on price relations between an exporting country and its competitors from other countries, with the target market of both being the world market. It will be shown empirically that aggregate cost differentials between countries are incompletely reflected in their relative export prices, reducing the short-run positive or negative impact on export performance. The discussion of the long-run impact, however, will be postponed until Chapter F, where the main point to be made is that investment in capacity responds positively to a country's competitiveness.

I. Defining Competitiveness

1. Is Competitiveness an Issue for Policy?

When the notion of competitiveness is applied to whole countries rather than single enterprises it is necessary to be more precise on the exact idea behind it. Even though it is right to say that a whole country cannot go bankrupt like enterprises do, since a country always possesses a comparative advantage somewhere and since its productive resources cannot disappear, it is not appropriate to characterize the debate about competitiveness as being "a matter of time-honored fallacies about international trade being dressed up in new and pretentious rhetoric," as

Krugman (1996) does.[32] There are, though, two reasonable and fruitful approaches to the notion of competitiveness of countries which are worth following.

The first approach comes from Dornbusch (1996), who modifies the assumption that a country's endowment with production factors is always fully utilized in production. More specifically, in case of unemployment of production factors in a country, a real devaluation may be warranted in order to restore aggregate price competitiveness. The rationale of this argument in the end is that it is the unused production factors which have to restore competitiveness in order to be employed again.[33] This way, competitiveness is conceived in an absolute rather than a relative dimension, because if one country is successful in being near full employment, no other country is hurt.

The second approach is from Siebert (2000b), who sees the main feature of international competition in the ability to attract internationally mobile production factors in order to improve productivity and the remuneration of the immobile factors. Only in this approach to competition, its relative or exclusive character is apparent to the extent that mobile resources are scarce and cannot be augmented easily from a single country alone. In contrast to Dornbusch's approach, which is a short-term or Keynesian approach, the second approach involves the long-term accumulation of production factors. Both approaches are used in this work. The short-term view will be used in this chapter, whereas the long-term view will be used in Chapter F.

In order to facilitate the discussion, one has to distinguish between the short-term and long-term horizon. If the short term is defined as the state in which at least some production factors are fixed, whereas in the long term, mobility between sectors or countries is an important issue, the modeling aproach of a representative producer, which will be developed in Chapter F, will be conditional on the time horizon. In the short run, the production capacity is given, with marginal costs of production being nearly constant until the capacity constraint is binding and marginal costs are edging upward. The decisions which the producers face concern the optimal price, or to put it differently, the optimal markup on marginal costs in the particular market considered, with the markup having to cover the costs of fixed production factors in the long term. Thus, in the short run, the focus is on how prices and quantities change as a result of cost shifts. Over the lon-

---

[32] See also Siebert (2000b).

[33] In particular, in the framework consisting of internal and external balance as put forward by Dornbusch (1996), nominal devaluations of the exchange rate are particularly effective if nominal wages are inflexible downward. If the situation is such that the internal balance necessitates an expansion, but the external balance cannot bear a budgetary expansion because there is already a current account deficit, then the aim of increasing export volume or market shares can be justified as restoring both full employment and at the same time improving the current account balance.

ger horizon, however, the condition for the fact that a particular product is produced is that profitability is maintained. If that is the case, real investments will be undertaken. These real investments shape the distribution of the capital stocks across sectors and countries.

2.   The Measurement of Competitiveness

The previous discussion has highlighted the role of the time horizon determining what production factors can be characterized as being variable in input. If the subject of analysis is the current employment of variable production factors such as low-skilled labor, then one would look at indicators which determine labor demand. If, however, the subject of analysis is long-term growth prospects and the attractiveness of a country as a location of production, the evolution of operating profits or the margin of prices over variable unit costs is of paramount importance.

Assume that one concentrates on the first subject of analysis, i.e., the current performance of the economy. The group of quantifiable variables will then be set on the one hand by activity or income variables which reflect the growth of the world economy or the state of the business cycle and, on the other hand, by determinants with respect to demand-switching effects between countries for the consumer of the product. Especially for small open economies, the first group of variables can be taken as exogenous, so as long as the realization of policy targets is concerned, only the second group of variables are of interest. They condition the proportion of world demand which is directed toward a particular country.

Since demand is generally modeled to be a function of relative prices which the consumer faces, it is straightforward to put special emphasis on relative export prices between producing countries competing for world market shares. However, as pointed out by Turner and Van't dack (1993) relative export prices suffer from some deficiencies. The more homogeneous the goods concerned are, the smaller the observed price differences between different producers given the same discrepancy in relative production costs. In the extreme case of completely homogeneous goods there is no scope for price discrimination between producers and the law of one price holds, so the measure of relative producer prices would be of little use. In Section D.II, a relatively high correlation was indeed found between Western German import and Western German producer prices for sectors with a high degree of product homogeneity such as paper and pulp and iron and steel, i.e., for goods which have been classified as belonging to the *A*-category. On the other hand, for differentiated products, which constitute the vast majority of exports of industrialized countries, it does make sense to use both relative price and relative cost indicators for measuring competitiveness.

Another problem with export prices is that they only cover those goods which are actually traded. They do not, however, take into account goods which are potentially tradable but which are not traded because they are lacking international competitiveness.[34] As a result, Turner and Van't dack (1993), after having compared a broad range of indicators of competitiveness, conclude that the real effective exchange rate based on relative unit labor costs is most useful. Golub (1994) investigates the effects of relative unit labor costs on sectoral trade balances and finds that the changes, but not the levels of trade balances can be explained by the evolution of unit labor costs. Carlin et al. (1999) examine the impact of relative unit labor costs on market shares for a number of OECD countries. The average long-run elasticity between relative costs and export market shares, which they calculated from a distributed lag model in first differences, is −0.27. They also find that, as far as long-run effects are concerned, the single components of relative unit labor costs such as the nominal exchange rate, nominal wages, and labor productivity do not have significantly different effects on export market shares. In addition, they also detect a nonnegligible positive effect of the relative investment share as a noncost factor on export market shares. However, since the topic in this work is the role of cost differentials between countries, investment and productivity will only be considered insofar as there may be repercussions from the costs side via the channel of profitability. Before this will be done in Chapter F, the topic of how export demand evolves to a changing environment of competitiveness will be treated first, since those results are used as input for the subsequent debate on the determinants of profit.

II.   Country Results for Cost and Price Competitiveness and National Export Performance

1.   The Empirical Picture

In order to test whether country-specific export prices deviate less from one another than their respective cost measures deviate from one another, quarterly data from 1975 through 1999 for OECD countries has been sampled from the OECD

---

[34]   In Chapter F.III, an integrative approach of modeling both export capacity and price setting will be advanced in order to highlight this aspect. In addition, the empirical results for unit root tests from Chapter F.III are supportive for the view that uncompetitive firms are forced out of the market so that there is an asymptotic tendency for the law of one price to hold internationally.

database on *International Trade and Competitiveness Indicators* (OECD 2000a). They contain for 28 OECD countries inter alia series of indices of relative unit labor costs for the manufacturing sector and indices of relative export prices of manufactured goods, both in a common currency. These indices are constructed by relating unit labor costs or the export price of country i to a weighted average of the competitors' series, with the group of competitors consisting of all OECD countries and a selection of developing countries with a significant world market share. The single weights are constructed by the OECD in first determining the import weights from all competitors $j = 1,..., N, j \neq i$ for each single target market $k = 1,..., N$ including the domestic market of country i itself, and then aggregating over all markets k. Since this measure represents competition on both the export market and the home market, this concept is denoted by the OECD as overall competitiveness.

Figure 22 graphs the respective series for OECD countries. The series are normalized to 100 in 1975, so that an index value of more than 100 signifies higher costs or prices than those of competitors, indicating that competitiveness has declined since 1975. The measure is thus tantamount to the concept of the real effective exchange rate based on unit labor costs or export prices, with an increasing index value representing a real appreciation of the national currency. As in Chapter D, it is still irrelevant whether a move in the real exchange rate is caused by nominal exchange rate adjustments or changes in the price (or cost) series which are used to construct the particular real exchange rate index. The use of relative export prices is warranted because price ratios often show a smaller degree of integration than nominal price series, provided that a certain cointegration relationship exists, as was already argued before.[35]

The general empirical picture concerning the movements of the relative export price series and the relative unit labor costs series vary between countries. As was already discussed above, large countries like the United States show only scarce evidence for pricing to market on their export side. This behavior is also reflected in the relatively large comovement of relative unit labor costs and relative export prices for the United States, therefore strengthening the case for the relatively large focus of U.S. producers on their home market. Thus, the rationale for stabilizing the amount of export quantities by adjusting prices seems to be lacking altogether. By contrast, for the majority of countries, and especially for Japan as the most outstanding case, one finds that relative export prices are more stable than relative unit labor costs, suggesting low pass-through and a high level of pricing to market. Looking at Japan in a more detailed fashion, it is striking that in periods of strong real appreciations of the yen in 1986 and from 1993

---

[35]   Tests for stationarity for relative export prices and relative unit labor costs are presented in Chapter F, when long-term adjustment mechanisms are discussed.

Figure 22: A Comparison of Relative Unit Labor Costs, Relative Export Prices, and OECD Market Shares for Selected Countries

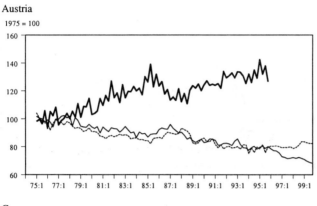

Austria

1975 = 100

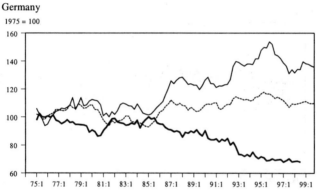

Germany

1975 = 100

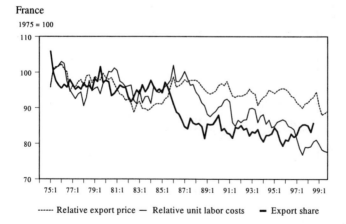

France

1975 = 100

------ Relative export price — Relative unit labor costs — Export share

Figure 22: continued

United Kingdom

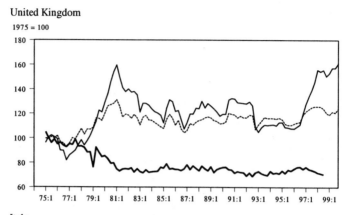

Italy

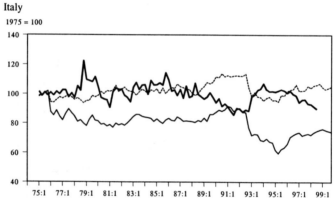

Japan

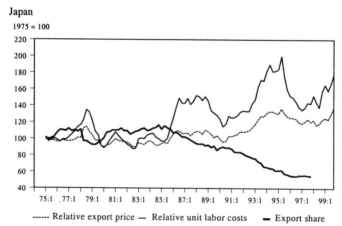

------ Relative export price — Relative unit labor costs — Export share

Figure 22: continued

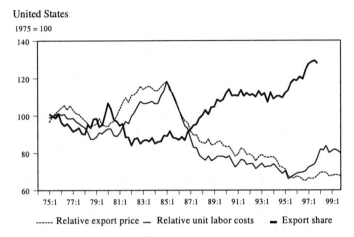

United States
1975 = 100

------ Relative export price — Relative unit labor costs ▬ Export share

Source: OECD (2000a).

through 1994, illustrated by strong upward movements of the relative unit labor cost series, export prices of Japanese exporters rose only slightly above the level of their competitors.

The situation is completely different for the case of Italy which suffered from a real appreciation in the beginning of the 1990s when it was a member of the European Monetary System (EMS) with its nominal exchange rate having a nearly fixed character relative to the other EMS members, whereas domestic prices and wages tended upward. It is interesting to realize that under these circumstances pricing to market or incomplete pass-through cannot be detected since relative unit labor costs and relative export prices show a large degree of comovement, at least in the 1990s. As was already discussed, determinants of the degree of pass-through are plenty, but the question is which factor is the main culprit for the practically 100 percent pass-through for Italy in that period. The solution might certainly lie in accounting for how the real exchange rate misalignment came about. If the source of the misalignment is long-term national wage or price inflation rather than an exchange rate shock, like in the Italian case, there is little ground for pricing to market as long as the foreign and domestic demand curves are not shifted against each other, as it happens when exchange rates fluctuate.

A similar reasoning may apply to Austria, where monetary policy was directed toward holding the value of its currency constant toward the German mark. Also for Austria, we indeed have a nearly one-to-one movement of relative unit labor costs and relative export prices suggesting that margins of Austrian exporters move in line with margins of foreign exporters. Note that a complete co-movement of relative export prices and relative unit labor costs does not imply that pass-through is full and that margins do not change. It does only show that margins of both groups of exporters move parallel to one another. As was derived by means of the theoretical model in Chapter C, there still can be justification for pricing to market even when exchange rates are fixed, for example when demand elasticities in the export market are larger than in the home market due to market shares or transport costs. Exchange rate volatility, especially when intervals of appreciations or depreciations are considered to be temporary, shifts both domestic production costs and the domestic demand curve against the foreign ones, so the markup in the export market changes more than in the home market.

Overall, one gets a fairly good confirmation of the imperfect pass-through hypothesis over a broad range of countries,[36] when pass-through is measured in terms of export prices relative to world export prices. This outcome is most visible when relative unit labor costs show strong and persistent increases or decreases. The outcome that small countries show a larger degree of pass-through into their import prices and more pricing to market themselves reflects both the theoretical finding and is also in line with empirical results from the comparison of export or import prices with domestic prices.

2.   Quantifying the Impact of Relative Unit Labor Costs on Relative Export Prices

In order to supplement the visual results by a thorough quantification of the effects of shifts in relative production costs on price competitiveness, some descriptive statistical measures for variances in the time series of relative export prices, relative unit labor costs, and export shares will be given next, analogously to the procedure in Chapter D, where the focus was on pass-through into import prices and the export price drift.

Since the absolute value of variances in the unit labor cost and export price series is determined by nominal exchange rate volatility in the first place, the variance of relative export prices is compared to the variance of relative unit labor costs by calculating the ratio of both measures. The hypothesis is that relative export prices are less volatile than relative unit labor costs if exporters pursue pricing to market at least to some extent. Table 16 presents some empirical statistics which are to prove this hypothesis. The first column shows the variance ratio of relative export prices to relative unit labor costs (*VRPU*), i.e., the ratio of the va-

---

[36] Graphs for further countries are presented in Chapter E.IV.

Table 16: Variances and Correlations between Relative Unit Labor Costs, Relative Export Prices, and Relative Consumer Prices[a]

	VRPU[b]	CPU[c]	CCU[d]	CRPC[e]
Australia	0.62	0.62	0.86	0.72
Austria	1.17	0.18	0.35	0.50
Belgium	0.60	0.47	0.84	0.56
Canada	0.47	0.50	0.84	0.59
Switzerland	0.80	0.76	0.87	0.87
Germany	0.45	0.57	0.67	0.86
Denmark	0.36	0.62	0.63	0.99
Spain	0.66	0.61	0.90	0.67
Finland	1.29	0.32	0.75	0.42
France	0.46	0.64	0.79	0.81
United Kingdom	0.46	0.80	0.93	0.86
Greece	1.88	0.12	0.56	0.21
Ireland	1.02	0.29	0.47	0.61
Iceland	0.79	0.13	0.78	0.16
Italy	0.50	0.48	0.76	0.62
Japan	0.33	0.80	0.92	0.87
South Korea	0.51	0.47	0.84	0.56
Mexico	0.42	0.22	0.95	0.23
Netherlands	0.76	0.66	0.78	0.85
Norway	1.33	0.12	0.44	0.27
New Zealand	0.69	0.50	0.91	0.54
Portugal	1.98	0.10	0.63	0.16
Sweden	0.36	0.50	0.63	0.79
Turkey	0.12	0.25	0.81	0.31
United States	0.79	0.79	0.87	0.91

[a]Relative unit labor costs and relative export prices are for the manufacturing sector. All original time series of relative prices or costs are computed relative to the weighted average of OECD countries reflecting their overall competitive position. The data is quarterly with the time period being 1975Q1 through 1999Q4. All original time series are indices, which have then been transformed into logs and differenced. For the computations of variances and correlation coefficients, a linear trend has been allowed for. – [b]VRPU is the variance ratio of relative export prices to relative unit labor costs. – [c]CPU denotes the correlation coefficient between relative export prices and relative unit labor costs. – [d]CCU denotes the correlation coefficient between relative consumption prices and relative unit labor costs. – [e]CRPC is the ratio of CPU over CCU.

Source: OECD (2000a).

riance of relative export prices to the variance of relative unit labor costs for OECD countries. In this table, however, the relative export price is not defined with respect to the domestic price index, which was the procedure in Chapter D, but with respect to the export price of all other exporters from the OECD countries. Indeed it is evident that for the majority of countries, this ratio is less than one, suggesting that the relative cost advantage is incompletely transmitted into a relative price advantage. The interpretation is analogous to what had been said for the corresponding graphs in Figure 22. Remembering the discussion of market shares in the pricing-to-market issue, it can be expected that small countries find it harder to pass through higher costs into higher prices. Pass-through is indeed smaller for some countries which depend largely on exports like Germany, Sweden, and in particular Japan, whereas the opposite holds for the United States. Unfortunately it is difficult to find this pattern for all countries in these data. The reason might be that since all variables have been detrended by differentiation, the implicit assumption of a linear trend might not be appropriate and thus might impact adversely upon the results, especially when growth rates show great differences between decades. In addition, countries with high and volatile price inflation and volatile exchange rates might show particularly unreliable results.

One possible approach to circumvent this problem is to use only those price components which are collinear to cost shifts. For this purpose, the correlation coefficient of relative export prices with relative unit labor costs (*CPU*) has been computed, and the corresponding figures are listed in the second column. The correlation is expected to be positive because the nominal exchange rate is a Common component of both relative unit labor costs and relative export prices. A large degree of pass-through, all other factors of influence being unchanged, is expected to result also in a large correlation coefficient. This might explain why countries taking part in the European Monetary System show smaller figures. Austria, which is doing a great deal of its external trade with Germany, to which it has already been tied via a de facto currency union long ago, enjoys a low volatility of its effective nominal exchange rate. For this reason the correlation coefficient in the second column is particularly low since the series of relative unit labor costs and relative export prices are driven by disturbances which are relatively uncorrelated to each other.

In order to isolate that part of the correlation which is due to exchange rate volatility, an analogous correlation coefficient has been computed with the consumption price index instead of the relative export price index (*CCU*). The ratio of column two over column three, i.e., the relative correlation ratio (*CRPC*), which is given in the last column, then should be a good measure of the pricing power in the export market. If that ratio is small, relative consumption prices show a larger comovement with relative unit labor costs than relative export prices. Indeed, column four of Table 16 is unanimously supportive of that view, since all countries have coefficients less than one.

If unit labor costs rise domestically more than in the rest of the world, then consumer prices at home rise more than abroad, and also the home country's export prices rise more than the other exporters' prices, but the rise in relative export prices is smaller than the rise in the country's relative consumption price index.

To conclude this analysis, the figures in the last column are most conclusive for the general pattern that smaller countries pass through a smaller amount of the shift in relative unit labor costs to the relative price of their products relative to the rest of the world. This behavior may be based on the positive impact of large market shares on pricing power. Alternatively, one can think of particularly small open economies, in which companies export a relatively large proportion of production and thus see a greater need to stabilize export quantities, and this is accomplished by incomplete pass-through. The next point of interest concerns the relationship of these measures with quantity measures such as the export share of a country relative to the group of all OECD countries.

3. Evidence for the Relation between Relative Unit Labor Costs and Export Performance

In order to obtain a measure of export performance in real quantities the OECD (2000a) computes in its database on *International Trade and Competitiveness Indicators* an indicator for export performance which represents, roughly speaking, the export volume of a country relative to the size of the world export market. The size of the export market, in turn, is the weighted average of import volumes of all other countries to which the respective country exports. A growth of the potential export market—for example, due to a positive business cycle evolution, long-term economic growth, or the dismantling of trade barriers, all leading to a rise in imports in those countries to which the respective country exports—is therefore already accounted for in the used measure of export performance. If export volumes evolve in a less than proportionate way relative to export market size, then export performance deteriorates, even if absolute exports may rise.

Figure 22 also contains this measure of export performance. The a priori expectation is that a decline in cost or price competitiveness represented by a hike in the respective series is followed by a decline in export performance. Looking at the graphs it is striking how close this relationship holds in reality. The shape of market share curve seems to be the same as those of price and cost measures for the majority of countries, the only difference being that it is reversed. It is also striking that this relationship does not only hold in the short run, but also reflects the secular evolution of export performance for a quite large number of countries. Indeed countries like the United Kingdom, Switzerland, Japan, and Germany show both deteriorating measures of competitiveness and actual export performance, whereas the opposite holds for Austria, Ireland, Korea, and the United States. Since the first group of countries, especially Germany and Japan, can be considered to be more open than the second one, the export sector for the first group of countries is more exposed to international factors of influence like the external value of the national currency or, to put it a bit differently, the price or cost measures of national competitiveness as discussed above. This might explain why trade shares of those countries respond to relative prices in the way which partial analysis suggests. Quite contrary, the second group of countries, with the United States as the most prominent example, show export sectors which are the mirror of relative dominant domestic economies and consequently can be better characterized as being residuals of national determinants like the current state of the national business cycle or the national consumption and saving decision. In these countries, where the export sector is small relative to the domestic one, the function of exports or imports as a valve for domestic excess demand or supply, or in general macroeconomic shocks, is more important than the matter of international competitiveness.

The bottom line of the country results just shown is that the issue of the real exchange rate has a nonnegligible impact on trade performance particularly for open economies, and will gain in concern as economies become more global.

III.   Sectoral Implications of Real Exchange Rate Movements

1.   The Real Exchange Rate and Comparative Advantage

I now turn to the question whether sectors are affected differently by real appreciations or depreciations of the national currency. To the extent that this hypothesis can be validated, the real exchange rate may impact upon a country's sectoral ranking of comparative advantage. However, it might be doubted that the interpretation of intersectoral price changes, when they are only due to aggregate national cost or exchange rate changes, does really make sense when related to the concept of comparative advantage. The assumption is that the country's currency appreciates in real terms. Then those sectors have a comparative disadvantage (measured in terms of prices) which pass through a larger proportion of the relative production cost increase—due to the currency appreciation—into the importer's price. However, this might not hold for the special case when goods are homogeneous. In this case, only little upward adjustment of prices is possible, and this sector's relative price is reduced thus signaling a rise in comparative advantage. Nonetheless, even though its price declined relative to other sectors, the loss in quantity and profit will be greater because demand is more elastic. The relative fall in profits will then attract only less than proportional investment in this sector thus leading to long-term declines of world market shares in this sector and higher long-term marginal costs of production.[37] It is then appropriate to state that comparative advantage has declined rather than increased. This is the rationale for incorporating profits and investment when assessing the impact of real exchange rate misalignments on the economic structure.

Drawing on the classification of goods into the groups *A*, *B*, and *C* from above, the argument is the following: The more the local price in a particular market is held stable, the less dominant fluctuations in quantities are, and vice versa. As a result, the profit per unit of output changes more than in the case of constant markups on variable production costs, but at the detriment of variation in quantities. If one assumes that profit margins are relatively small so that a given absolute adjustment of margins has a large impact on relative margins, the variation of relative variable profits is also large, since the price effect outweighs the counteracting quantity effect on variable profits. This pattern should hold for the case of relatively homogeneous goods (*A*-goods), where the world market price is preset for producers, and margins of prices above variable costs are relatively small. If those margins are squeezed, investments would be suppressed and the long-term production possibility of this sector as a whole is on the decline. As a result, both short-term and long-term competitiveness of production in a particular location will be sharply decreased if there is an upward cost shift relative to the reference group of countries.

On the other hand, for *B*-goods prices are also quite invariable due to the stabilizing pricing-to-market effect, but margins of prices above variable costs should be larger compared to *A*-goods because producers incur fixed costs of product development which account for the comparatively large degree of observed product differentiation. Consequently, the relative fluctuation of margins is less, since its average level is higher, which dampens the variability of profits. Moreover, since prices in local markets are quite inflexible, demand and therefore profits are also stabilized. In the end, both the effect of short-term and long-term competitiveness in *B*-sectors is less than in the *A*-sector when macroeconomic cost shifts occur. If *C*-goods as the third category are also taken into consideration, the impact on competitiveness, both short-term and long-term, is even less than with *B*-goods, since local demand for *C*-goods is even more inelastic than in the case of for *B*-goods. This reduces the impact on quantities and profit margins even further.

So what did we learn from this analysis for the evolution of absolute and comparative advantage? A positive macroeconomic country-specific cost shock de-

---

[37] It is implicitly assumed that output is a function of two production factors, one of them being capital, which is substitutable in the long run, whereas capital is fixed in the short term. A larger capital stock therefore reduces the share of variable production factors.

creases the absolute comparative advantage of all sectors *A*, *B*, and *C*, but hitting
A-sectors the most and *C*-sectors the least. Accordingly, their relative position in
long-term comparative advantage changes, since *C* gains relative to *A*, both in
terms of short-term quantity of production and in terms of long-term attractiveness of investment. It would therefore be of interest to investigate empirically
what the effect of real appreciations or depreciations is on sectoral comparative
advantage in terms of exported quantities. However, this venture becomes quite
ambitious, since trade flows differ across sectors, and business cycles in target
regions as a predominant determinant of exports to these target regions would se-
riously blur the picture. This is why shares in the world market rather than absolute export quantities are investigated next.

2.   Empirical Results for Sectoral Cost Competitiveness and Sectoral World Market Shares

It has been argued that sectors differ in their price elasticities of world demand
for a country's exports, which causes exporters to choose sector-specific pass-
through rates. As these sector-specific pass-through rates have already been giv-
en for Germany in Table 9 and Figure 19, a multi-country approach would now
be appropriate in order to cover both the sectoral and international dimension of
pass-through. Unfortunately, there is only scarce data on sectoral export prices
on a comparable basis for OECD countries, so an indirect approach by using relative unit labor costs is warranted.

The OECD (1999) database *Main Industrial Indicators* contains sectoral relative unit labor costs for OECD countries, complemented by quantity data on export performance defined as a country's share of total OECD exports, which will
be used in the following empirical analysis. The sectoral unit labor costs can be
regarded as sector-specific real effective exchange rates based on unit labor cost
indices, with the weights of partner countries having been calculated on sector-
specific trade weights. The database thus contains data across countries and sectors.

The export share of a particular industry *z* as used by the OECD is defined as
the value of a country *A*'s exports in this industry relative to the exports of all
OECD countries in the same industry:

$$(E.1) \quad z_s^A \equiv \frac{p_s^A x_s^A}{P_s X_s},$$

where *p* denotes export prices and *x* real export quantities. The superscript *A* refers to the export country which is a particular OECD country. Capital letters *P*

and X denote aggregate export price and real quantity indices for the entity of all OECD countries, and the subscript s stands for the sector. Note that all prices and costs are expressed in the same currency. It does not matter which curency is used, since only relative prices and relative costs are considered. As a result, relative unit labor costs for a country may rise for a variety of reasons which are all covered by this relative cost measure: It might be the case that the currency of A appreciates relative to the OECD average, i.e., the nominal effective exchange rate changes. It might also apply that labor remuneration per employee rises relatively more in country A than in the OECD as a whole. It might also hold that the growth of labor productivity as the ratio of constant price value added to the number of employees engaged falls behind the OECD-wide growth rates. It is not investigated in further detail how much each of these factors account for possible disequilibria in that relative cost measure. The focus is on how value shares of exports evolve, given a particular pattern of relative cost movements. Note that market shares are always measured in terms of value shares.

The estimated elasticity of export share with respect to relative production costs on the left-hand side of (E.2) is the product of the elasticity of export share with respect to relative prices (first factor on the right-hand side) times the pass-through elasticity (second factor on the right-hand side), where the pass-through elasticity indicates the percentage change in relative export prices when relative production costs change:

$$(E.2) \quad E\left(z_s^A, \frac{c_s^A}{C_s} \right) = E\left(\frac{p_s^A \, x_s^A}{P_s X_s}, \frac{c_s^A}{C_s} \right) = E\left(\frac{p_s^A \, x_s^A}{P_s X_s}, \frac{p_s^A}{P_s} \right) \times E\left(\frac{p_s^A}{P_s}, \frac{c_s^A}{C_s} \right),$$

where c denotes unit labor costs as a proxy for total production costs and C denotes aggregate unit labor costs.

The elasticity of the export share with respect to relative prices, in turn, is one plus the elasticity of the quantity share with respect to relative export prices, where the latter elasticity is a measure for the underlying price elasticity of world demand for a country's exports (right-hand side of (E.3)):

$$(E.3) \quad E\left(\frac{p_s^A x_s^A}{P_s X_s}, \frac{p_s^A}{P_s} \right) = 1 + E\left(\frac{x_s^A}{X_s}, \frac{p_s^A}{P_s} \right).$$

The elasticity of the quantity share with respect to relative export prices can be obtained from the observed elasticity of z in the denominator—by substituting (E.3) into (E.2) and solving for the elasticity of the quantity share with respect to relative export prices—and an estimate of the pass-through elasticity (numerator on the right-hand side of (E.4)):

$$(E.4) \quad E\left(\frac{x_s^A}{X_s}, \frac{p_s^A}{P_s}\right) = \frac{\left.E\left(z_s^A, \frac{c_s^A}{C_s}\right)\right\} \in [-\infty, 1]}{\left.E\left(\frac{p_s^A}{P_s}, \frac{c_s^A}{C_s}\right)\right\} \in [0,1]} - 1 \right\} \in [-\infty, 0].$$

However, the *Main Industrial Indicators* database (OECD 1999) does not contain relative export prices in order to compute pass-through elasticities. Because the possible range in pass-through is between zero and plus one, the obtained coefficients from Table 17 as estimates of the elasticity of z with respect to relative unit labor costs can be interpreted indirectly as the elasticity of quantity share with respect to relative prices.

An estimate for the observed price elasticity of z in (E.2) of value zero signifies an isoelastic demand schedule, no matter how much the pass-through is. A negative estimate always implies elastic demand, but the absolute value of the demand elasticity is underestimated if pass-through is incomplete. If pass-through is incomplete, the unobservable elasticity of the quantity share with respect to prices (E.4) is larger in absolute value, since a one-percent relative cost change, which is the basis in the empirical implementation, entails a less than one-percent change in relative export prices, thus making the denominator in (E.4) smaller, and the elasticity of the quantity share (left-hand side of (E.4)) larger in absolute value. A large negative elasticity of z (the value share of exports) with respect to relative unit labor costs, or a moderate one combined with small pass-through, both signify large elasticities of the quantity share with respect to relative prices.

On the other hand, a positive coefficient indicates that demand is inelastic. It does not imply, though, that the real export share in terms of physical units is increasing, but that the value share of exports with respect to all OECD countries is increasing. This increase in value is due to a price increase of national producers relative to all other OECD producers since an increase in relative unit labor costs is transmitted into an increase in relative export prices with respect to the other OECD countries.

In order to focus on the sectoral components the variables have been pooled across countries and a panel data estimation has been employed with country-specific fixed effects. Table 17 displays a regression of world market shares against relative unit labor costs on the basis of (E.5). Because one cannot expect the adjustment of world market shares to be instantaneous and in order to account for possible unit roots in the data, an error-correction specification is used to determine for each sector s separately the long-term dependency of country-specific export shares (z_s) in total OECD exports of this sector from relative unit

Table 17: Panel Data Estimation of World Market Shares against Relative Unit Labor Costs[a]

Industry code	Sector (s)	LNRULC	$-a_S$	DW
3100	Food, beverages, & tobacco	−0.548 (−8.107**)	−0.445 (−5.764*)	1.957
3200	Textiles, apparel, & leather	−0.408 (−1.850)	−0.250 (−5.717*)	1.855
3300	Wood products & furniture	0.029 (0.368)	−0.379 (−5.638*)	1.930
3400	Paper, paper products, & printing	−0.742 (−1.931)	−0.287 (−5.674*)	1.995
3510	Industrial chemicals	0.162 (1.084)	−0.475 (−7.696**)	1.849
3520	Other chemicals	−0.465 (−1.816)	−0.214 (−4.126)	1.505
3534	Petroleum refineries & products	0.307 (2.465)	−0.238 (−4.587)	1.812
3534	Rubber & plastic products	−0.451 (−2.287)	−0.357 (−6.259**)	1.845
3600	Nonmetallic mineral products	−0.122 (−0.923)	−0.310 (−6.445**)	2.032
3710	Iron & steel	−0.279 (−2.103)	−0.416 (−6.857**)	2.057
3720	Nonferrous metals	0.228 (1.563)	−0.315 (−5.626*)	1.883
3810	Metal products	−0.078 (−0.559)	−0.344 (−5.972**)	1.780
3820	Nonelectrical machinery	0.002 (0.675)	−0.322 (−4.510)	1.896
3830	Electrical machinery	0.089 (0.068)	−0.397 (−7.250**)	1.822
3840	Transport equipment	−0.444 (−3.954)	−0.345 (−5.402*)	2.002
3850	Professional goods	0.364 (4.243)	−0.216 (−3.899)	1.926
Summary statistics	Low-technology industries	−0.803 (−7.682**)	−0.333 (−5.448*)	1.922
	Total manufacturing	−0.448 (−2.023)	−0.327 (−5.413*)	1.908

[a]Estimated coefficients refer to (E.5) with $q = r = 1$. Only coefficients of the error-correction term are given. Estimates are based on yearly mean-adjusted data from 1980 through 1997. Included are 9 counties: Belgium, France, Western Germany, Italy, Japan, Spain, Sweden, United Kingdom, United States. The total number of observations for each sector is 135. World market shares are defined as exports of a certain industry for a given country as a percentage of exports of this industry for the OECD as a whole, with both export values being converted into U.S. dollars using nominal exchange rates. Source of data: OECD (1999), *Main Industrial Indicators*. ** and *: significant at 5 and 1 percent, respectively. The critical values at the 5 and 1 percent level of significance are −5.35 and −5.77 for $T = 10$ and $N = 10$ according to Levin and Lin (1992). DW: Durbin–Watson test statistic. t-statistics in parentheses.

labor costs (*LNRULC*) as the ratio of unit labor costs of a country relative to the weighted average of all OECD countries with respect to this sector:

$$(E.5) \quad d\ln z_s = c_s - a_s\left[\ln z_{s,t-1} - \overline{b}_s \ LNRULC_{s,t-1}\right] + \sum_{j=0}^{q} b_{sj}\Delta LNRULC_{s,t-j}$$

$$+ \sum_{j=1}^{r} d_{sj}d\ln z_{s,t-j} + \varepsilon_{st}.$$

Concerning the properties of the error terms, a cross-sectional dependency has necessarily to be assumed since a gain in one country's share has to be a loss somewhere else, even though not the full sample of all OECD countries could be included in the sample due to data availability. Estimation by SUR is appropriate to account for this effect. The critical values of the coefficients in the error-correction term are from Levin and Lin (1992) in order to take account of possible unit roots in the data which have to be expected from the visual inspection of the graphs in Section E.II.1.

It is apparent from column 2 of Table 17 that the coefficients on *LNRULC* in the long-term relationship vary across sectors, but are negative for total manufacturing thus representing elastic world demand for the country-specific exports. Particularly negative coefficients have been found for food, paper products, other chemicals, rubber and plastic products, and transport equipment, whereas even positive coefficients have been obtained for industrial chemicals, nonferrous metals, petroleum refineries, and professional goods. Unfortunately, the standard levels of significance of the coefficients are only reached for food, beverages, and tobacco, which is probably due to the short regression period.

C-goods, for which the sector of professional goods is a prominent example, are characterized by little possibilities of substitution on the demand side. If products are scarcely substitutable, allowing producers to be a kind of monopolistic supplier within their specific product variant, then demand is relatively unresponsive to relative price changes, even when price changes are large and a positive impact on market share would result. The coefficient for professional goods is indeed quite positive, but it is insignificant.

For the category of *B*-goods, for example, wood products, textiles, and transport equipment, representing the group of pricing-to-market goods, no clear direction of market share response is expected a priori, since the result depends on how much prices in the local target markets are stabilized in the event of cost changes. In fact, regression results are more in favor of a negative bias, but coefficients are sometimes insignificant.

The *A*-goods themselves, which are only relatively sheltered from competition due to the presence of transport costs when the countries' products are not particularly differentiated from substitutes produced in the rest of the world. Transport costs therefore establish a band of inaction in which relative prices may fluctuate without causing substantial shifts in demand. When costs rise to a sufficiently high level, thus also entailing an increase in export prices, this band may be left, demand elasticity rises, and the producer's optimal markup is cut down causing pass-through to be incomplete.

As a summary statistic, the database also includes data for the aggregated sector of low-technology industries, which is a composition of only those industries with a relatively low level of technology.[38] It is striking how significantly negative the coefficient is for this aggregated sector. This result reflects the combination of two factors: Firstly, the large degree of product homogeneity in the low-technology industries makes demand more elastic thus contributing to the larger switching effect of expenditure between the exporting country and its competitors. Secondly, not only the response to the price adjustment, but also the adjustment of relative prices to relative costs itself is sharper because markup margins are generally lower because sunk costs incurred by research and development can be expected to be less important in this sector.

This last important result can be taken to conclude briefly the chief findings of Section III of this chapter. It has been shown that the real exchange rate impacts differently on sectors when adjustment of prices to costs and world market shares are concerned, thus justifying a disaggregated approach. Low-technology industries are particularly vulnerable to real exchange rate appreciations, but also benefit most when a depreciation occurs.

The sectoral findings complement the country-specific results which point toward small open economies being more tied to given world market prices than large economies. The question which remains to be answered is what the adjustment process of real exchange rate deviations is like and how the real economy is affected by this adjustment. As will be shown in the next chapter, a crucial variable in this process is investment which is driven by profitability.

---

[38] The database *Main Industrial Indicators* (OECD 1999) also contain high, medium-high, and medium-low technology industries, but unfortunately these other summary sectors exhibit missing values for nearly all OECD countries.

IV.   Appendix

Figure A4: A Comparison of Relative Unit Labor Costs, Relative Export Prices, and OECD Market Shares for Further Countries

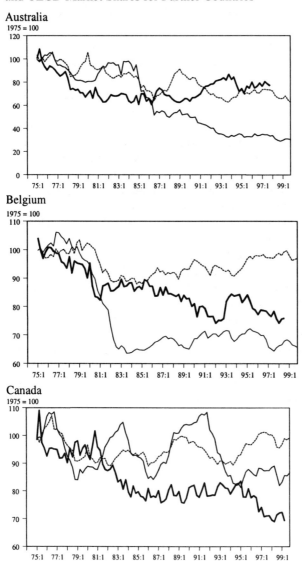

Figure A4: continued

Switzerland

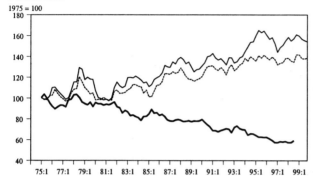

Denmark

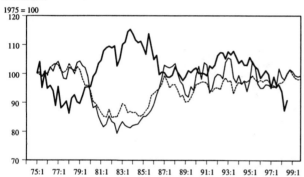

Spain

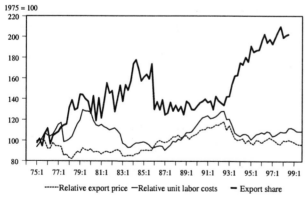

------Relative export price ―Relative unit labor costs ― Export share

Figure A4: continued

Finland

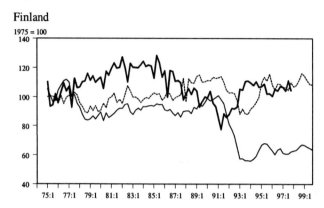

Greece

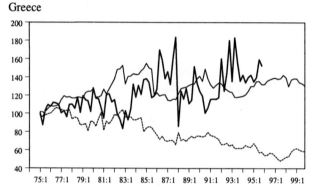

Ireland

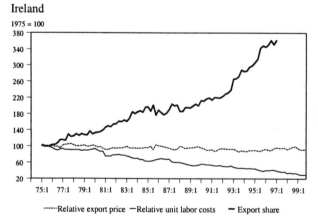

------Relative export price ─Relative unit labor costs   ━ Export share

Figure A4: continued

Iceland

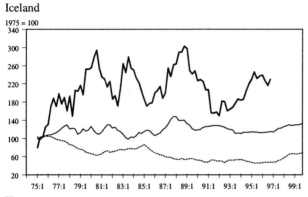

Korea

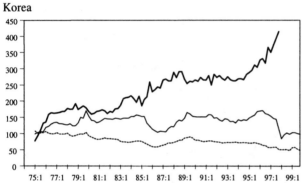

Mexico

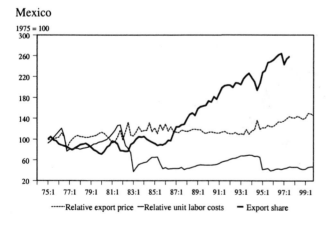

······Relative export price ──Relative unit labor costs ── Export share

176

Figure A4: continued

Netherlands

Norway

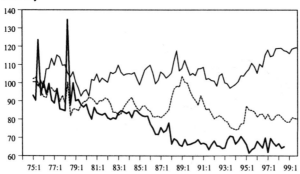

New Zealand

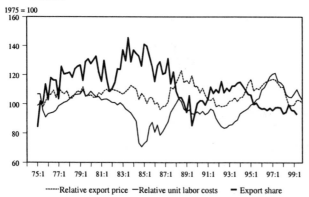

-----Relative export price —Relative unit labor costs ▬ Export share

Figure A4: continued

Portugal

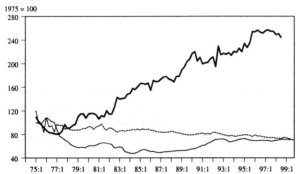

Sweden

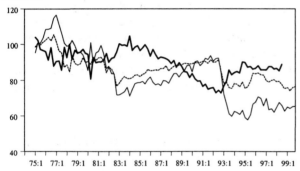

Turkey

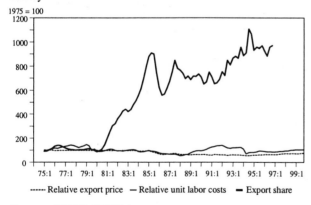

----- Relative export price   — Relative unit labor costs   ▬ Export share

Source: OECD (2000a).

F. The Law of One Price and Adjustments of the Real Economy

The previous chapter dealt with how and to what extent relative cost competitiveness has an impact on export market shares. As has already been discussed, the kind of mechanism behind this impact is conditional on the time horizon which one is interested in. Figure 23 illustrates this idea. The short-run impact on export quantities depends upon pass-through of relative production costs to relative export prices, which causes a demand switching effect toward or away from national exports. Note that this impact only works through the transmission chain if at least a part of relative cost changes is reflected in relative export price adjustments. The long-run impact, on the other hand, is less conditional on the particular value of the pass-through elasticity, since it is working through the evolution of profits and the supply decision of producers. The value of the pass-through elasticities will be shown to be as relevant as the elasticity of demand,[39] with both elements bearing upon the magnitude of profit margin adjustment when cost competitiveness changes.

Figure 23: The Transmission of Relative Cost Shifts into Export Prices

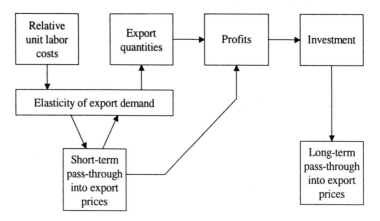

---

[39] For a complete account of factors which determine pass-through, see Chapter C.

The general relationship between (1) pass-through, profitability, and investment and (2) national cost differentials driven predominantly by exchange rate shifts will also be shown. Then the aspect of entry and exit of producers in the export market will be treated. The basic hypothesis is that real appreciations force the most inefficient firms out of the market, thus restoring aggregate competitiveness of one country at least partly and narrowing the gap in export prices between countries. This final adjustment in export prices, after reallocations on the supply side have been allowed for, constitutes the long-term pass-through, which is supposed to be smaller in magnitude, since international price differentials disappear in the long run.

I. Does the Law of One Price Hold Asymptotically for Export Prices and for Unit Labor Costs?

1. The Motivation for Unit Root Tests

Another approach to determine whether pass-through of exporters is incomplete, additional to variance and regression analysis, is to test what the time series behavior of relative export prices is. If the series of countries' export prices relative to their worldwide competitors is stationary, a tendency for mean reversion exists which constrains exporters in the long run not to deviate from export prices of their competitors. One would expect a priori that the series for the real exchange rate based on relative unit labor costs will also show less signs of mean reversion since labor as a geographically incompletely mobile production factor is not exposed to direct competition across borders, but only indirectly through the working of product market competition.

If, starting from a hypothetical equilibrium, wages in a particular country rise once and for all to a permanently higher level with everything else being unchanged, export prices relative to all other world exporters also rise, but only less than proportionally. This would imply that without any real adjustment mechanism, variable profits, i.e., gross profits minus variable costs, would be squeezed permanently. This holds for products sold on export markets, and, to a lower degree, also for domestic sales because of import competition. It is straightforward that this profit squeeze is not sustainable, so that an adjustment will occur. The first channel of adjustment is of course a devaluation of the nominal exchange rate, provided the country's exchange rate regime allows for flexibility between currencies. If this is the case, both relative unit labor costs and relative export prices would be restored to equilibrium. However, empirical studies generally find only slow rates of mean reversions of real exchange rates. Even if an adjustment does occur, it would often be done by the working of the world capital market.

The second channel of adjustment, which is dealt with in the next chapter, is that productivity is increased after the real exchange rate has appreciated. This is accomplished via the allocation process of factor inputs. Since a country produces not only for the export market but for the home market as well, and since often a substantial part of the value-adding process consists of activities which are nontradable (such as local distribution and marketing activities, which are excluded from international competition), an equalization of unit labor costs or consumer prices is not easy to detect. The reason is that only for tradable goods, a forceful adjustment mechanism is at work which eliminates price differences by competition.

That is why in the following the use of relative export prices is opted for in testing for mean reversion. If the relative export price series, i.e., the ratio of a country's export price relative to that of its competitors in the world market, is stationary, then this finding can be taken as evidence that producers are price takers in the end. The ability of passing through a part of a local cost shock can then be seen to be more or less temporary, and is then at least partly reversed, so in the long run the tendency is toward incomplete pass-through or pricing to market in the absence of any further shocks. If this holds for each single country, and country-specific export prices converge when measured in the same currency, then the notion of pricing to market, which was applied only with respect to a single target market and with a short-run horizon, has a long-run interpretation as "pricing to the world market." Interestingly, the long-run tendency of a reduction of pass-through has also been established in the two-period theoretical approach where a permanent cost or exchange rate shock makes the second-period pass-through less than the first-period one. The finding of a reduction of pass-through toward the world markets when time is passing can also be interpreted as an increase in the long-run price elasticity of world demand relative to the short-run elasticity. This in turn makes quantity responses in the long run greater than in the short run, a consequence which is to be highlighted in one of the next sections when also investment behavior will be shortly looked at.

For now, the task is to determine whether relative export prices of a country relative to the world show a tendency of mean reversion. For that purpose the OECD (2000a) database on *International Trade and Competitiveness Indicators* will be used. Since the panel encompasses several countries which are members of the European Monetary Union or formerly took part in the European Exchange Rate Mechanism, their effective nominal exchange rates are correlated, because their single rates move as a bloc against outside currencies, e.g., the U.S. dollar. To take just two country pairs as examples, as Tables 18 and 19 show, the growth rate of German and Dutch relative unit labor costs, and also relative ex-

Table 18: Time Series Correlations between Relative Export Prices of Selected OECD Countries[a]

	AUS	BEL	CAN	CHE	DEU	DNK	FRA	GBR	ITA	JPN	NLD	NZL	USA
AUS	1	–0.12	0.52	–0.28	–0.22	–0.24	–0.10	0.14	–0.04	–0.34	–0.11	0.48	0.13
BEL	–0.12	1	–0.19	0.01	0.50	0.45	0.18	–0.32	0.28	0.17	0.30	–0.30	–0.33
CAN	0.52	–0.19	1	–0.11	–0.17	–0.10	–0.05	0.18	–0.03	–0.18	–0.15	0.32	–0.10
CHE	–0.28	0.01	–0.11	1	0.28	0.37	0.19	–0.08	0.01	0.21	0.28	0.02	–0.28
DEU	–0.22	0.50	–0.17	0.28	1	0.73	0.17	–0.18	0.24	0.01	0.59	–0.30	–0.52
DNK	–0.24	0.45	–0.10	0.37	0.73	1	0.32	–0.28	0.32	0.09	0.51	–0.26	–0.41
FRA	–0.10	0.18	–0.05	0.19	0.17	0.32	1	–0.25	0.43	0.14	0.20	–0.10	–0.30
GBR	0.14	–0.32	0.18	–0.08	–0.18	–0.28	–0.25	1	–0.11	–0.15	–0.09	0.19	–0.11
ITA	–0.04	0.28	–0.03	0.01	0.24	0.32	0.43	–0.11	1	0.00	0.18	–0.11	–0.17
JPN	–0.34	0.17	–0.18	0.21	0.01	0.09	0.14	–0.15	0.00	1	–0.02	–0.20	–0.38
NLD	–0.11	0.30	–0.15	0.28	0.59	0.51	0.20	–0.09	0.18	–0.02	1	–0.13	–0.45
NLZ	0.48	–0.30	0.32	0.02	–0.30	–0.26	–0.10	0.19	–0.11	–0.20	–0.13	1	0.20
USA	0.13	–0.33	–0.10	–0.28	–0.52	–0.41	–0.30	–0.11	–0.17	–0.38	–0.45	0.20	1

[a]The country abbreviations are: Australia (AUS), Belgium (BEL), Canada (CAN), Switzerland (CHE), Germany (DEU), Denmark (DNK), France (FRA), United Kingdom (GBR), Italy (ITA), Japan (JPN), Netherlands (NLD), New Zealand (NLZ), United States (USA). – Data are quarterly from 1975Q1 through 1999Q4.

Source: Own calculations based on OECD (2000a, 2000b).

Table 19: Time Series Correlations between Relative Unit Labor Costs of Selected OECD Countries[a]

	AUS	BEL	CAN	CHE	DEU	DNK	FRA	GBR	ITA	JPN	NLD	NZL	USA
AUS	1	–0.23	0.27	–0.11	–0.28	–0.25	–0.06	0.04	0.10	–0.16	–0.31	0.19	0.28
BEL	–0.23	1	–0.12	0.35	0.13	0.49	0.17	–0.19	–0.12	0.15	0.69	–0.02	–0.25
CAN	0.27	–0.12	1	–0.04	–0.12	–0.07	–0.09	0.00	0.05	–0.36	–0.11	0.15	0.10
CHE	–0.11	0.35	–0.04	1	–0.14	0.24	0.22	0.02	–0.09	0.32	0.42	0.01	–0.34
DEU	–0.28	0.13	–0.12	–0.14	1	0.24	–0.05	–0.29	–0.30	–0.08	0.22	0.11	–0.21
DNK	–0.25	0.49	–0.07	0.24	0.24	1	0.28	–0.26	–0.13	0.17	0.48	–0.06	–0.19
FRA	–0.06	0.17	–0.09	0.22	–0.05	0.28	1	–0.15	–0.13	0.13	0.21	–0.07	–0.16
GBR	0.04	–0.19	0.00	0.02	–0.29	–0.26	–0.15	1	0.14	0.00	–0.11	0.13	–0.17
ITA	0.10	–0.12	0.05	–0.09	–0.30	–0.13	–0.13	0.14	1	–0.09	–0.09	–0.14	0.02
JPN	–0.16	0.15	–0.36	0.32	–0.08	0.17	0.13	0.00	–0.09	1	0.13	–0.10	–0.53
NLD	–0.31	0.69	–0.11	0.42	0.22	0.48	0.21	–0.11	–0.09	0.13	1	0.00	–0.32
NLZ	0.19	–0.02	0.15	0.01	0.11	–0.06	–0.07	0.13	–0.14	–0.10	0.00	1	0.05
USA	0.28	–0.25	0.10	–0.34	–0.21	–0.19	–0.16	–0.17	0.02	–0.53	–0.32	0.05	1

[a]For the country abbreviations, see Table 18. – Data are quarterly from 1975Q1 through 1999Q4.

Source: Own calculations based on OECD (2000a, 2000b).

port prices, are positively correlated with a correlation coefficient of 0.22 and 0.59, respectively for the reason just mentioned. On the other hand, for Germany and the United States the correlation coefficient of those series is –0.21 and –0.52, suggesting that, as both countries hold a dominant position in world trade, when Germany gains competitiveness relative to all other countries the United States lose and vice versa.

As O'Connell (1998) shows, when disturbances are not identically and independently distributed (iid), as is the case when there is cross-sectional dependence, then critical values for unit root tests in panels, notably those computed by Levin and Lin (1992), are biased in terms of rejecting too often the null of nonstationarity, thus concluding perhaps erroneously that mean reversion exists. O'Connell also shows that if estimated by generalized least square (GLS), and provided that the number of countries is much smaller than the number of observations, the power of the test is close to the conventional panel unit root test when the disturbances are iid.

Following this, the GLS estimator was employed to account for cross-country correlation and country-specific autocorrelation of disturbances. In contrast to most other studies, I employ multilateral effective time series for real exchange rates based on unit labor costs, and, as a second series, the series on the relative export price, also calculated on a multilateral basis for each country. The problem of correlation between the series of different countries is here less severe than in panel studies where bilateral pairs are used and where the computed pairs of real exchange rates are all with respect to one and the same country, for example the United States. A real appreciation of the U.S. dollar would cause practically all other currencies to depreciate in real terms against the United States at the same time, so a strong positive correlation between all real exchange rates would be the result. This problem can be overcome when multilateral real exchange rates are used for each single country, because, on average, countries which appreciate and those which depreciate should cancel out each other, so the correlation on average should be nearly zero. Indeed the average value of correlation coefficients for the group of 21 OECD countries used in this study is 0.005 for the relative export price series and 0.019 for relative unit labor costs. However, when only partial country groups are formed, the problem is still relevant, so the GLS estimate should still be more efficient, since the information on the bilateral correlation structure is used.

Another advantage of using multilateral time series is that competitor countries are weighted according to their actual importance as competitors for the respective countries when country-specific trade shares are used in the weighting procedure. For example, variables pertaining to big world exporters such as the United States, Germany, or Japan as competitor countries should be given more weight in the regressions than the series for Iceland or Austria. This is however not the case when bilateral pairs are considered equally.

2. The Empirical Approach

Pooling countries together for the estimation of common coefficients has the disadvantage that the relationship might not hold for all countries so that outlier detection is an important first step (Hansen 2000). For that purpose the estimation has first been done by allowing coefficients to vary freely between countries, but taking account of cross-section correlation of the disturbances by means of the SUR (seemingly unrelated regression) estimator. Let x be the log of the variable for which the unit root test will be conducted, and i and t indexing the country and time, respectively. For the specification $a_i = 0$ unit root tests are implemented without any constant, taking account of the proposition that deterministic trends are not compatible with the law of one price holding in the long run. The regression equation for a particular country is

$$(\text{F.1}) \quad \Delta x_{it} = a_i + (\rho_i - 1)\, x_{i,t-1} + \sum_{j=1}^{p} b_{ij}\, \Delta x_{i,t-j} + \varepsilon_{it}, \quad i = 1,\dots, N;\ t = 1,\dots, T.$$

Subsequently, the panel estimation is done with data pooled over all OECD countries and the adjustment coefficients being restricted to be identical, i.e. all ρ_i are equal to ρ. In order to account for cross-sectional differences in means, the panel model has also been estimated with country-specific constants:

$$(\text{F.2}) \quad \Delta x_{it} = a_i(1-\rho) + (\rho - 1)x_{i,t-1} + \sum_{j=1}^{p} b_j\, \Delta x_{i,t-j} + \varepsilon_{it}, \quad i = 1,\dots,N;\ t = 1,\dots,T.$$

Following Hansen (2000), this specification ensures that fixed effects disappear in the case of unit roots ($\rho = 1$). Concerning the error term ε_{it}, the approaches in the literature for unit root tests in panels of real exchange rates differ in the assumptions that were made about the properties of the disturbances. Whereas Papell (1997) argues that serial correlation can affect the critical values of unit root tests, Hakkio (1984) and Abuaf and Jorion (1990) take into account explicitly the cross-sectional behavior of the error terms. In this approach both elements are accounted for.

3.   Empirical Results

Table 20 gives the results of the SUR estimation method applied to two kinds of country-specific variables. The first one is the relative export price as the export price index of the respective country relative to the export price of this country's competitors, which is computed by the OECD in weighting import shares of those competitors in the most important export markets and then aggregating. The second variable is the relative unit labor cost series being constructed by the same method, but with unit labor cost indices instead of export prices. Table 20

Table 20: Unit Root Tests for Relative Export Prices and Relative Unit Labor Costs

	Relative export price		Relative unit labor costs	
	coefficient	t-statistic	coefficient	t-statistic
Australia	−0.057	−2.80**	−0.011	−1.07
Austria	−0.086	−2.75**	−0.020	−0.19
Belgium	−0.040	−1.52*	−0.440	−6.83**
Canada	−0.102	−3.78**	−0.057	−2.55*
Switzerland	−0.058	−2.59**	−0.030	−1.47
Germany	−0.051	−3.13**	−0.023	−1.36
Denmark	−0.075	−3.76**	−0.074	−2.62**
Spain	−0.044	−1.51	−0.066	−2.18*
Finland	−0.185	−3.56**	−0.027	−1.62
France	−0.104	−2.81	−0.043	−1.52
United Kingdom	−0.139	−4.05**	−0.053	−2.35*
Greece	−0.031	−1.31	−0.114	−2.99**
Ireland	−0.212	−3.65**	−0.005	−0.54
Iceland	−0.037	−5.03**	−0.160	−4.07**
Italy	−0.078	−2.06**	−0.085	−2.84**
Japan	−0.033	−1.55	−0.060	−3.34**
Korea	−0.051	−2.63**	−0.132	−4.08**
Mexico	−0.126	−2.35**	−0.054	−2.02*
Netherlands	−0.054	−2.80**	−0.013	−1.52
Norway	−0.152	−3.55**	−0.148	−2.62**
New Zealand	−0.225	−2.94**	−0.105	−3.57**
Portugal	−0.035	−0.93	−0.048	−3.72**
Sweden	−0.093	−2.84**	−0.048	−1.96*
Turkey	−0.029	−2.69**	−0.074	−2.17*
United States	−0.017	−2.44**	−0.023	−1.88

[a] ** and * denote significance at the 1 and 5 percent level, respectively, for which the asymptotic critical values are −2.56 and −1.94 according to McKinnon (1994).

gives the results for the individual countries for $a_i = 0$, because when constants are included, they are insignificant for nearly all countries. For both series and the majority of countries, the critical values are sufficiently negative in order to reject the unit root hypothesis. This suggests that deviations from the long-term stationary mean of that variable cause adjustments toward that mean. For this particular problem the outcome can be interpreted as evidence for the law of one price to hold in many cases. Moreover, since this tendency seems to be stronger for relative export prices than for relative unit labor costs, the integration of product markets does explain this difference in results. If it were the case that export prices were determined from domestic factors without any correcting force from world markets, the tendency of mean reversion would be about the same. The results for relative unit labor costs indicate that particularly smaller economies exhibit mean reversion, with their t-statistics being significant, in contrast to big economies like the United States, Germany, and France with insignificant t-statistics, which obviously are less subject to adapt to external forces.

The tests are repeated by restricting ρ to be identical over all countries, the results of which are presented in Table 21. Concerning the constant, three different kinds of restrictions have been implemented. The first row shows the regression results when no constant is included, as it is the case when ρ is estimated for each country separately. This specification thus restricts the law of one price to hold asymptotically. As a result, strong mean reversion is detected for both series, with the relative export price revealing a larger absolute value of the adjustment coefficient than for relative unit labor costs. This suggests again that the adjustment in export prices is faster than in the real exchange rate based on unit labor costs.

Repeating the regression with a constant common to all countries reveals a similar result. The constant itself is not very different from zero, thus justifying the restricted specification. The estimation with individual-specific intercepts does not serve to increase the value of the t-statistic of the single adjustment coefficient ρ, but only leads to higher critical values which have to be applied, so that the border of significance is just met. With the exception of Ireland in the unit labor cost estimation, county coefficients (not shown in the table) are insignificant.

What is now the bottom line of all these results so far? The question whether a deterioration or an improvement in cost competitiveness (in terms of relative unit labor costs) also implies a corresponding evolution of price competitiveness (i.e., export prices relative to the world) is important for the transmission of shocks since price-setting determines the quantity outcome with respect to world market shares. It was argued that price competitiveness in the short run will be relatively unaffected by movements in cost competitiveness when countries are small and relatively open, when only nominal exchange rates change, and when product and market characteristics allow for pursuing pricing-to-market strategies. The adjusting variables under these circumstances are markups and therefore profits, as has been derived in Chapter B. In the long run, a permanent deviation of profits from the equilibrium market value cannot be sustained, and at the same time the price elasticity of demand increases because the lock-in effect with regard to a particular product variety on the consumption side is smaller. The group of possible strategies followed by exporters can be delineated by two extreme limiting cases. The first one is that profit margins per quantity sold are kept up, implying that a positive cost shock is reflected in a permanent increase of the relative export price without any tendency of adjustment. The second one suggests that, because the international price relationship is working, producers follow world market prices in the long run but reduce production and sales for the export market in the wake of the reduction in profitability. The evidence for mean reversion in relative export prices together with the less strong result for relative unit labor costs suggests that producers are indeed constrained in their price setting in the long run, since there is a tendency for export prices of producers located in different countries to converge.

Table 21: Panel Unit Root Tests for Relative Export Prices and Relative Unit Labor Costs[a]

Coefficient, t-statistic[b], and critical value	Relative export prices	Relative unit labor costs
Without constant		
ρ	−0.044	−0.035
t_ρ	−7.79	−8.30
Critical value for t_ρ	−2.41 (−1.74)	−2.41 (−1.74)
With constant		
ρ	−0.040	−0.033
t_ρ	−7.64	−8.23
Critical value for t_ρ	−2.58 (−1.91)	−2.58 (−1.91)
a	−0.0008	−0.0007
t_a	−3.95	−2.31
With constant		
ρ	−0.040	−0.031
t_ρ	−7.66	−8.12
Critical value for t_ρ	−8.27 (−7.69)	−8.27 (−7.69)

[a]Coefficients as defined in the text. $T = 96$, $N = 25$. – [b]Critical values for t_ρ are from Levin and Lin (1992), Tables 1, 2, and 4 for $T = 100$ and $N = 25$ at the level of significance of 1 (5) percent.

II. The Role of Profit and Investment as Adjusting Tools to Real Exchange Rate Disequilibria

The next question one is led to ask is if the empirical picture in terms of market share, profits, and investment is also conclusive for this kind of adjustment mechanism. For this purpose it will shortly be shown how the variables which are crucial in the adjustment process behave after imbalances in international cost competitiveness have been established. In order to distinguish between short-term and long-term effects, an error correction mechanism has also been accounted for in the regressions.

1. The Approach of Campa and Goldberg

Since the evolution of expected profits is a pivotal element in the investment process, the dependency of profits on international cost competitiveness, capturing exchange rate and production cost developments, will be investigated first. For this purpose a representative firm in the domestic country A will be considered, which produces a good for the home and the export market, country B. Drawing on the same kind of notation as in Chapter C, gross profits[40] of the representative firm in the domestic country A can be expressed in static form as:

$$(F.3) \quad \Pi_t\left(K_t, e_t\right) = \max_{x_t^{AB}, L_t^A, L_t^B} p_t^{AA}\left(x_t^{AA}\right)x_t^{AA} + e_t p_t^{AB}\left(x_t^{AB}\right)x_t^{AB} - w_t^A L_t^A$$

$$- e_t w_t^B L_t^B,$$

subject to

$$(F.4) \quad x_t^{AA} + x_t^{AB} = f\left(K_t, L_t^A, L_t^B\right).$$

where x_t^{AA} and x_t^{AB} are the quantities sold in the home and export market, L_t^A is the quantity of domestic labor input as being representative for all domestic variable inputs, and L_t^B is the counterpart sourced from the foreign country, with w_t^A and w_t^B being the corresponding factor prices for both variable inputs. Capital K_t as a quasi-fixed factor is the third production factor, the stock of which is determined at the end of the previous period. In order to better illustrate the relation between demand elasticities and profits, and following Campa and

---

[40] Gross profits are defined as export and home market revenues minus costs of variable production factors.

Goldberg (1995, 1999), general demand functions which are decreasing in price are used for domestic and export sales.

As an instrument for introducing shifts in competitiveness between the two countries the nominal exchange rate will be used as the exogenous shock variable. Changes in the nominal exchange rate determine profits in three ways. Firstly, the export revenue changes because of varying export quantities and, when exchange rate pass-through is imperfect, adjustments in the producer's export price. Secondly, domestic revenue is also affected via import competition, but the effect is smaller than for the export market because the domestic producer's cost curve only shifts against those of his foreign competitors, leaving the location of the demand curve relative to domestic cost curves unaltered. Moreover, the market share of the domestic producer is larger in his own national market than in the export market, and markups and profits are less vulnerable to exchange rate changes, since it has been established in Chapter C that a larger market share implies more pass-through. Thirdly, the foreign input cost component also depends on the exchange rate, so the use of internationally traded inputs dampens the effect of nominal exchange rate changes on competitiveness because of the resulting positive correlation between total input costs of the representative domestic and foreign producer. For these three reasons profits from sales in the domestic market compared to those from exports are less volatile when the real exchange rate moves.

Following Campa and Goldberg (1999), the investment process of the representative firm is determined as the maximization of the expected stream of future net profits which are net of investment and capital adjustment costs. The maximized firm value V in period t is

$$(\text{F.5}) \quad V_t\,(K_t,e_t) = \max_{\{I_t\}_{\tau=t}^{\infty}} \exists \left\{ \sum_{\tau=0}^{\infty} \varpi^{\tau} \big[\Pi(K_{t+\tau},e_{t+\tau}) - g\big(I_{t+\tau}\big) - I_{t+\tau} \big] \Big| \Im_{\tau} \right\},$$

$$0 < \varpi < 1$$

subject to

$$(\text{F.6}) \quad K_{t+\tau} = (1-\delta)K_t + I_t, \quad 0 < \delta < 1$$

with K_t being the stock of capital which has to be built at the end of period t, when the exchange rate in $t+1$ is not yet known, but the firm has full information about realizations of the exchange rate and profits in period t. The capital stock depreciates by the rate δ, and ϖ denotes the discount rate. Investment in period t, I_t, is the argument of the capital cost adjustment function g, with v and ι being constant, and adjustment costs assumed to be increasing in I_t. In particular, a quadratic relationship is assumed between investment and adjustment costs of the usual form:

(F.7) $g(I_t) = \dfrac{v}{2}(I_t - \iota)^2$, with the parameters $v, \iota > 0$.

The exchange rate e is defined as the amount of currency units of the exporting country A for a currency unit of the importing country B, and $\exists(\cdot \mid \mathfrak{I}_t)$ is the expectation operator, whereby expectations are assumed to be formed subject to the information set available at time t, $\mathfrak{I}_t$. The only variable over which expectations have to be formed is the exchange rate, all other variables are deterministic and are part of the information set of the representative firm. Concerning the particular expectation with regard to the exchange rate process, Campa and Goldberg assume static expectations, i.e., the expected realization of the exchange rate in period $t + 1$ is the actual value of the exchange rate in period t.[41]

The general first-order condition for the optimal volume of investment is

(F.8) $\exists\left[\dfrac{\partial V_t}{\partial I_t}\middle| \mathfrak{I}_t\right] = 1 + \dfrac{\partial g(I_t)}{\partial I_t}$.

It is profitable for the firm to expand investment by one monetary unit as long as the investment expenses on the right-hand side of (F.8) (which consist of the one currency unit spent for investment itself plus the marginal cost of investment) is smaller than the increase in the value of the firm net of investment expenditure. The optimum will be reached if equality holds.

The marginal increase in firm value of one unit of investment in period 0 is the sum of the marginal increase in profits in all future periods from period 1 onward since the investment does not affect the current capital stock and current profits in period 0. The marginal increase of firm value itself is given as

(F.9) $\dfrac{\partial V_t}{\partial I_t} = \sum\limits_{\tau=1}^{\infty}[\varpi(1-\delta)]^{\tau}\left[\dfrac{\partial \Pi(K_{t+\tau}, e_{t+\tau})}{\partial K_{t+\tau}}\right]$.

---

[41]   In the model accounting for exit and entry below, I assume that the log of the exchange rate follows a random walk with the shock in each period being a random variable with a normal distribution, combined with rational expectations of the profit-maximizing producer. In linear profit (or log profit) equations both assumptions yield the same property that the realization of current profits is taken in the place of unknown future profits.

The effect on profits in each future period is getting smaller with increasing time horizon into the future. The reasons for this are twofold: firstly, the present value of future profit is smaller because the discount factor ϖ^τ decreases with τ. Secondly, the impact of one unit of investment on the capital stock is smaller for more distant periods, since only the fraction $1 - \delta$ of the invested capital survives to the next period due to depreciation.

Under quadratic adjustment costs as specified above, the first-order condition can be solved for I_t:

$$(F.10) \quad I_t = \iota' + \frac{1}{v} \, \Im \left[\left. \frac{\partial V_t}{\partial I_t} \right| \Im_t \right] = \iota' + \sum_{\tau=1}^{\infty} \varpi'^\tau \, \Im \left[\left. \frac{\partial \Pi \, (K_{t+\tau}, e_{t+\tau})}{\partial K_{t+\tau}} \right| \Im_\tau \right]$$

with $\iota' = \iota - \dfrac{1}{v}$ and $\varpi' = \dfrac{\varpi(1-\delta)}{v^{1/\tau}}$.

Under the assumption of static expectations with regard to the exchange rate the expected marginal profitability of capital in each future period is the value of the current marginal profitability:

$$(F.11) \quad \Im \left[\left. \frac{\partial \Pi (K_{t+\tau}, e_{t+\tau})}{\partial K_{t+\tau}} \right| \Im_t \right] = \frac{\partial \Pi (K_t, e_t)}{\partial K_t}.$$

The optimal investment then depends only on the current realization of marginal profits as the expected values for all future marginal profits, of which the discounted sum determines the marginal increase in firm value of a unit of investment:

$$(F.12) \quad I_t = \iota' + \frac{\varpi}{v[1 - \varpi(1-\delta)]} \frac{\partial \Pi (K_t, e_t)}{\partial K_t}.$$

The next step is to determine the marginal profitability of capital, as given by $\partial \Pi (K_t, e_t) / \partial K_t$. Differentiation of the profit function (F.3) with respect to K_t yields

$$(F.13) \quad \frac{\partial \Pi \, (K_t, e_t)}{\partial K_t} = \left[1 + \left(E \left(x^{AB}, p^{AB} \right) \right)^{-1} \right] e_t \, p_t^{AB} \, \frac{\partial f}{\partial K_t}.$$

The impact of one additional unit of capital on profits is equal to the physical profitability of capital times a factor that depends on the price elasticity of demand since, in the general case of imperfect competition, the firm has to lower the price in order to be able to sell the additional units that have been produced with the increased capital stock. Considering now the linear homogeneous production function (F.4), the physical productivity of capital in turn is related to the productivity of the two other production factors via Euler's theorem:

$$(\text{F.14}) \quad \frac{\partial f}{\partial K_t} K_t + \frac{\partial f}{\partial L_t^A} L_t^A + \frac{\partial f}{\partial L_t^B} L_t^B = x_t^{AA} + x_t^{AB}.$$

The marginal productivity of capital depends on the factor intensities of the other production factors, the input of which can be obtained implicitly from the profit function (F.3). Making use of the Euler equation and the fact that factor prices equal the value of their marginal productivities according to

$$(\text{F.15}) \quad w_t^A = \left[1 + \left(E\left(x^{AB}, p^{AB}\right)\right)^{-1}\right] e_t \, p_t^{AB} \, \frac{\partial f}{\partial L_t^A} \quad \text{and}$$

$$(\text{F.16}) \quad e_t w_t^B = \left[1 + \left(E\left(x^{AB}, p^{AB}\right)\right)^{-1}\right] e_t \, p_t^{AB} \, \frac{\partial f}{\partial L_t^B},$$

the profit function (F.3) can be rewritten in terms of the physical productivity of capital as

$$(\text{F.17}) \quad \Pi_t = p_t^{AA}\left(x_t^{AA}\right) x_t^{AA} + e_t \, p_t^{AB}\left(x_t^{AB}\right) x_t^{AB}$$
$$- \left[1 + \left(E\left(x^{AB}, p^{AB}\right)\right)^{-1}\right]\left(e_t \, p_t^{AB} x_t^{AB} - K_t \frac{\partial f}{\partial K_t}\right).$$

After having solved for the physical productivity of capital, the resulting expression can be substituted into (F.13), which yields

$$(\text{F.18}) \quad \frac{\partial \Pi\left(K_t, e_t\right)}{\partial K_t} = \frac{\Pi_t}{K_t} - \frac{p_t^{AA} x_t^{AA} + e_t \, p_t^{AB} x_t^{AB}}{K_t}$$
$$+ \left[1 + \left(E\left(x^{AA}, p^{AA}\right)\right)^{-1}\right] p_t^{AA} x_t^{AA} + \left[1 + \left(E\left(x^{AB}, p^{AB}\right)\right)^{-1}\right] e_t \, p_t^{AB} x_t^{AB}.$$

Replacing Π_t with the definition of profits and canceling terms the resulting equation for the marginal profitability of capital is

$$(\text{F.19}) \quad \frac{\partial \Pi\left(K_t, e_t\right)}{\partial K_t} = \frac{1}{K_t}\left\{\left[1 + \left(E\left(x^{AA}, p^{AA}\right)\right)^{-1}\right] p_t^{AA} x_t^{AA}\right.$$
$$\left. + \left[1 + \left(E\left(x^{AB}, p^{AB}\right)\right)^{-1}\right] e_t \, p_t^{AB} x_t^{AB} - w_t^A L_t^A - e_t \, w_t^B L_t^B \right\}.$$

Knowing the marginal profitability of capital, the investment equation (F.12) can be expressed in terms of observable variables as

(F.20) $I_t = \iota' + \dfrac{\varpi}{v\,[1 - \varpi\,(1-\delta)]K_t}\left\{\left[1 + \left(E(x^{AA}, p^{AA})\right)^{-1}\right]p_t^{AA}x_t^{AA}\right.$

$\left. + \left[1 + \left(E(x^{AB}, p^{AB})\right)^{-1}\right]e_t\,p_t^{AB}x_t^{AB} - w_t^A L_t^A - e_t\,w_t^B L_t^B\right\}.$

Simplifying terms, this relation can be rewritten as

(F.21) $I_t = \iota' + \dfrac{\Gamma}{K_t}\left\{\left[1 + \left(E(x^{AA}, p^{AA})\right)^{-1}\right]p_t^{AA}x_t^{AA}\right.$

$\left. + \left[1 + \left(E(x^{AB}, p^{AB})\right)^{-1}\right]e_t\,p_t^{AB}x_t^{AB} - w_t^A L_t^A - e_t\,w_t^B L_t^B\right\}.$

with $\Gamma = \dfrac{\varpi}{v\,[1 - \varpi\,(1-\delta)]}$.

This is the fundamental relationship which determines investment. Investment is an increasing function of the value of output and decreases with a rise in variable costs, all other things being equal. However, the value of output is discounted by one plus the inverse of the elasticity of demand. The impact of an exchange rate change depends on how each of the components in the investment equation is affected. If the exporter's currency depreciates, i.e., e_t rises, the value of exports in the exporter's currency rises unambiguously if pass-through is between zero and one. The export price in the producer's currency rises as well as the quantity exported. This effect itself has a larger impact on overall sales of the producer, the larger the share of exports in total sales. On the input side, a large fraction of imported inputs lets domestic costs rise when the currency depreciates, acting negatively on profits and investment. So far, the result that a currency depreciation is more favorable for a domestic producer, the larger his export share and the smaller the share of imported inputs is quite intuitive.

By contrast, the effect of the elasticity change is a bit less straightforward, since the magnitude of the demand elasticity is not independent of price-setting behavior. This relationship will be investigated in greater detail in the next subsection.

2.   How the Competitive Structure of Goods Markets Determines the Evolution of Profits

Specifically, under the assumption that the demand function conjectured by the producer is identical to the market demand, i.e., that there are no interdependencies like in the Cournot model, observed prices are set as a markup over variable costs, with the markup factors M_t^{AA} and M_t^{AB} being conditional on the elasticity of demand as follows:

(F.22) $\quad M_t^{As} = \dfrac{1}{1 + \left(E\left(x^{As}, p^{As}\right)\right)^{-1}}$, $\quad s = A, B.$

The equation for marginal investment is then as follows:

(F.23) $\quad I_t = \iota' + \dfrac{\Gamma}{K_t}\left[\left(M_t^{AA}\right)^{-1} p_t^{AA} x_t^{AA} + \left(M_t^{AB}\right)^{-1} e_t\, p_t^{AB} x_t^{AB} - w_t^A L_t^A - e_t\, w_t^B L_t^B\right].$

In order to cast some more light on the interrelationship between prices, marginal costs, and markups, and their adjustment to exchange rate changes, which is more detailed than the treatment of Campa and Goldberg (1999) on this subject, some specific assumptions concerning the kind of market structure and price setting behavior have to be made.

Consider the export market. Since the markup factor is also defined as the ratio of price over marginal costs (MC_t), here both expressed in the currency of the importer, it also holds for the markup factor that

(F.24) $\quad M_t^{AB} = \dfrac{p_t^{AB}}{MC_t/e_t}.$

If the currency of the exporter appreciates, i.e., if e falls, at least one of the remaining three variables like markup, export price in the importer's currency, or marginal costs has to adjust. The pattern of adjustment is crucial in determining the magnitude of profit response to exchange rate changes.

To start with those goods which have been classified into the A-category above and which correspond to the case of perfect competition, the markup factor is assumed to be one, and prices equal marginal costs evaluated in the same currency. The currency appreciation leaves import prices unaltered, so marginal costs have to adjust downward via a reduction in production and export volume:

(F.25) $\quad \overline{p_t^{AB}} = \dfrac{1}{e_t \downarrow} MC_t \downarrow \quad$ (A-goods).

The next benchmark are B-goods which are related to A-goods in that competition is high on the demand side and prices in the importer's currency are held constant because of pricing-to-market strategies. The difference is that on the production side the existence of fixed costs imply a markup factor over marginal costs larger than one, and it is this markup which takes the burden of adjustment.

Import prices and quantities, at least in the benchmark model of extreme pricing to market, are unaltered:

(F.26) $\overline{p_t^{AB}} = M_t^{AB} \downarrow \dfrac{1}{e_t \downarrow} \overline{MC_t}$ (B-goods).

The last category consists of C-goods, which are indicative of perfect pass-through and unchanged markups. These are features which also apply to Dixit–Stiglitz type demand schedules of monopolistic competition where producers enjoy some flexibility in price setting for their specific product variant:

(F.27) $p_t^{AB} \uparrow = \overline{M_t^{AB}} \dfrac{1}{e_t \downarrow} \overline{MC_t}$ (C-goods).

As a comparison of the effects of exchange rate changes on profits and thus investment, Table 22 depicts the differential impact on those components which appear in (F.23). It depends on the good type which of the three endogenous variables in that equation adjusts to an exchange rate shock. For the extreme benchmark case of an A-good, it is the marginal cost which has to adapt, for B-goods the markup changes, and for C-goods it is the price in the importer's currency which adjusts.

For A-goods, which are produced and sold under perfect competition, marginal costs adjust. This is achieved by a one-to-one reduction in the producer's export price as a result of a currency appreciation which entails necessarily a parallel downward adjustment of production and export quantity until marginal

Table 22: The Impact of a Currency Appreciation on the Components of Marginal Profit and Investment[a]

Type of good	Adjusting variable	Endogenous variables			
		$e_t\,p_t^{AB}$	M_t^{AB}	x_t^{AB}	I_t
A	MC_t	↓	→	↓↓	↓↓↓
B	M_t^{AB}	↓	↓	↓	↓↓
C	p_t^{AB}	→	→	↓	↓

[a]The second column indicates the variable which bears the adjustment (or the main part of it). The next three columns indicate the effect of an appreciation of the exporter's currency on the producer's export price, the markup, and the export quantity. For B-goods and C-goods it is assumed that demand is never totally inelastic, and for B-goods that there is at least some pass-through. The last column shows the effect of an appreciation on investment.

costs equal the reduced producer price for the last marginal unit produced. Because of the strong reduction of the export price in the producer's currency and the cut in production, profits are squeezed to a substantial degree.

B-goods, by contrast, show a strong adjustment of the markup instead of leaving the burden of adjustment alone to export prices in the importer's currency. The reduction in demand is cushioned compared to *A*-goods, and it might still be profitable to maintain a relatively high output level as long as variable costs are covered. This implies that profits are hit to a lower degree compared with *A*-goods. The interrelationship between adjustments in markup and changes in demand elasticities perceived by the producer has already been discussed theoretically when incomplete pass-through was justified by changing values of demand elasticities to exchange rate or relative cost changes conjectured by the producer. Specifically, one feature of the demand schedule in Chapter C was that a decrease in cost competitiveness of the domestic producers relative to foreign ones results in a squeeze of the markup of prices on marginal costs. A slight modification applies to the case when prices are determined on the basis under the Cournot assumption, which states that the decisions of each agent are taken on the assumption that the competitors do not respond. In that case, the absolute value of the conjectured elasticity of demand is larger than when price adaptations of competitors are taken into account. As has been discussed, in case of an appreciation of the exporter's currency, competitors will follow with price increases so that a smaller proportion of demand switches to competing product variants. In the end, the ex post elasticity of demand which accounts for mutual responses until the new equilibrium is established is smaller than the elasticity conjectured by the producer. The consequence is that the markup (F.24) does no longer apply for the Cournot model, since the rise in prices is partly due to a subsequent move of competitors. The squeeze of the markup is therefore smaller than the theoretical reduction of the markup calculated on the basis of the demand elasticity perceived by the producer. Now what does this result mean for marginal profits and investment? From (F.17) it is apparent that if the rise in prices outweighs the factor mirroring the change in the perceived elasticity of demand, i.e., if the relative rise in p^{AB} is larger than the relative fall in the expression $(1 + E(x^{AB}, p^{AB})^{-1})$, a positive net component is left for profits. This counteracts the primary valuation effect which is negative because export revenue is less valuable in the domestic currency due to the appreciation. As a result, the negative impact of a currency appreciation on investment is substantially smaller for *B*-goods compared to *A*-goods.

For *C*-goods in their pure form, the markup does not change, and prices in the exporter's currency are unaltered. The only effect on profits as a result of a currency appreciation is the reduction in the quantity exported because full or nearly complete pass-through into prices of the importer's currency leads to a reduction of demand for exports. The impact of exchange rate changes on investment therefore depends solely on the elasticity of demand. In the extreme case of a perfectly inelastic demand the export quantity would be completely unaltered, and together with unchanged export prices in the producer's currency, this would imply that marginal profits and investment are totally unaffected by exchange rate changes.

3.   The Role of the Demand Elasticity for the Magnitude of Profit Fluctuations

It was shown that demand and market structure characteristics are important for the effect of exchange rate changes on investment. Since the export price in the producer's currency, the markup, and marginal costs are interrelated, a unified framework will next be advanced in order to develop a kind of reduced form. In particular, when the producer's currency appreciates, his export revenues fall, but the absolute value of the price elasticity of export demand conjectured by the producer may be higher, resulting in a larger correction factor $(1 + E(x^{AB}, p^{AB})^{-1})$ on the value of output. In the following, it will further be assumed that the producer produces only for the export market and that all input factors are domestic, in order to make those interdependencies costs more tractable. It is also supposed that there is no difference between conjectured and ex post elasticity of demand. If that is the case, prices will be set as a markup over variable costs, with the markup M_t^{AB} being determined in (F.22). Using the definition of the markup from (F.24), the investment equation can then be rewritten as

$$(F.28)\quad I_t = t' + \frac{\Gamma}{K_t}\underbrace{\left[MC_t\, x_t^{AB} - w_t^A L_t^A\right]}_{Z_t}.$$

In order to abbreviate terms, Z_t is a shorthand notation for the bracket in (F.28).

$$(F.29)\quad Z_t = x_t^{AB}\left(p_t^{AB}(e_t)\right) MC_t\left(x_t^{AB}\left(p_t^{AB}(e_t)\right)\right)$$

$$- x_t^{AB}\left(p_t^{AB}(e_t)\right) VUC_t\left(x_t^{AB}\left(p_t^{AB}(e_t)\right)\right).$$

The variable costs, which are considered in (F.29) as variable unit costs (*VUC*) times the quantity produced, are equivalent to the value of domestic variable input factors used in production. In order to tackle the central problem of how investment responds to a change of the exchange rate, this function will be differenced with respect to the exchange rate, allowing for export prices to reflect incomplete pass-through and optimal quantities to adjust to exchange rate shocks:[42]

$$(F.30) \quad \frac{\partial Z_t}{\partial e_t} = \frac{\partial x_t^{AB}}{\partial p_t^{AB}} \frac{\partial p_t^{AB}}{\partial e_t} MC_t + x_t^{AB} \left(\frac{\partial MC_t}{\partial x_t^{AB}} \frac{\partial x_t^{AB}}{\partial p_t^{AB}} \frac{\partial p_t^{AB}}{\partial e_t} \right)$$

$$- \frac{\partial x_t^{AB}}{\partial p_t^{AB}} \frac{\partial p_t^{AB}}{\partial e_t} VUC_t - x_t^{AB} \left(\frac{\partial VUC_t}{\partial x_t^{AB}} \frac{\partial x_t^{AB}}{\partial p_t^{AB}} \frac{\partial p_t^{AB}}{\partial e_t} \right).$$

Substituting the change in variable unit costs by

$$(F.31) \quad \frac{\partial VUC_t}{\partial x_t^{AB}} = \frac{1}{x_t^{AB}} (MC_t - VUC_t)$$

and cancelling terms the resulting expression is

$$(F.32) \quad \frac{\partial Z_t}{\partial e_t} = \frac{\partial x_t^{AB}}{\partial p_t^{AB}} \frac{\partial p_t^{AB}}{\partial e_t} x_t^{AB} \frac{\partial MC_t}{\partial x_t^{AB}}$$

or, in elasticity terms,

$$(F.33) \quad \frac{\partial Z_t}{\partial e_t} = \frac{x_t^{AB} MC_t}{e_t} E(MC_t, x_t^{AB}) E(x_t^{AB}, p_t^{AB}) E(p_t^{AB}, e_t).$$

The investment equation then becomes

$$(F.34) \quad \frac{\partial I_t}{\partial e_t} = \frac{\Gamma}{K_t} \frac{x_t^{AB} MC_t}{e_t} \underbrace{E(MC_t, x_t^{AB})}_{>0} \underbrace{E(x_t^{AB}, p_t^{AB})}_{<0} \underbrace{E(p_t^{AB}, e_t)}_{\leq 0}.$$

The impact of an exchange rate appreciation (i.e., a decline of e) on investment is either negative or zero. The response of investment is greater, the more complete pass-through is, the larger the price elasticity of export demand is, and the more marginal costs rise if output is increased. The positive elasticity of marginal costs with respect to output is due to the assumption that the production function has the property of constant returns to scale. With capital being a quasi-

---

[42]   The following algebra deviates from the procedure of Campa and Goldberg (1999) in making use of the relation between prices and costs, so that net effects are easier to interpret.

fixed production factor, output can only be increased by augmenting the variable input, of which the marginal productivity decreases thus leading to increasing marginal costs. This elasticity term increases marginal revenue and investment because optimal prices are based on marginal costs rather than average costs. The more marginal costs increase, the larger the distance of marginal costs above average costs, so the larger the operating profit per unit produced. The operating profit, in turn, is used to compute the profitability of the quasi-fixed factor, thus determining the investment decision. The effect on marginal profitability and investment is also greater in sectors where demand is more elastic or where exchange rate pass-through is higher. The next task will be to complement this analysis by empirical figures.

4.   Some Empirical Evidence on Real Exchange Rates, Profits, and Investment for Main Industrial Sectors

In order to shed some light onto the relationship between the real exchange rate, profits, and investment, the last two variables which are to be explained are regressed on the real exchange rate. Since adjustment is expected to take some time, an error-correction specification analogous to the sectoral market share regression in (E.1) is chosen. Before the actual estimation can be advanced, the difficult task of operationalizing the measurement of profits has to be solved. Since the OECD database on competitiveness is across sectors and countries, a viable solution is to construct an approximation for profits from variables of that dataset. Since the labor share of value added s_L is covered by the database, the profit share s_K can be calculated as the residual $1 - s_L$. The estimated equation in logarithms follows the usual error-correction specification:

$$(F.35) \quad d \log s_{Kt} = c_s - a_s \left[\ln s_K - \bar{b}_s \log RULC_{s,t-1} \right] + \sum_{j=0}^{q} b_{sj} \, \Delta \log RULC_{s,t-j}$$

$$+ \sum_{j=1}^{r} d_{sj} \, d \log s_{K,t-j} + \varepsilon_{st} \, .$$

Similarly, the investment equation states

$$(F.36) \quad d \log I_t = c_s - a_s \left[\log s_K - \bar{b}_s \, LNRULC_{s,t-1} \right] + \sum_{j=0}^{q} b_{sj} \, \Delta \, LNRULC_{s,t-j}$$

$$+ \sum_{j=1}^{r} d_{sj} \, d \log I_{t-j} + \varepsilon_{st} \, .$$

Panel estimations are done for each sector separately, but pooled over all countries. The long-term coefficients of both regressions are presented in Tables 23 and 24. For each sector, we obtain a negative, and in most of the cases significant, long-term coefficient, which is indicative of a compression of profits. The effect is significant and strongest in the sectors of textiles and paper, paper products and printing, but also in transport equipment and nonelectrical machinery. Generally speaking, sectors which are most vulnerable to a relative deterioration of competitiveness in terms of unit labor costs are either those which dominantly use domestic inputs, as it is the case for the first two of the four sectors mentioned, or those which are subject to quite elastic demand, as it applies for sectors which practice pricing to market, like the sector of transport equipment.

For interpretation of the results one has to consider that relative unit labor costs are a relative concept, since they are expressed relative to other countries, whereas profits are not. In addition, it is less the development of wages than shocks to the exchange rate which account for innovations in the relative unit labor costs series. By contrast, the profit share applies only to one single country. It is thus not a tautology that a rise in relative unit labor costs in a country relative to others, primarily brought about by a nominal appreciation, causes value added in that country to develop only less than proportionally relative to unit labor costs, thus acting unfavorably on profits. The fact that value added in nominal terms and evaluated for a single country cannot keep up with rising wage income is because a value and quantity effect is operating. The value effect is just another name for incomplete pass-through of costs into the producer's prices in his currency. The quantity effect is due to a decline of sales when the competitive position is deteriorating. This explains the outcome when sectors are ranked according to their exposure in terms of profit shares.

As to the inference for investment, country shares of investment in research and development relative to the entity of all OECD countries are given for each sector by the same OECD database. It can be stated that the results from Table 24 show only scarce evidence of effects of deteriorations in cost competitiveness on investment. Coefficients show the postulated negative dependency, but the error-correction terms are more or less insignificant in each case. Interestingly, low-technology industries show a somewhat stronger response compared to the whole aggregate, which is in line with expectations based on theoretical deductions from above.

As a final task, it remains to close the circle by turning to the implications of a decline in the return to capital in selected national and sectoral industries, especially with regard to the adjustment process toward equilibrium.

Table 23: The Impact of Shifts in Relative Unit Labor Costs on Profits[a]

Industry code	Sector description	$-a_s$	LNRULC	DW[b]	XDEP[c] 1980	XDEP[c] 1995
3100	Food, beverages, & tobacco	−1.316 (−1.848)	−0.820 (−5.842**)	1.918	9.14	11.36
3200	Textiles, apparel, & leather	−1.814 (−1.899)	−0.979 (−9.668**)	1.837	16.33	24.86
3300	Wood products & furniture	−0.842 (−7.357**)	−0.663 (−6.619)	1.981	9.16	12.08
3400	Paper, paper products, & printing	−0.945 (−5.983**)	−0.893 (−8.838**)	1.788	10.12	11.91
3510	Industrial chemicals	−0.570 (−4.308)	−0.446 (−5.014)	1.966	30.88	41.74
3520	Other chemicals	−0.387 (−0.498)	−0.735 (−5.657*)	1.929	18.14	23.68
3534	Petroleum refineries & products	−0.456 (−1.663)	−0.163 (−3.191)	1.900	8.08	9.14
3556	Rubber & plastic products	−0.951 (−2.969)	−0.666 (−3.825)	1.846	11.62	12.95
3600	Nonmetallic mineral products	−0.572 (−4.459)	−0.762 (−8.134**)	1.840	9.40	12.19
3710	Iron & steel	−0.621 (−8.901)	−0.491 (−7.163**)	1.814	14.20	16.01
3720	Nonferrous metals	−0.125 (−4.676)	−0.500 (−6.826**)	1.842	20.13	21.08
3810	Metal products	−0.244 (−3.314)	−0.760 (−8.608**)	1.880	13.56	14.89
3820	Nonelectrical machinery	−0.158 (−5.669*)	−0.886 (−6.858**)	1.859	28.83	37.31
3830	Electrical machinery	2.039 (0.452)	−0.832 (−6.992**)	1.787	21.14	29.48
3840	Transport equipment	−1.159 (−5.757*)	−0.895 (−12.816**)	2.022	29.11	32.81
3850	Professional goods	−2.326 (−2.288)	−0.695 (−2.851)	1.842	26.06	42.20
Summary statistics	Low-technology industries	−1.540 (−0.512)	−0.998 (−8.165**)	1.822	10.79	13.66
	Total manufacturing	−0.875 (−0.502)	−0.846 (−8.196**)	1.945	17.37	22.82

[a]Estimated coefficients refer to (F.36) with $q = r = 2$. Only coefficients of the error-correction term are given. Estimates are based on yearly data from 1980 through 1995. Countries include: Belgium, France, Western Germany, Ireland, Italy, Japan, Spain, Sweden, United Kingdom, United States. The total number of observations for each sector is 120. – [b]Durbin–Watson test statistic. – [c]Export dependency ratio which is defined as the share of exports relative to domestic production. Source of data: OECD (1999), *Main Industrial Indicators.* ** and * denote significance at levels of 1 and 5 percent, respectively, with values obtained from Levin and Lin (1992) for $N = 10$ and $T = 10$.

Table 24: The Impact of Shifts in Relative Unit Labor Costs on Relative Expenditure on Research & Development[a]

Industry code	Sector description	*LNRULC*	$\bar{b}_s$	DW[b]
3100	Food, beverages, & tobacco	−0.154 (−2.844)	−0.406 (−0.408)	1.948
3200	Textiles, apparel, & leather	−0.286 (−4.156)	−1.366 (−2.741)	1.718
3300	Wood products & furniture	−0.243 (−4.944)	−4.179 (−2.126)	1.707
3400	Paper, paper products, & printing	−0.650 (−7.659**)	0.341 (3.422)	1.614
3556	Rubber & plastic products	−0.483 (−5.801**)	−0.591 (−0.522)	1.718
3600	Nonmetallic mineral products	−0.285 (−4.515)	−0.418 (−0.144)	1.909
3710	Iron & steel	−0.287 (−5.844**)	−0.654 (−0.293)	1.837
3720	Nonferrous metals	−0.301 (−4.884)	−0.470 (−0.061)	1.952
3810	Metal products	−0.337 (−6.215**)	−0.473 (−0.785)	1.954
3820	Nonelectrical machinery	−0.230 (−5.178)	0.758 (4.822)	1.916
3830	Electrical machinery	−0.130 (−4.493)	−0.282 (−2.381)	1.851
3840	Transport equipment	−0.226 (−4.408)	−0.667 (−4.061)	1.903
3850	Professional goods	−0.291 (−7.996**)	−1.281 (−2.303)	1.902
Summary statistics	Low-technology industries	−0.140 (−2.439)	−1.609 (−2.628)	1.863
	Total manufacturing	−0.152 (−4.436)	0.057 (2.880)	1.818

[a]Estimated coefficients refer to (F.36) with $q = r = 1$. Only coefficients of the error-correction term are given. Estimates are based on yearly data from 1980 through 1995. Countries include: Belgium, France, Western Germany, Ireland, Italy, Japan, Spain, Sweden, United Kingdom, United States. The total number of observations for each sector is 130. The dependent variable is the sectoral investment in research and development of a country as a share of all OECD countries in the same sector. Source of data: OECD (1999), *Main Industrial Indicators.* ** denotes significance at levels of 1 percent, with values obtained from Levin and Lin (1992) for $N = 10$ and $T = 10$. — [b]Durbin–Watson test statistic.

III.   An Integrative Approach of Modeling the Decision to Enter and Exit in the Export Market and Price Setting

It will be shown in the following simple model that producing and exporting activities which are not profitable in the long term in the country of interest will not
be pursued any further as long as fixed costs do not cause firms to continue their
export supply. If fixed costs are irrelevant in the long run, firms which are not
competitive because their costs are too high in order to leave a nonnegative profit
margin will exit the export market. This, in turn, causes aggregate export prices
to come down, since only the "cheap" suppliers are left which are still profitable
because of higher productivity. In order to illustrate this reasoning, there must be
some heterogeneity introduced for the productivity between single firms. One
way to allow for this is to argue that each single firm stands for only one particular production activity of a variant of a differentiated product, which is characteristic of a specific mix of input factors such as labor of certain qualifications and
specific technical knowledge. These underlying determinants may be distributed
unequally between the country of interest and a second country which is representative in the model for the rest of the world. In addition, each product variant
is assumed to differ in the intensity of using of each of these factors. In order to
keep statements general, in the following I will refer to the notion of "activities,"
because this assumption may not only hold for product varieties, but also for single elements in the production chain. It then becomes possible to construct a
ranking of all activities i produced in the country according to their productivity
which combines the heterogeneity of all those factors between variants in one parameter θ_i. To make the model tractable, it is assumed that only labor of a homogeneous kind with the common factor price w is used as the only variable production factor and that the productivity parameter θ_i, which reflects all other
kinds of heterogeneity, denotes the log of labor productivity.

For variable costs, it holds that

(F.37) $\log c_i = \log w - \theta_i , \quad i = 1, \dots, N.$

On the demand side, all variants face symmetric demand schedules from the
world. In order to make things simple, only export supply is considered here.
One can think of all variants being produced for the home market anyway because transport costs are sufficiently high or home demand is biased toward
home produced products, which shields domestic products from outside competition in the domestic market in such a way that production is necessarily profitable. For the export market, however, the producer is assumed to incur a fixed
cost F in advance in order to being able to export at maximum one unit of output
in the following period. This can be justified by the use of resources for estab-

lishing a distribution network or gaining consumer confidence in the quality of the product. The producer thus has the option to export in period $t+1$, when having spent F in period t as long as variable costs are covered. For the sake of simplicity, it shall be assumed that the producer cannot spend more than F and cannot export more than one unit per time period. Another simplifying assumption is that the option to export is only valid for the following period, which means the decision to invest does not depend on the past decisions. By this assumption path dependencies are excluded which simplifies analysis.

The exchange rate e in terms of national currency units, say the euro, per unit of foreign currency, say the U.S. dollar, in order to make references simpler by using specific names, transforms domestic costs c_i into the U.S. dollar equivalent. Because the model shall also allow for imperfect pass-through without specifying the exact demand schedule, it is assumed that the optimal export price in U.S. dollars is determined as follows:

(F.38) $\quad \log p_i^{AB} = (1-v)\log p^B + v(\log c_i - \log e), \quad 0 < v < 1,$ or

(F.39) $\quad \log p_i^{AB} = (1-v)\log p^B + v(\log w - \log e - \log \theta_i),$

where p^B is representing foreign costs and the foreign prices of substitutes which enter the exporter's pricing schedule as an aggregate variable in addition to the domestic cost component. The parameter v is the pass-through coefficient, and the pricing rule has thus the feature of being homogeneous of degree 1 in both components. The export price increases with a rise in the nominal wage level in the exporting country, a rise in the price level in the importing country, an appreciation of the exporter's currency, or a reduction of the productivity parameter θ_i.

The relative operating profit OP_i in U.S. dollar as the markup factor of the export price on variable costs can be determined as:

(F.40) $\quad \log OP_i = \log p_i^{AB} - (\log c_i - \log e).$

Substitution of the export price and variable cost expressions yields

(F.41) $\quad \log OP_i = (1-v)(\log p^B + \log \theta_i + \log e - \log w).$

The operating profit is thus higher for those activities which are more productive and show a larger parameter θ_i. Naturally, it also increases when labor costs of the exporter fall, when his currency depreciates, or when the price level in the export market increases.

The fixed cost F for entering the export market has to be covered with the operating profit so that export activity becomes remunerative. The producer decides to incur those costs only if the following relation, expressed in the importer's currency and in nonlogarithmic terms, is satisfied:

(F.42) $p_i^{AB} - \dfrac{c_i}{e} \geq F_i$,

or expressed in relative terms, the markup factor of price over marginal costs must at least be as great as the ratio of total costs over variable costs:

(F.43) $\dfrac{p_i^{AB}}{\dfrac{c_i}{e}} \geq \dfrac{\left. F_i + \dfrac{c_i}{e} \right\}\ \text{total costs}}{\left. \dfrac{c_i}{e} \right\}\ \text{variable costs.}}$

In order to keep the relation of variable to fixed costs unaltered in terms of U.S. dollars when the exchange rate changes, it is assumed that the fixed costs are proportional to the U.S. dollar equivalent of variable unit costs with $\varXi$ denoting the scaling factor:

(F.44) $F_i = \varXi \left(\dfrac{c_i}{e} \right).$

or, expressed in logarithms with ξ being defined as the log of total costs including fixed costs over variable costs:

(F.45) $\xi = \log(\varXi + 1),$

(F.46) $\log p_i^{AB} - (\log c_i - \log e) \geq \log(\varXi + 1) \equiv \xi.$

Suppose now that as in the general investment model treated before the future realization of the exchange rate is not known by the producer, but that he has to decide whether or not to invest in export capacities one period in advance. It is therefore necessary for the producer to build rational expectations with respect to the exchange rate process which is assumed to follow a random walk with the innovation in each period ξ_t being a random variable with mean zero and variance σ_ξ.

(F.47) $\log e_t = \log e_{t-1} + \xi_t,\quad \xi_t \sim N(0, \sigma_\xi).$

The expectation of the exchange rate in period $t+1$ is thus the current realization of the exchange rate in period t:

(F.48)　$E_t(\log e_{t+1}) = \log e_t$.

The condition for entering into or staying in the export market when all other variables are constant can now be refined for a risk-neutral producer by explicitly accounting for the time structure. Under the assumption of zero interest rates it must then hold that the expected value of operating profits is larger than the amount of fixed costs, which he has to pay one period in advance:

(F.49)　$E_t(OP_{t+1}) = OP_t \geq \xi$.

The condition that the producer invests in export capacity in period t can be expressed in terms of labor productivity as

(F.50)　$\theta_i > \theta^* \equiv \log w + \dfrac{\xi}{1-\upsilon} - \log p^B - \log e_t$.

When nominal wages will rise in the future period, the price level in the importing country falls, or the currency of the exporting country depreciates, then the productivity of the marginal variety, for which the break-even condition is fulfilled, has to rise and a smaller range of varieties will be exported.

Concerning the current period, only variable costs have to be covered by the export revenue, so the short-term condition for the decision to export can be obtained by setting the expression for fixed costs in (F.50) to zero.

(F.51)　$\theta_i > \tilde{\theta} \equiv \log w - \log p^B - \log e_t$.

Figure 24 illustrates this relationship. In the upper-right sector all activities are ranked according to their labor productivities.[43] The more activities are to be exported, the higher is the sum of all single activity-specific fixed costs which have to be spent, which corresponds to an increase in export capacity depicted on the right axis. Each productivity corresponds to a specific value for unit labor cost in foreign currency, with the negative relationship being shown in the upper-left sector with the slope of the line being minus 1. For the initial right-hand line, the value of $\log w - \log e$ has been arbitrarily equated to θ_{max}. The line $\log OP = 0$ denotes the transformation of costs into prices and thus reflects the pass-through relationship. Since pass-through lies between zero and one, the absolute value of the slope of this line is smaller than one. The line to the right delineates those

---

[43]　It is assumed for simplicity that labor is the only variable production factor with constant returns to scale, so that it is justified to equate marginal and average labor productivity.

Figure 24: The Simultaneous Determination of Export Capacity and Export Prices

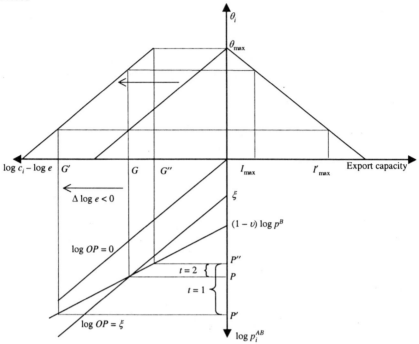

price-cost combinations for which the fixed costs are covered ($\log OP = \xi$). It is the graphical counterpart of (F.42). All combinations to the right or below this line are profitable. An analogous interpretation applies to the left-hand line, the only difference being that only short-term variable costs are considered. For the producer it is optimal in the long run to export all activities up to the price P, where the pass-through line and the long-term profitability line intersect. Since the lowest price possible is $(1-v)\log p^B$, the range of the prices for the continuum of activities is within those points.

Suppose now that this represents an equilibrium realization of the exchange rate in period 0 with $\log e_{t=0} = \log e_{t=-1}$. The equilibrium values for the price and the marginal cost in the currency of the importing country are P and G, respectively. The corresponding export capacity is I_{max}. The currency of the exporter then appreciates in period 1, i.e., $d\log e_{t=1} < 0$ and stays there up to period 2, so that we deal with a permanent exchange rate shock. This is reflected in an outward shift of the line in the upper left sector. The maximum price is now P'. If the amount of the appreciation is smaller than $\log F/(1-v)$, as it is depicted in the graph since, when P' holds, the price-cost combination is on the right to the $\log OP = 0$ line, so variable costs are still covered for all export activities for which fixed costs have been spent a period before. For each activity, the export price in period t increases according to (F.39) by $-vd \log e_t > 0$, since pass-through is positive but imperfect. As a result, the aggregate export price in period t increases by the same proportion v of the currency appreciation and the range of possible prices is given the interval $P' P''$.

However, this is not a long-term equilibrium, since for all points between P and P', the markup of price over marginal cost is insufficient to cover the fixed costs. If the exchange rate does not move any further, i.e., the shift in period 1 is once and for all, then producers will revise their investment decision in period 1 and do not prolong investment in those activities which fall out of the range of expected positive long-term profitability. Specifically, they will exit from the export market with all those activities which are between P and P' in period 2. This brings aggregate export prices down because that part of export activities cannot be sustained which are the least price competitive, i.e., which are related to the lowest values of θ and which have revealed the highest export price in period t. As a result, a part of the increase in export prices has been reversed by the exit of the most expensive firms, and long-term pass-through is smaller than short-run pass-through in the absence of any further exchange rate shocks.

This analysis has shown that the fact that pass-through is incomplete can have two different interpretations, depending on the relevant time horizon. In the short run, it is a reflection of the optimization process for prices, whereas in the long run, it can be interpreted as the outcome of a selection process in which the inefficient activities leave the market. The model thus complements the empirical evidence that the international price interrelationship is stronger than that for unit labor costs, and gives a possible explanation with regard to the causality. Price competition in the goods market is the driving force for also closing the gap of relative production costs between countries. Parallel to prices, the average production costs fall in the country where production is more expensive, and vice versa. An important feature of the adjustment process is that investment is shifted away from the country which suffers from an overvalued currency toward the region in which production is cheaper by an international comparison. If these flows of investment are accompanied by portfolio capital, having in turn a substantial impact on the equilibrium exchange rate, then the exchange rate may also contribute to convergence toward equilibrium, since money flows are directed away from the overvalued currency and toward the more competitive region.

G. Concluding Remarks: Is the Real Exchange Rate an Issue for National Policy?

This work tries to shed some light on two central problems. The first one is the determination of prices of internationally tradable goods as a function of relative production costs of the exporting countries, and the second one is the role of this price-setting pattern for the adjustment process in the real sector.

Concerning the first problem which focuses on the discrepancy arising from real exchange rate movements on the one hand, leading to shifts in aggregate cost and price levels between countries or currency areas and thus altering their competitive position, and, on the other hand, the fact that goods (and also certain types of services) can be traded between countries, so that the possible arbitrage inherent in trade flows should constrain cross-country price differentials of tradable goods to be limited. There are three benchmark price-setting patterns to dissolve this discrepancy, with the actual outcome being somewhere between the extreme cases and the relative position depending on the characteristics of the good, the market, the country, and the demand features.

The first pattern is that competition is nearly perfect so that the law of one price tends to hold across countries, which generally applies to the case of homogeneous goods in the absence of market imperfections. However, a differential relative to the prices of nontradable production factors, notably labor, then necessarily emerges in at least one country when costs move asynchronously between countries, leading to adjustments in margins.

To the extent that price discrimination between target markets, such as export and home markets, is a viable option, the pricing-to-market outcome can be observed as the second pricing pattern. A company which, for example, offers Internet access in multiple national target markets can set prices in each local market independently, and in the extreme case each price may move proportional to some local cost or price index. This independent price setting in local markets also leads, like the first case, to adjustments in the markup over the producer's marginal costs in his home currency after a shock.

The third price-setting pattern is that the producer can pass through the cost differential into the prices of all target markets by the same amount, a feature which may be due to some kind of monopolistic position made possible by the existence of sufficiently differentiated product variants, which inhibit, to some degree, substitution on the consumption side.

Empirical results for price setting, presented in Chapter D, generally support the main relationships proposed in the theoretical part in showing that sectors differ considerably concerning the adjustment of prices as a result of exogenous shocks. Moreover, in developing a unified framework which reflects all the main features which in the literature have been discussed only separately, a two-dimensional framework for the ranking of sectors was established. The first dimension considers the scope for price differentials by focusing on the degree of substitutability of product varieties. The other dimension ranks sectors according to how much of an increase in production costs of a producer relative to its worldwide competitors gets passed through into a relative price increase. This ranking can thus be conceived as representing the degree of market power. The overall empirical picture from the German manufacturing sector is that the third price-setting pattern in its pure form is extremely rare, suggesting that pricing power of producers of manufactured products is indeed limited.

To the degree that pass-through of nominal exchange rate shocks into import prices is muted, domestic monetary policy in the importing country remains to be quite effective in achieving price stability. Inflation would be far more difficult to control to the extent that external forces have a greater impact on import prices. Short-term pricing to market therefore reduces the international transmission of monetary shocks and allows each country to follow its independent monetary policy according to national preferences.

The finding that world market shares are important for the degree of pass-through has also consequences for the European Monetary Union. As was shown in Chapter C, where the role of market shares was discussed, pass-through into local prices in the importing countries is high if the proportion of producers subject to the same shock is large. This implies that a single EMU member country is less forced to adapt export prices to a shock common to the whole EMU area, such as an appreciation or depreciation of the euro, than it would be when only its own national currency were subject to the exchange rate shock. Similarly, import prices will show a smaller response to devaluations in a large currency area. The empirical results obtained for the United States are particularly conclusive for these hypotheses, and the European Monetary Union can be expected to behave similarly in the future. The projection of a possibly larger correlation of export and import prices with domestic prices complements the general expectation that the euro will increase in importance as a currency of denomination in international trade.

The analysis of the second main problem addressed in this work, the implications of price setting for the real economy, has also generated some important insights. It can be argued that trade flows are substantially cushioned from short-term exchange rate volatility to the extent that it is rational for exporters to keep prices in the importing countries stable. The poor immediate response of trade flows to real exchange rate disequilibria has several consequences.

Firstly, these results help to explain why real exchange rate disequilibria are not reversed immediately through the working of trade flows but can persist over sometimes quite long intervals. This observation is congruent with frequent findings that national trade balances are predominantly driven by the timing of the national business cycle relative to main trading partners rather than by the real exchange rate.

Secondly, to the extent that exchange rate pass-through is incomplete in the longer run, too, countries which opt to save or dissave as a whole, for example because of the rationale of intertemporal consumption smoothing, which in turn is tantamount to the incidence of a surplus or a deficit in the current account, will need a much larger variation in the real exchange rate in order to generate a sufficient response of the trade balance. This explains both why real exchange rates sometimes show very large movements, but that it is at the same time difficult for a single country to separate the decision on investment and saving from one another. The phenomenon that national savings show a high correlation with national investment can thus partly be attributed to the incomplete adjustment of trade prices.

Thirdly, the role of a fixed exchange rate regime or a currency area as a catalyst of promoting trade is probably overstated in the public discussion. As was argued, shocks which are seen to be reversed shortly, as it applies particularly for exchange rate volatility, are absorbed largely by adjustments in the exporters' profit margins. Since the efficiency of financial markets has reached a sufficiently high level nowadays that it is possible for producers to hedge exchange rate risks at very low costs, there is no justification to regard revenue from exporting as being inherently risky. This risk is even further reduced if export markets are multiple or if companies are multinationals, with the ability to distribute production activities across several markets, so that exchange rate movements should tend to average out in their impact on overall profits. The importance of the European Monetary Union for the creation of further trade must therefore be questioned.

Chapter E has shown that even though pass-through has indeed been found to be incomplete in nearly all cases, there is still an important part of shifts in relative cost competitiveness transmitted to prices, so that world market shares are affected particularly in the long run. However, even though the response of prices often does not fully reflect the development of costs, market shares can be affected to a substantial degree. This can be explained by also taking into account the location decisions of multinational companies, so that the consideration of relative production costs in a particular country is even more relevant if production activities can easily be shifted across countries.

When disequilibria in production costs between countries occur, only those production activities survive in which the country still has an absolute advantage, restoring the average export price back to equilibrium. In addition, portfolio capital flows which accompany real investment opportunities work toward a nominal depreciation of the overvalued currency relative to the other, thus making the adjustment process complete. The empirical result from Chapter F that relative unit labor costs across countries show mean reversion, but at a somewhat smaller pace than relative export prices, lends support to this hypothesis.

Lastly, an implication for European Monetary Union is that a cost shock in a single member country, for example a nominal wage rise which exceeds the development of labor productivity, is now perceived to be more or less permanent, since it cannot be reversed by a nominal depreciation of the national currency. The expectation that an adverse cost shock deteriorates the competitive position of a country permanently not only induces exporters' prices to reflect a larger degree of pass-through, because future exports from that country are seen to be less valuable than if the shock is expected to reverse soon. What is more, the country also risks to cut down on its productive capacity, as was concluded in Chapter F, where the investment process has been highlighted as an important element of the adjustment mechanism in closing the price gap between countries in the wake of persistent real exchange rate shifts when the exchange rate can no longer be used as an adjustment tool to restore equilibrium.

These findings contribute to the explanation of why real exchange rate misalignments cannot persist forever and are reversed, even though trade flows play a negligible role in the foreign exchange market relative to portfolio capital. Overall, the general message is that international goods arbitrage works toward the ruling of the law of one price in tradable goods, but also acts indirectly on the equalization of production costs, notably unit labor costs, by means of the adjustment process.

References

Abuaf, N., and P. Jorion (1990). Purchasing Power Parity in the Long Run. *Journal of Finance* 45(1): 157–174.

Anderson, S.P., and V.A. Ginsburgh (1994). Price Discrimination with Costly Consumer Arbitrage. CORE Discussion Paper 9439. Université catholique de Louvain, Louvain-la-Neuve.

Athukorala, P., and J. Menon (1994). Pricing to Market Behaviour and Exchange Rate Pass-Through in Japanese Exports. *Economic Journal* 104(423): 271–281.

Athukorala, P., and J. Menon (1995). Exchange Rates and Strategic Pricing: The Case of Swedish Machinery Exports. *Oxford Bulletin of Economics and Statistics* 57(4): 533–546.

Banerjee, A.B., J.J. Dolado, and R. Mestre (1998). Error-Correction Mechanism Tests for Cointegration in a Single-Equation Framework. *Journal of Time Series Analysis* 19(3): 267–283.

Blanchard, O.J., and A. Melino (1986). The Cyclical Behavior of Prices and Quantities: The Case of the Automobile Market. *Journal of Monetary Economics* 17(3): 379–407.

Bloch, H., and M. Olive (1997). Pass-Through Elasticities for Production Costs and Competing Foreign Prices: Evidence from Manufacturing Prices in Seven Countries. Working Paper 97.08. School of Economics and Finance, Curtin University of Technology, Perth.

Bodnar, G.M., B. Dumas, and R.C. Marston (1997). Pass-Through and Exposure. Les cahiers de recherche 628. Chambre de Commerce et d'Industrie, Paris.

Brauer, H. (1999). Price Setting in International Markets. Kiel Working Paper 915. Kiel Institute for World Economics, Kiel.

Campa, J.M., and L.S. Goldberg (1995). Investment in Manufacturing, Exchange Rates and External Exposure. *Journal of International Economics* 38(3/4): 297–320.

Campa, J.M., and L.S. Goldberg (1999). Investment, Pass-Through, and Exchange Rates: A Cross-Country Comparison. *International Economic Review* 40(2): 287–314.

Campa, J.M., and H.C. Wolf (1998). Goods Arbitrage and Real Exchange Rate Stationarity. Working Paper 29. Oesterreichische Nationalbank, Vienna.

Carlin, W., A. Glyn, and J. Van Reenen (1999). Export Market Performance of OECD Countries: An Empirical Examination of the Role of Cost Competitiveness. IFS Working Paper W99/22. Institute for Fiscal Studies, London.

Clarida, R.H. (1997). The Real Exchange Rate and US Manufacturing Profits: A Theoretical Framework with Some Empirical Support. *International Journal of Finance and Economics* 2(3): 177–187.

Clark, P.B., and H. Faruqee (1997). Exchange Rate Volatility, Pricing to Market and Trade Smoothing. IMF Working Paper 97/126. International Monetary Fund, Washington, D.C.

Crowder, W.J. (1996). Purchasing Power Parity When Prices Are I(2). *Review of International Economics* 4(2): 234–246.

Cumby, R.E. (1996). Forecasting Exchange Rates and Relative Prices With the Hamburger Standard: Is What You Want What You Get With McParity? NBER Working Paper 5675. National Bureau of Economic Research, Cambridge, Mass.

Davidson, R., and J.G. McKinnon (1993). *Estimation and Inference in Econometrics.* New York: Oxford University Press.

De Gregorio, J., A. Giovannini, and H.C. Wolf (1994). International Evidence on Tradables and Nontradables Inflation. *European Economic Review* 38(6): 1225–1244.

Dickey, D.A., and W.A. Fuller (1979). Distribution of the Estimators for Autoregressive Time Series With a Unit Root. *Journal of the American Statistical Association* 74(366): 427–431.

Dixit, A.K., and J.E. Stiglitz (1977). Monopolistic Competition and Optimum Product Diversity. *American Economic Review* 67(3): 297–308.

Dornbusch, R. (1987). Exchange Rates and Prices. *American Economic Review* 77(1): 93–106.

Dornbusch, R. (1996). The Effectiveness of Exchange Rate Changes. *Oxford Review of Economic Policy* 12(3): 26–38.

Engle, R.F., and C.W.J. Granger (1987). Co-integration and Error Correction: Representation, Estimation, and Testing. *Econometrica* 55(2): 251–275.

Eurostat (2000). *Intra- and Extra-EU Trade* (Combined Nomenclature). CD-ROM. Edition 1/2000. Luxembourg.

Faruqee, H. (1995). Pricing to Market and the Real Exchange Rate. *IMF Staff Papers* 42(4): 855–881.

Feenstra, R.C. (1989). Symmetric Pass-Through of Tariffs and Exchange Rates under Imperfect Competition: An Empirical Test. *Journal of International Economics* 27(1/2): 25–45.

Feenstra, R.C., J.E. Gagnon, and M.M. Knetter (1996). Market Share and Exchange Rate Pass-Through in World Automobile Trade. *Journal of International Economics* 40(1): 187–207.

Feinberg, R.M. (1986). The Interaction of Foreign Exchange and Market Power Effects on German Domestic Prices. *Journal of Industrial Economics* 35(1): 61–70.

Frankel, J.A. (1986). International Capital Mobility and Crowding-Out in the U.S. Economy: Imperfect Integration of Financial Markets or of Goods Markets? In R.W. Hafer (ed.), *How Open Is the U.S. Economy?* Lexington, Mass.: D.C. Heath and Company.

Frankel, J.A. (1991). Quantifying International Capital Mobility in the 1980s. In B.D. Bernheim and J.B. Shoven (eds.), *National Saving and Economic Performance.* Chicago: University of Chicago Press.

Frankel, J.A., and A.K. Rose (1995). Empirical Research on Nominal Exchange Rates. In G.M. Grossman and K. Rogoff (eds.), *Handbook of International Economics.* Volume 3. Amsterdam: Elsevier.

Froot, K.A., and P.D. Klemperer (1989). Exchange Rate Pass-Through When Market Share Matters. *American Economic Review* 79(4): 637–654.

Froot, K.A., and K. Rogoff (1995). Perspectives on PPP and Long-Run Real Exchange Rates. In G.M. Grossman and K. Rogoff (eds.), *Handbook of International Economics.* Volume 3. Amsterdam: Elsevier.

Ghosh, A.R., and H.C. Wolf (1994). Pricing in International Markets: Lessons from The Economist. NBER Working Paper 4806. National Bureau of Economic Research, Cambridge, Mass.

Giovannini, A. (1998). Exchange Rates and Traded Goods Prices. *Journal of International Economics* 24(1/2): 45–68.

Gly, A. (1997). Does Aggregate Profitability Really Matter? *Cambridge Journal of Economics* 21(5): 593–619.

Goldberg, P.K., and M.M. Knetter (1997). Goods Prices and Exchange Rates. What Have We Learned? *Journal of Economic Literature* 35(3): 1243–1272.

Goldstein, M., and M.S. Khan (1985). Income and Price Effects in Foreign Trade. In R.W. Jones and P.B. Kenen (eds.), *Handbook of International Economics.* Volume 2. Amsterdam: North Holland.

Golub, S. (1994). Comparative Advantage, Exchange Rates, and G-7 Sectoral Trade Balances. IMF Working Paper 94/5. International Monetary Fund, Washington, D.C.

Hakkio, C. (1984). A Reexamination of Purchasing Power Parity. *Journal of International Economics* 17(3/4): 265–277.

Hansen, G. (1998). The Mark-Dollar Exchange Rate and Purchasing Power Parity: Some Empirical Evidence. In H.P. Galler and G. Wagner (eds.), *Empirische Forschung und wirtschaftspolitische Beratung.* Frankfurt/Main: Campus.

Hansen, G. (2000). Puzzles in Panel Unit Root Tests of Purchasing Power Parity. Manuscript. Institute of Statistics and Econometrics, Christian-Albrechts-University, Kiel.

Hooper, P., and C.L. Mann (1989). Exchange Rate Pass-Through in the 1980s: The Case of U.S. Imports of Manufactures. *Brookings Papers on Economic Activity* 1989(1): 297–329.

Huizinga, J. (1987). An Empirical Investigation of the Long-Run Behavior of Real Exchange Rates. In K. Brunner and A.H. Meltzer (eds.), *Empirical Studies of Velocity, Real Exchange Rates, Unemployment and Productivity*. Carnegie-Rochester Conference Series on Public Policy. Volume 27. Amsterdam: Elsevier.

Johansen, S. (1988). Statistical Analysis of Cointegration Vectors. *Journal of Economic Dynamics and Control* 12(2/3): 231–254.

Kasa, K. (1992). Adjustment Costs and Pricing-to-market: Theory and Evidence. *Journal of International Economics* 32(1): 1–30.

Kim, C. (1998). Wechselkursänderungen und Außenhandelsstruktur in der Bundesrepublik Deutschland. *Jahrbücher für Nationalökonomie und Statistik* 217(2): 161–184.

Klemperer, P.D. (1995). Competition When Consumers Have Switching Costs. An Overview with Applications to Industrial Organization, Macroeconomics, and International Trade. *Review of Economic Studies* 62(4): 515–539.

Knetter, M.M. (1993). International Comparisons of Pricing-to-market Behavior. *American Economic Review* 83(3): 473–486.

Knetter, M.M. (1995). Pricing to Market in Response to Unobservable and Observable Shocks. *International Economic Journal* 9(2): 1–25.

Kreinin, M.E. (1977). The Effect of Exchange Rate Changes on the Prices and Volume of Foreign Trade. *IMF Staff Papers* 47(2): 207–229.

Krugman, P.R. (1986). Pricing to Market When the Exchange Rate Changes. NBER Working Paper 1926. National Bureau of Economic Research, Cambridge, Mass.

Krugman, P.R. (1996). Making Sense of the Competitiveness Debate. *Oxford Review of Economic Policy* 12(3): 17–25.

Levin, A., and C.-F. Lin (1992). Unit Root Tests in Panel Data: Asymptotic and Finite-Sample Properties. Working Paper. 92-23. University of California, San Diego La Jolla, CA.

Lorz, J.O. (1998). Capital Mobility, Tax Competition, and Lobbying for Redistributive Capital Taxation. *European Journal of Political Economy* 14(2): 265–279.

Lothian, J.R., and M.P. Taylor (1996). Real Exchange Rate Behavior: The Recent Float from the Perspective of the Past Two Centuries. *Journal of Political Economy* 104(3): 488–509.

Marston, R.C. (1990a). Pricing to Market in Japanese Manufacturing. *Journal of International Economics* 29(3/4): 217–236.

Marston, R.C. (1990b). Systematic Movements in Real Exchange Rates in the G-5: Evidence on the Integration of Internal and External Markets. *Journal of Banking and Finance* 14(5): 1023–1044.

McKinnon, J.G. (1994). Approximate Asymptotic Distribution Functions for Unit-Root and Cointegration Tests. *Journal of Business and Economic Statistics* 12(2): 167–176.

Meese, R.A., and K.S. Rogoff (1988). Was It Real? The Exchange Rate-Interest Differential Relation over the Modern Floating-Rate Period. *Journal of Finance* 43(4): 933–948.

Menon, J. (1996). *Exchange Rates and Prices: The Case of Australian Manufactured Imports*. Berlin: Springer.

Ohno, K. (1989). Export Pricing Behavior of Manufacturing: A US-Japan Comparison. *IMF Staff Papers* 36(3): 550–579.

O'Connell, P.G.J. (1998). The Overvaluation of Purchasing Power Parity. *Journal of International Economics* 44(1): 1–19.

OECD (1992). OECD's Indicators of International Trade and Competitiveness. OECD Working Paper 120. Organisation for Economic Co-operation and Development, Paris.

OECD (1999). *Main Industrial Indicators*. OECD Statistical Compendium on CD-ROM. Edition 02/1999. Paris.

OECD (2000a). *International Trade and Competitiveness Indicators*. OECD Statistical Compendium on CD-ROM. Edition 01/2000. Paris.

OECD (2000b). *Main Economic Indicators*. OECD Statistical Compendium on CD-ROM. Edition 01/2000. Paris.

Oliveira-Martins, J., S. Scarpetta, and D. Pilat (1996). Mark-Up Ratios in Manufacturing Industries: Estimates for 14 OECD Countries. OECD Working Paper 4(24). Organisation for Co-Operation and Development, Paris.

Osterwald-Lenum, M. (1992). A Note with Quantiles of the Asymptotic Distribution of the Maximum Likelihood Cointegration Rank Test Statistics. *Oxford Bulletin of Economics and Statistics* 54(3): 461–471.

Pantula, S.G., G. Gonzales-Farias, and W.A. Fuller (1994). A Comparison of Unit-Root Test Criteria. *Journal of Business and Economic Statistics* 12(4): 449–459.

Papell, D.H. (1997). Searching for Stationarity: Purchasing Power Parity under the Current Float. *Journal of International Economics* 43(3/4): 313–332.

Prakash, G., and A.M. Taylor (1997). Measuring Market Integration: A Model of Arbitrage with an Econometric Application to the Gold Standard, 1879–1913. NBER Working Paper 6073. National Bureau of Economic Research, Cambridge, Mass.

Rogoff, K.S. (1996). The Purchasing Power Parity Puzzle. *Journal of Economic Literature* 34(2): 665–668.

Sachverständigenrat zur Begutachtung der gesamtwirtschaftlichen Entwicklung (1996). *Reformen voranbringen. Jahresgutachten 1996/97*. Stuttgart: Metzler-Poeschel.

Shaked, A., and J. Sutton (1990). Multiproduct Firms and Market Structure. *Rand Journal of Economics* 21(1): 45–62.

Siebert, H. (1997). An Institutional Order for a Globalizing World Economy. Kiel Working Paper 807. Kiel Institute for World Economics, Kiel.

Siebert, H. (1999). *The World Economy*. London: Routledge.

Siebert, H. (2000a). *Außenwirtschaft.* 7th Edition. UTB für Wissenschaft. Stuttgart: Lucius & Lucius.

Siebert, H. (2000b). The Paradigm of Locational Competition. Kiel Discussion Paper 367. Kiel Institute for World Economics, Kiel.

Siebert, H., and H. Klodt (1999). Towards Global Competition: Catalysts and Constraints. In OECD (ed.), *The Future of the Global Economy: Towards a Long Boom?* Paris: Organisation for Economic Co-operation and Development.

Summers, R., and A. Heston (1991). The Penn World Table (Mark 5): An Expanded Set of International Comparisons, 1950–1988. *Quarterly Journal of Economics* 106(2): 327–368.

Sutton, J. (1991). *Sunk Costs and Market Structure: Price Competition, Advertising, and the Evolution of Concentration.* Cambridge, Mass.: MIT Press.

Sutton, J. (1995). The Size Distribution of Business. Part I: A Benchmark Case. Discussion Paper EI/9. The Economics of Industry Group, STICERD, London School of Economics.

Turner, P., and J. Van't dack (1993). Measuring International Price and Cost Competitiveness. BIS Economic Papers 39. Bank for International Settlements, Basle.

Wei, S.-J., and D.C. Parsley (1995). Purchsing Power Disparity during the Floating Rate Period. Exchange Rate Volatility, Trade Barriers and Other Culprits. NBER Working Paper 5032. National Bureau of Economic Research, Cambridge, Mass.

Symposia and Conference Proceedings

Horst Siebert, Editor

Towards a New Global Framework for High-Technology Competition
Tübingen 1997. 223 pages. Hardcover.

Quo Vadis Europe?
Tübingen 1997. 343 pages. Hardcover.

Structural Change and Labor Market Flexibility
Experience in Selected OECD Economies
Tübingen 1997. 292 pages. Hardcover.

Redesigning Social Security
Tübingen 1998. 387 pages. Hardcover.

Globalization and Labor
Tübingen 1999. 320 pages. Hardcover.

The Economics of International Environmental Problems
Tübingen 2000. 274 pages. Hardcover.

The World's New Financial Landscape: Challenges for Economic Policy
Berlin . Heidelberg 2001. 324 pages. Hardcover.

Economic Policy for Aging Societies
Berlin . Heidelberg 2002. 305 pages. Hardcover.

Economic Policy Issues of the New Economy
Berlin · Heidelberg 2002. 251 pages. Hardcover.

Berlin · Heidelberg: Springer-Verlag (http://www.springer.de)
Tübingen: Mohr Siebeck (http://www.mohr.de)

KIELER STUDIEN · KIEL STUDIES

Kiel Institute for World Economics

Editor: *Horst Siebert* · Managing Editor: *Harmen Lehment*

312. **Der Euro als Ankerwährung. Die mittel- und osteuropäischen Beitritts-länder zwischen Transformation und Integration,** *Rainer Schweickert*
Berlin · Heidelberg 2001. 123 pp. Hardcover.

313. **Noise Trading, Central Bank Interventions, and the Informational Content of Foreign Currency Options,** *Christian Pierdzioch*
Berlin · Heidelberg 2001. 207 pp. Hardcover.

314. **Internationale Diversifikation in den Portfolios deutscher Kapitalanleger. Theorie und Empirie,** *Susanne Lapp*
Berlin · Heidelberg 2001. 176 pp. Hardcover.

315. **Subsidization and Structural Change in Eastern Germany,** *Katja Gerling*
Berlin · Heidelberg 2002. 208 pp. Hardcover.

316. **Complementarities in Corporate Governance,** *Ralph P. Heinrich*
Berlin · Heidelberg 2002. 234 pp. Hardcover.

317. **Globalisierung der Automobilindustrie. Wettbewerbsdruck, Arbeitsmarkteffekte und Anpassungsreaktionen,** *Julius Spatz, Peter Nunnenkamp*
Berlin · Heidelberg 2002. 117 pp. Hardcover.

318. **Sozialhilfe, Lohnabstand und Leistungsanreize. Empirische Analyse für Haushaltstypen und Branchen in West- und Ostdeutschland,** *Alfred Boss*
Berlin · Heidelberg 2002. 201 pp. Hardcover.

319. **Schooling and the Quality of Human Capital,** *Ludger Wößmann*
Berlin · Heidelberg 2002. 228 pp. Hardcover.

320. **Climate Policy in a Globalizing World. A CGE Model with Capital Mobility and Trade,** *Katrin Springer*
Berlin · Heidelberg 2002. 293 pp. Hardcover.

321. **Die neue Ökonomie: Erscheinungsformen, Ursachen und Auswirkungen,** *Henning Klodt et al.*
Berlin · Heidelberg 2003. 248 pp. Hardcover.

322. **The Real Exchange Rate and Prices of Trade Goods in OECD Countries,** *Holger Brauer*
Berlin · Heidelberg 2003. 239 pp. Hardcover.

More information on publications by the Kiel Institute at http://www. uni-kiel.de/ifw/pub/pub.htm, more information on the Kiel Institute at http://www.uni-kiel.de/ifw/

Berlin · Heidelberg: Springer-Verlag (http://www.springer.de)